HAIRCUTS & LEAGUE CUPS

THE RISE AND FALL OF CARSON YEUNG

Daniel Ivery and Will Giles

Book design by David Turner
www.mrdeetee.co.uk

Cover Photography by Gareth Sambridge
www.garethsambridge.co.uk

Cartoons by Harry Harrison

UK ISBN Number 978-0-9929549-0-1
HK ISBN Number 978-988-13480-0-5
Printed and bound in the Peoples Republic of China.

GHI's policy is to use papers that are natural, renewable and recyclable products and made from wood grown in sustainable forests.

GHI
2 Warwick Court, Saxon Business Park, Bromsgrove
United Kingdom

1401 China Insurance Group Building
141 Des Voeux Road Central
Hong Kong

For Swiss Jonny and all the Blues Fans
who have experienced joys and sorrows
during the Carson Yeung reign

Author Profiles

DANIEL IVERY

Daniel was born in Marston Green, Birmingham in 1978 and grew up in Chelmsley Wood. Introduced to Blues at an early age (much to the consternation of his grandfather who supported rivals Aston Villa), Daniel has been a Birmingham City season ticket holder for the majority of the last fifteen years.

He has run the "Often Partisan" website since its founding in April 2012 and has written extensively for his website, the Birmingham Mail and various internet outlets about Birmingham City, Carson Yeung and in particular Carson's money laundering trial.

Now living in Kingshurst, Birmingham, Daniel has a daughter who is also a season ticket holder.

WILL GILES

Will was born in Elburton near Plymouth in 1962 but grew up in Essex where he attended Bancroft's School, Woodford Green. He studied law at Sheffield University and became a solicitor in 1987, working in the City with Berwin Leighton. In 1990 he moved to Hong Kong where he continues to live with his wife Julie and children Oli, Harriet, Guy and Alice. He works with his good friends Andrew Hart and Peter Mills in their law firm Hart Giles.

A life-long Spurs fan his only recollection of seeing Birmingham City play was with his schoolmates Dave Johnstone and Pissy Pembery in the 5th round of the FA Cup in 1980 when his favourite player Glenn Hoddle scored twice in a 3-1 victory at the Lane before a crowd of 49,936. He looks forward to seeing a Blues v Spurs game at St. Andrew's in the Premier League with his good friend Daniel Ivery in the near future.

Authors' Acknowledgements

The authors would like to thank their friends in the press, in particular Barclay Crawford, Greg Torode, Shai Oster, Kelvin Chan, Aaron Tam, Alexandra Hoegberg, Neil Moxley, Tom Ross, Chris Lepkowski and Colin Tattum and all their friends in the Hong Kong legal community – we hope you're not too offended.

Much appreciation to Janice Ng for her great research and additional material. Enormous gratitude to Oliver Giles for his editing – we know how difficult it was.

We are indebted to Neil Brown whose organisation kept us on the straight and narrow; Chris Munn and Robin McLeish for their advice and guidance; Harry Harrison for his glorious "Carsoons", Emma Woollcott and Leyla Linton of Mishcon de Reya for their legal expertise; and to David Turner and Mash Chudasama for their help with the design and layout of the book.

Great credit should be given to Lee Yiu-tung, Vico Hui and Zhou Dan for agreeing to be interviewed for the book along with the countless people who cannot be named but who have helped so much.

A special thanks to Ian Danter and Professor John Samuels for providing the Forewords.

WILL GILES

Will would like to thank his wife Julie and his children Oliver, Harriet, Guy and Alice for all their support during this lengthy project and pay tribute to his Mum and Dad for his upbringing in a wonderful literary household.

DANIEL IVERY

Daniel would like to thank his long suffering parents Elaine and Malcolm, his sister Emma, his auntie Susan and uncle Steve and his cousins John and Lucy, who were all a massive inspiration to him and whose words of encouragement were much needed. He would also like to pay tribute to his grandfather Ron, who sadly passed away on Boxing Day 2013 and who was a big influence on his life – even if he did end up supporting the wrong team – and without whose input into his early life he'd never have gotten anywhere near to thinking about this book.

Daniel is also indebted to his friends Anita Mueller, Connor Cameron, Andy Webb, Sarah Kaye, Sara Murzynski, Vikki Buntain, Ray Markham and Alexandra Stepanof, Matthew Elliot, January Wellington, Roya Shams, Kat Bennett and Beth amongst many others for their words of support.

Daniel would also like to thank Brendon Davis, Peter Lewis, Stuart Bannister, Ian Bowater, Kevin Kelly, Roger Woodcock and Gary Cooper for their support in this venture. There are many more football fans who helped give their support to this venture before publication and their names are listed in the roll of honour at the end of this book.

Most of all, Daniel would like to thank his daughter Rachel – may your times as a Bluenose have more joys than sorrows.

THERE ARE NO VACANCIES IN THE PRISON BARBER'S BUT WE'VE THOUGHT OF SOMETHING ELSE YOU MIGHT BE GOOD AT...
PRISON LAUNDRY
HARRY

CONTENTS

FOREWORD BY IAN DANTER

When you become a fan of a football club, you rarely choose your choice – more often than not, it is simply a birth right; a hereditary disease, if you will, passed down from generation to generation.

The Danter family was no exception to this rule with Birmingham City FC. I was a Bluenose before I was on solid foods and possessed the power of speech – my first ever trip to St Andrew's with Dad & Grandad at the age of 5 was perhaps the ideal introduction to the reality of following the Blues - a 3-0 defeat to Stoke City with Jimmy Greenhoff, a former striker of ours, scoring a brace on his return.

In the ensuing decades, I saw 'Superboy' Trevor Francis play at his dizzying peak, the side Jim Smith built with the money from Francis' sale to Nottingham Forest (ironically, a Blues team who would surely have won something with Francis still there amongst them), the relegations, the promotions, the violence, the two occasions where we plummeted into the old Third Division and in doing so, witnessed more drama than a Christmas Eastenders omnibus played on a constant loop. Indeed, as I type, fans are still recovering from a 93rd minute Paul Caddis header that has kept Birmingham City safe in the Championship at Bolton Wanderers when all looked lost 5 minutes beforehand.

Birmingham City simply does not do mediocrity.

It must be desperately easy to be a Manchester United, Chelsea or Manchester City supporter, but I wasn't brought up there, and I was always taught by my Dad to 'support your local team'. So that is that. However, far from being annoyed at not having my pick of allegiance, the last 45 years supporting Blues have been a real treat of an emotional rollercoaster, culminating in the greatest day I shall ever have as a football nut – Sunday February 27th 2011 – Obafemi Day - the day the club beat Arsenal at Wembley to win the League Cup, a major trophy that no sane fan of the club would ever have considered likely at any point. It's just what we've become used to.

Everyone knows the club song 'Keep Right On' and it's usually pretty trite when a Blues fan correlates their own life and experiences with this traditional tune (adopted by the club in the last century during an FA Cup run). But in the current climate of mistrust, misinformation and missing millions, it is lyrically as apposite as ever; the 'joys' of League Cup triumph and the ensuing Europa League campaign, swiftly engulfed by the 'sorrows' of financial instability following relegation, of established players being sold off like the family silver and the constant 'cloak and dagger' approach of the Yeung administration's PR machine that alienated fans in droves.

I remember the day when the current regime was unveiled at a St Andrew's press conference – I sat with my colleague from BBC WM Mike Taylor in an upstairs suite, as Carson Yeung delivered an initial statement for live TV & Newspapers before he was scheduled to do radio interviews with the likes of us. I can clearly recall the look Mike and I gave each other as Carson blurted out mid-statement that he was giving the manager £40M to spend in the transfer market. It was a look that required no words and yet spoke volumes;

"This guy is a successful businessman, and yet he's telling everyone at the outset exactly how much he has to spend???"

It made for great copy in all media outlets, but it should have served as a warning that those in charge were not as savvy as the previous incumbents. In fact when it soon came to light that Yeung had paid David Gold & David Sullivan over £80M to acquire the club, more alarm bells sounded. I love Birmingham City with all my heart, but come on - we were never worth £81M at any stage, even after the League Cup win and imminent return to European competition.

Not long after Carson was charged and was set to face trial, I heard a stat (us football types love a stat) that 100% of money laundering cases in Hong Kong judicial history had gone the way of prosecution lawyers. That was a sign right there of what was to come.

Whilst the quite extraordinary commercial staff at BCFC back in Brum continued to keep the club ticking over with the essential match day revenues that are the lifeblood of any football club, the owners merely dealt in vague rhetoric and delayed releasing accounts time and time again, raising suspicions all the more as to the shifting sands on which Blues' finances were built. Whilst no court case outcome can ever be seen as a fait accompli, the holes in the defence case seemed leakier than the defence on the pitch as the club slid dangerously towards 3rd tier oblivion - and there would've been no right of appeal had that happened.

In my position as a national radio broadcaster with talkSPORT, my opinion on such matters appears to be of great importance to those that follow me on social media. I don't pretend (and never have) to be a journalist in the traditional sense, and there are many in newspapers - both local and national - who are far better placed to obtain information about Blues and put it into the public domain. That said, the secrecy that has surrounded Birmingham City Football Club since Carson Yeung & Peter Pannu assumed control has led to a situation where those in power have rarely proffered salient information to any intrepid news gatherer. This leads to frustration for writers and broadcasters and just as much for fans, whose salacious demand for information has grown and grown disproportionately with the small amounts of rhetoric Messrs Yeung & Pannu have delivered over time.

These men have absolutely no comprehension whatsoever of the blind allegiance I and many thousands of other Blues fans have for BCFC and they have no interest in the raw emotion we've felt during the last few years of their administration. They are probably unaware of the growing in-fighting as fans, desperate for scapegoats, use social media to attack journalists and broadcasters who they perceive are not working hard enough to uncover what they see as 'the truth' about the Yeung administration – worse still, some in the media have been accused of deliberately siding with those in the Far East, thus protecting their connection to the club.

This is, of course, utter tripe. But that's the thing with Twitter, Facebook et al – everyone has a voice and the ones who shout loudest and longest tend to get heard most. In amongst the (righteous) angst Blues fans have been feeling lately, it's been hard to find supporters with a saner grasp of the club's plight.

Daniel Ivery is one such sane individual. His website (Often Partisan) has developed and blossomed over the last few years into a go-to source for information, knowledge and balanced opinion on BIHL, HKSE, BCFC... and many other acronyms! Such has been his influence that he was front and centre in Hong Kong during vital stages of the Carson Yeung money-laundering trial, writing opinion pieces with well-researched comment on the financial machinations of the club's holding company and the mysterious individuals therein. Ably assisted by his friend Will Giles, Daniel was able to explain the complex legal procedures surrounding the trial to the fans back in Birmingham.

This book, therefore, is an essential epitaph – if that is indeed where we're currently at – to a regime that, whilst it did preside over Birmingham City's first ever major trophy, also caused such major heartache to those of us who constantly seek 'the end of the road' – owners who seem to this day to be utterly unrepentant as to the way in which they have systematically dismantled the club that I love.

Keep Right On
Ian Danter
talkSPORT

May 2014

FOREWORD BY PROFESSOR JOHN SAMUELS

The relationship between the owners of the football club and its fans has always been complex, usually acrimonious. This has become more of a problem following the globalisation of the English game. This process has resulted in an inflow of foreign players, foreign managers and foreign owners. The fans have usually found it easy to welcome the foreign players and the managers but many of the new owners have led to conflict.

Success in football is now built on money. The inequality in the game is increasing. The bigger clubs are becoming bigger and the others struggle to compete. Owners can buy success. Where do they get the money from? In some cases we do not know, in other cases it is from private equity funds based in tax havens and in other cases it is sovereign (government) funds. There are many clubs witnessing the clash between those who provide the money and the fans. To the local fans the club is an important part of their day to day life, a big part of their identity. The owners are usually not emotionally involved. Their objectives vary, they might be to boost their own status, to earn respect and global recognition, to promote a country's name and even, on some occasions to make a financial gain. There are bound to be conflicts of interest.

This season we have seen disputes at Hull and at Cardiff. At the end of the season the fans at the one club may have been happy but not so those at the other club. At a local level Coventry City continue with a clash between their fans and their owners, a Cayman Island hedge fund. At Aston Villa after four disappointing seasons the fans are not happy, neither is the owner, and the club is up for sale. At BCFC the major shareholder is in jail and the club is up for sale.

When Carson Yeung and his associates acquired 29.9% of the shares in the club in 2007 we were told that Yeung was a billionaire, a top businessman with an interest in and knowledge about football. We were told he and his fellow investors were going to sell the Blues in the huge under-exploited Chinese market and would turn the Blues into one of the top clubs in the World.

To those who thought about it, it seemed a bit too good to be true. BCFC were a club that had won very little, did not have a strong brand name and it would need a large financial backing to turn them into one of the elite. Yeung himself had faced criminal charges in the past but the football regulators in England were satisfied with him. One mystery was why he had paid two to three times more to buy the club than it appeared to be worth. Another unknown was how he could sell an average club to consumers in China.

The Blues fans have been lucky in that amongst their 12,000 or so loyal supporters there is Daniel Ivery who with the support of his co-author Will Giles has been able to keep us informed about what has been happening 5,000 miles away in the Courts of Law in Hong Kong. We were able to find out about strange land deals and about mysterious ladies who owned casinos in Macau.

The communication between the owners of a club and the fans, is often poor. To be fair to Yeung and to other foreign owners this division between owners and fans is not new. It occurred before globalisation. The owners of the Blues from 1993 had been David Sullivan and the Gold brothers. Fans should have been grateful as they purchased the club out of administration. They did invest in the ground and the team enjoyed some success. It was, however, not long before the fans and owners fell out, culminating in a nasty confrontation near the directors box at one home match. Sullivan wanted to sell and he was lucky to find Yeung who had access to money that he wanted to spend.

Before Sullivan and Gold the club had been owned by the Kumar brothers, low price clothing manufacturers from Manchester and a scrap metal merchant from Walsall. Who in fact does a football club belong to? Is it the legal owners, the manager, the players or the fans? The owners of the club come and go, each with their own objectives. Nowadays the managers and players do not stay long. Many players are on loan contracts and a manager's position is now very insecure. It is the fans that provide the passion, who are the soul of the club.

The then Tottenham Hotspur manager recently said, "It's their (the fans) team, their passion and they don't trade it for anything else, not like Alan Sugar who trades it for money." At the time of making this statement André Villas-Boas was seeking to protect his own position as manager. He was perhaps with the fans in order to try and keep his job.

Football mirrors what is happening in the rest of society. The power in the game is now with those who provide the money. When wealth captures policy making the rules tend to favour the rich, often to the detriment of everyone else. The Economist newspaper recently commented that in football "good management matters but not as much as money does." The link between the amount spent on wages and the number of points won by a team in a season is strong. The wealthy global investors, the large multinational companies and the sovereign funds wish to be associated with successful clubs. Unfortunately the Birmingham clubs are not successful and they cannot attract the big money.

It is in fact now the amount of commercial income which is earned by clubs which results in the inequality,that and the income that comes to the few clubs that qualify for European competitions. It is now commercial revenue that is key to the wealth of clubs, that is income from corporate sponsors and partners, advertising and hospitality. The inequality is dramatic. In 2012/13 the commercial revenue of Manchester City was £143M. That of West Bromwich Albion £10M. Manchester United have 35 official sponsors, usually top name multinational companies. Their new shirt sponsorship deal is said to be worth £69M per annum. The income from just this one sponsor is equal to the total annual revenue of Stoke City. How can such teams compete on equal terms?

The fans hope that a new owner will appear who will invest enough to enable their team to compete at the highest level. Unfortunately such a possibility is very very slim. Recent studies have shown that the competitive balance in the game in England has declined over the last 20 years. The top teams have become more dominant year by year.

The position in England is in fact worse from the point of view of the fans of the majority of clubs, than in all the other major European footballing nations.

There is much talk about UEFA's financial fair play rules. There is hope that they will end some of the excesses in the game. There is talk of levelling the playing field. But their rules only apply to teams taking part in their competitions and most people agree that they will help maintain the status quo. Little chance therefore of things changing for the fans of the majority of clubs. What about the position in the lower leagues? The annual revenue of teams outside the Premiership is exemplified at Bolton £35M, £32M at Wolves and £24M at BCFC; small sums compared with just the commercial income of the top clubs.

Unfortunately as the game has become globalised with money considerations the driving force, the local fans have become of less importance (financially). In the first year of the Premier League (1992/93) total gate receipts and season ticket income accounted for 48% of total turnover. This was the income provided by the fans. By 2011/12 match day receipts were only responsible for 23% of the total turnover of the clubs and not all of this match day revenue was coming from traditional fans. Much of it was corporate hospitality expenditure. The importance of the local fans had declined dramatically - the age of the cyber fan, the new consumer is with us. The multinational corporations are interested in supporting football clubs because a club's success helps them sell their products all over the world, the local fans are of minor interest.

Another revealing statistic showing the change in the finances of the game is that in the first year of the Premier League gate receipts were sufficient to fund 73% of the wage bill of the average club. This indicates that at that time the local fan was very important to the players. By 2011/12, however, gate receipts could only finance 30% of the average club's wage bill. Local fans were providing the atmosphere at the matches but not the money.

Business interests have hijacked the game. It is the interests of business that lie behind decisions that are made by top administrators, regulators and the owners. The media in its own interests continues to hype the game. It is left to the fans of the clubs to keep an eye on what is happening and if necessary to expose the problems. At a national level such bodies as Supporters Direct offer guidance. At a local level it is people like Daniel Ivery who seek to protect the soul of the game.

There is an historical link between the club and its fans. Traditionally it was a working class game, there was a bond between fans, players and the club. The owners were often local. There was a socio-geographical connection. Now the important relationships are all based on money. The product is only sold to those who can afford to pay. The owners of the football businesses want the consumers to pay and keep quiet. But fortunately some supporters will not keep quiet.

Professor John Samuels
Emeritus Professor (of Business Finance), University of Birmingham
Author of "The Beautiful Game is Over: The Globalisation of Football"

INTRODUCTION BY DANIEL IVERY
THE ROLLERCOASTER RIDE OF BEING A BLUES FAN

It's never easy being a Birmingham City fan. For as long as I can remember we've yo-yoed between divisions and yes, we've almost always been in the shadows of our "more illustrious" neighbours. We've had owners who insisted that all the lights were switched off at the end of the day to save electricity; owners who lost everything in the BCCI crash and owners who made money from fans selling watches via a premium rate phone line.

Carson Yeung was in a class of his own though. We've had larger than life owners whose apparel was an extension of their extrovert personalities before, but there hadn't been anyone who used his chequebook in the same manner. We've had owners who lost almost everything due to financial incompetence but this was the first time we've had an owner display the kind of financial acumen that would make Peter Ridsdale blush. Carson was at once both the most successful owner we've had in my lifetime – he delivered a major trophy and a ninth place finish in the top flight – but he's also been the worst – he has left the club in the most dire financial situation it has been in for at least 20 years, even arguably worse than when the club was an hour away from liquidation after the Kumar brothers lost their fortune in 1991.

When Carson rocked up in 2009, having finally completed his protracted takeover Blues were stable financially but stale from a football perspective. The former owners, Ralph and David Gold along with David Sullivan had long lost interest in their troublesome charges and were more than happy to cut and run when Carson came a-calling with what seemed at the time a ludicrous offer for the club. He promised us riches and ambition – more money than ever to be spent on players. It was hard not to feel excited at the prospect.

Since relegation in 1986, even just achieving top-level football was all Blues fans craved. When Sullivan and Gold had taken over the club in 1993, it was only an hour from going out of existence and for the first few years of their tenure Birmingham City spent time bouncing between the second and third tiers before slowly consolidating their place in the Championship under

Trevor Francis and then pushing to become a Premier League club, which they completed via the playoffs at the fourth time of asking in May 2002.

In the period immediately before Carson's initial investment in the club, Blues had stabilised somewhat as a Premier League team. There had been a couple of blips when the team had managed to get itself relegated despite having some of the better players we'd seen down at St Andrew's for years but on the whole the club was steady. Managers stayed for longer periods, the fans got used to top-flight football and wins over the mob from across the expressway. For the first time after a long hiatus, we had almost caught our neighbours, and you could start to feel that with the right investment, the potential was finally there to overtake them: to make them see how it felt being the second team in the second city.

The trouble was that ambition was going to cost a lot of money – and any return on that investment was nowhere near as predictable as the jump from the Championship to the Premier League. The vast increase in television rights given to clubs in the Premier League ensure that money spent on promotion is more than paid back on achieving that goal. Merit payments increase on attaining a higher placing in the top flight but the cost of transfers and players' wages rise exponentially in the Premier League and a return is by no means guaranteed. Sullivan and the Gold brothers are shrewd operators and it seemed that they had come to realise that – although an extra few places higher in the Premier League would please the fans – it wouldn't bring in enough extra cash to fund the higher transfer fees and wages it would no doubt cost them. Blues started to stultify and the fans got increasingly edgy, so much so when Blues once again relinquished their position in the top flight at the end of the 2007/08 season their tempers boiled over into a full-scale pitch invasion and near riot. Whilst it ended up as nothing more than a bunch of unhappy fans singing ribald songs towards the directors' area and some vandalism to the goals when a crossbar was snapped, the damage had been done. The camel's back was well and truly broken and Sullivan and the Gold brothers had decided enough was enough.

Carson cut a strange figure at the time. He had arrived – seemingly out of nowhere, as no one knew a thing about him – and bought a 29.9% stake in the club at the start of the 2007/08 season; he intended to complete the purchase of the remainder of the club, but for some reason it did not transpire. There were a few demands in the press for a proxy for Carson to sit on the BCFC board but the incumbents knew they held all the cards, so were happy to refuse Carson any board representation or control even though his company was the club's single largest shareholder.

It took him another year and a half to return to complete the deal. It was in the summer of 2009 after Blues had bounced back to the top flight at the first time of asking that Carson came back with an offer Sullivan and the Golds just couldn't refuse: a quid a share. All the Blues fans who had shares believed all their Christmases had come at once – it represented a huge premium on the price most had paid for their shares and to most fans at the time it was double, maybe treble what the club was worth. I don't think I'm exaggerating when I say that Sullivan et al literally ran all the way to the bank with the cheque, hardly believing that they'd managed to get such a massive profit out of something which they had decided was a millstone around their collective necks.

So you can imagine that Carson taking full control represented an exciting time. There were a few people preaching caution; as time has gone by more and more have said with perfect hindsight that they were the voice of reason maintaining that they had seen something iffy with the deal, but at the time I can't remember many people dissenting at the prospect of the transfer coffers being inflated by a massive wad of Hong Kong dollars. Most of us fans had dollar signs in our eyes as we dared to dream that the time for Birmingham City finally had come – and with the old board being so stale and disenchanted it felt like the dawn of a new era.

The fans had been assured by the previous incumbents that the new owners were kosher; as rich as Croesus with enough dough in the bank to bankroll the football club right to the top.

That view seemed to be backed up by Carson offering to fund the club £5M to complete a transfer (Tuncay Sanli) before he completed the purchase of the club itself – an offer that wasn't taken up. At their first press conference on 15 October 2009 Carson and his happy gang told the waiting media that they had their chequebooks ready and they were willing to splash out as much as £40M in transfer fees and wages, something the media reported with glee.

There was the normal cynicism amongst the fans; we'd heard it all before from various boards about money being spent and I guess it had reached the stage where it was the boy who cried wolf; you couldn't believe that they were going to splash the cash until you could see the players standing on the Kop, holding a scarf aloft and smiling in the glare of the flashbulbs. However, the board quickly ingratiated themselves with the fans, dropping ticket prices to watch games and doing what they could to improve lines of communication by reinstating the fans' forums that had been abandoned by the previous owners. They told us that the club was to be like a family once again and they wanted the fans to be a key part of Carson's vision for the future.

We had all seen what had happened at Manchester City. In September 2008 Sheik Mansour bin Zayed Al Nahyan had taken control of the Citizens via his Abu Dhabi United Group and proceeded to pour untold sums of petrodollars into the club, transforming them into a powerhouse in the top flight and ensuring that once again they could compete at the top end of the Premier League with their city rivals. Abramovich had poured millions into Chelsea, Peter Coates on a smaller scale at Stoke City – the top flight was awash with multi-millionaires and billionaires indulging their playthings. Although I don't think anyone expected Carson to have quite the same monetary clout as some of these major players, there was a definite level of hope and optimism that Carson really was as minted as had been made out and that Blues too would soon be splashing out huge sums of money on transfer fees for top quality players.

At the time, not many people really wondered out loud if Carson and his band of merry men should have been more thoroughly vetted – either by the game's regulatory bodies or by the people selling the club. I think it's fair to say that most people assumed all was rosy but we all know now with 20:20 hindsight that there should have been alarm bells ringing. Indeed, it emerged in Carson's trial on money laundering charges that Kingston Securities were fully aware that Carson was being investigated for that crime when they lent him and BIH (Birmingham International Holdings) the money to complete the purchase; had "The Owners and Directors Test" required any kind of positive vetting, the footballing authorities could have found out too, or at least asked appropriate questions.

Carson's reign has reflected all the emotions of being a Blues fan. We've had incredible highlights – winning a major trophy in a Wembley final, playing in European competition along with a run in the Premier League that saw the team achieve their best finish for fifty years. However, we've also seen the lows – relegation, a team taken apart to pay the bills followed by the harsh reality of having to sell the best prospects to come through the academy for forty years for peanuts to stave off threats of administration. I think it's the last bit that stuck in the craw of fans the most; for so long the Academy had failed to produce a real star and then all of a sudden we had nineteen-year-old England international keeper Jack Butland and seventeen-year-old local-born winger Nathan Redmond who were making the big clubs sit up and take notice... and yet we sold both for less money than it cost to buy Nikola Zigic.

It's quite bizarre, but Carson almost immediately became a hated figure on the terraces after his arrest (along with his right hand man Peter Pannu), notwithstanding the absolute joys we had enjoyed only a few months previously. This was a man who had mortgaged his family home to put money into Birmingham City and all he got in return was to be compared to a manual DIY enthusiast and an Anglo-Saxon word for a part of the female anatomy on a regular basis at a football club he couldn't even visit due to his bail restrictions.

I found it difficult from a personal point of view to join in the vitriolic chants against our erstwhile President; as much as his business ethics seemed to have been massively at fault, I couldn't help but see a man who had sunk almost everything he had into the club trying to make it better.

It didn't help that the evidence points to Carson being just like any other football fan in private. In videos I've seen of him at home, he's like any other bloke on a Sunday afternoon – munching on a sandwich, playing with his dogs, watching a bit of Sky Sports News. The difference is that his house is worth many millions and there are half a dozen expensive sports cars on the driveway but – essentially – Carson was just a fan like us on the terraces. When I met him during the court case he was more than happy to discuss the last football game, commiserate on the result and talk about how he had faith that the team could do better. The fact is that apart from anything else, Carson is a football fan and it's entirely possible that this was part of his undoing – that he ran the club as a football fan and not as a businessman.

Of course, it has since emerged it wasn't just his money that he was sinking into the club. It's one thing to be done for money laundering in the years prior to his buying of the club; it's another for it to emerge that the money he had loaned the club hadn't come from him but from various unknown sources with no paper trail, no documentation and no clues as to whether the money was clean or dirty. In the end BIH has had to assume or "novate" the debt for itself and to exchange it for further equity issued to Carson in order to wipe it from the football club's books because that "loan debt" had become so toxic and was affecting any potential sale of the club.

The fact is that the seeds of his downfall were very much sown during Carson's meteoric rise. It was almost as inevitable as gravity that Carson's fortunes would plummet back to earth because those fortunes were never his in the first place – it was disclosed in his trial that during both takeover attempts Carson had borrowed money from Kingston Securities to enable him to buy his required proportion of the rights issues involved.

There was only so long he could continue to act in the manner he did before he was going to get caught. For every moment that he spent swanning around in his bearskin coat quaffing champagne and living the dream of being a football club owner, it was a moment closer to the net closing around him.

Rumours had started almost immediately after the League Cup win in 2011 that the money fans assumed was going to be available for new players in the summer wouldn't be there; I'm of the firm belief that even if Blues had managed to pick up more than the solitary point in their last six Premier League games and stayed up, players would still have been sold in the summer. BIH were required by the HKSE (The Hong Kong Stock Exchange) to announce in March 2011 that Carson had mortgaged his house on The Peak, Hong Kong Island to provide liquidity for the company – for whatever reason, someone had turned the tap off and funds available to the club were no longer forthcoming.

I started writing the Often Partisan website in April 2011, having spent the previous eight months writing sporadically about Blues on my own personal blog. One of the things that always struck me was the absolute dearth of information about Carson, so I made it my mission to try and track down what I could, using my "google-fu" skills and a very basic grasp of traditional Chinese characters. I'm a believer that the fans deserve to be given all the information possible to make up their own minds about what is happening at their club and, as such, transparency and openness should be key. I'm a season ticket holder at the club (along with my daughter) and everything that I have ever tried to do with my website has been to try and inform other fans, and to help the club that I hold dear to my heart.

Having been given the opportunity to visit Hong Kong, Macau and China for myself (thanks to the generosity of some of the people who helped me write this book) to talk to people surrounding BIH along with building close links with the club itself I found that answers just presented more questions and, as these questions emerged, we realised that there was a story in all this: a story of how a former hairdresser who grew up in a poor area of Kowloon made it big, bought a football club and then brought it to its knees all in a matter of a few years.

However, this is more than a story. There is also a lesson to be learned by the footballing authorities as to what steps should be taken to vet potential new owners as fit and proper persons. Recent years have seen bigger and bigger clubs fall into administration and worse – Portsmouth being the first Premier League club to fall into administration, who have ended up three years later in League Two and in danger of falling out of the Football League entirely, having been forced at one point to get rid of every single player contracted to the club and to endure a lengthy second administration of more than a year. Indeed, in Portsmouth's case the agony could have been prolonged further had the Football League not finally taken action and forced the sale of the club to its fans.

Although the Carson era has now ended, I think there are also lessons for football fans – be careful what you wish for. If you make a Faustian pact with the Devil as you stand praying for a miracle at Wembley stadium, then you have to accept that you're going to reap the agony as well as the ecstasy. Spending massive amounts of money on players is exciting and shows ambition; however, ultimately the gravy train will come to an end at some point. Carson came to England from Hong Kong an unknown and left Birmingham in infamy – this is the story of how he had it all and lost it.

1

THE LUCKY AND LARGER
THAN LIFE HAIRDRESSER

Carson Yeung Ka-sing was born in Hong Kong on 27 February 1960 to Yeung Chung and Yung Sau Mui. As is usual with Chinese families, Carson was given a Chinese name that reflected his parents' hopes for his future. "Ka" is a common first part, meaning "home" or "family", whereas "Shing" means "truthful" or "honest". There is a rather delicious irony in Carson's name implying honesty given his current predicament.

Carson was his father's first son by his second wife; he has one full sister, Yeung Kai-yi, and has a multitude of half-siblings from his father's previous marriage including three older half-brothers who were estranged from their father at the time of his death. Kai-yi is married to Victor Ma Shui-cheong, who is Vice Chairman of BIH, an Executive Director of Birmingham City and Vice Chairman of Sing Pao Media. She is also known to have nursed their father through the last stages of bladder cancer before he died in 2012. The elder Yeung's death deprived Carson the opportunity to ask his father to give evidence in his court case about their shared investments – something that undoubtedly hindered his defence.

Carson grew up in a public housing estate in Wong Tai Sin, in the shadow of Lion Rock Hill in Kowloon. His upbringing was similar to that of a child growing up in a council estate in the UK; a working class area living in social housing – by no means "the ghetto" but not a middle class suburb either. The area is famous for the temple of the same name where Taoist worshippers go to hear their fortunes and pray for success and luck. It's not hard to imagine a young Carson kneeling before the altar with the kau cim sticks seeking guidance from the Great Immortal Wong on how to be a success, or how to proceed when faced with a difficult choice – particularly bearing in mind how his life would progress.

Carson's father ran a fruit and vegetable stall called "Yeung Kee Vegetable Stall" in Lok Fu[1], Kowloon and was apparently quite a successful businessman – Carson gave evidence in his trial that he was bailed out by his "daddy" when he lost his money in the stock market crash of 1978.

1. HKSAR v Yeung Ka Sing, Carson DCCC860 of 2011 (DJ Douglas Yau) para 215

Yeung Chung ran his business until 1988 when he handed management duties to a Mr Cho, who subsequently assigned the business to a third party.

Carson spent his school life at New Method College, a secondary school with four campuses across Kowloon. New Method was known for its relatively liberal teaching methods, concentrating on non-core subjects and preparing its students for a life working abroad. Its list of famous alumni is long, including the founders of Chong Hing Bank Liu Lit-mo and Liu Lit-chi[2], and the school is considered to have been a good finishing ground for many children who didn't quite fit into Hong Kong's educational mainstream. It's no surprise that students at the college were well known for being "tearaway types". Carson left school at the age of fifteen after completing Form 5[3] – two years earlier than usual – and went to serve an apprenticeship as a hairstylist.

His first job was at the Excelsior Hotel in Causeway Bay where he worked as an apprentice stylist in the salon concession. Carson spent his first year as an apprentice cutting, dying and crimping hair at the salon, learning his trade before becoming a fully-fledged stylist. He continued for two more years as a qualified hairdresser. He then moved on to the well-known "Le Salon" in the Central district, working there for four years and steadily building his reputation.[4] From a young age he was clearly considered something of a talent; claiming in court during his testimony that he picked up a wage including tips of HK$50,000-HK$60,000 per month whilst at Le Salon – a hefty salary in the early eighties for someone in his profession. Le Salon manager Ricky Kwok, a former colleague of Carson, remembers him as being very thin, very talkative and greatly loved by the rich female clientèle. Kwok went on to say that Carson loved to drink and dance back then, but he claimed Carson left Le Salon after less than a year due to a lack of clients.[5]

In 1983, Carson visited Europe for twelve months, ostensibly to learn from the masters of the hairdressing trade in London and Paris, before returning to Hong Kong.

2. Oliver Chou, "The last bell", *South China Morning Post*, 29 July, 2012
3. *HKSAR v Yeung Ka Sing, Carson* DCCC860 of 2011 (DJ Douglas Yau) para 212
4. Ibid, para 212
5. *Next Media*, 6 March 2014

How he spent his time in Europe is not well documented, although he later confirmed in court he enhanced his trade over in the Old World by taking a couple of advanced courses. There isn't much more information available as to where and for whom he worked – there are some rumours that he worked in London during that time but nothing that has been independently verified. One thing that is clear is that Carson's spoken English is still limited. There remains a gap in public knowledge of Carson's life between 1984 and 1988,[6] a period not covered in his trial.

Carson opened his first salon by the name of "Vole" in the Royal Pacific Hotel in Tsim Sha Tsui in July 1989 at a cost of around HK$4M,[7][8] which Carson told the court in his evidence that he had saved up from his work as a hairdresser. Within a month, he opened a second salon – partnering a lady Alice Chan – in the exclusive Peninsula Hotel in Kowloon, putting up another HK$1.5M in personal savings for a 50% stake, eventually buying out his partner in 1990 for around HK$1M.[9] When giving evidence regarding his hairdressing career he claimed he was very successful, earning HK$3M annually from each establishment. Business was booming and Carson was raking it in. He was forced to close the Vole Peninsula in February 1991 when the hotel underwent a renovation and sold the Vole Royal Pacific in March 1994 for close to HK$4M.

Around the same time, Carson and his father Yeung Chung invested in a hotel in Dongguan, an industrial city up the Pearl River from Hong Kong near Guangzhou.[10] Yeung Chung operated the hotel along with his nephew Yang Wu Jun for four years until the Yeungs sold up in 1994.

Eight months after setting up Vole Peninsula, Carson opened a salon called "Vanity" with business partner Denis Shek in the Royal Garden Hotel, Tsim Sha Tsui, putting up HK$1.75M for a 50% stake.[11] Carson bought out Shek in March 1994, operating the salon as sole owner of the business until 1999.

6. HKSAR v Yeung Ka Sing, Carson DCCC860 of 2011 (DJ Douglas Yau) Para 214
7. Ibid para 221
8. Note for all financial transactions, we have used an exchange rate of HK$12.5 - £1 regardless of time period
9. Ibid para 226
10. Ibid para 243
11. Ibid para 232

Carson claimed he earned between HK$2-2.5M annually from the Vanity hair salon.

In March 1993, Carson opened another salon, also called Vole – his fourth, although by then Vole Peninsula had been closed – in the Sun Plaza mall, Tsim Sha Tsui, Kowloon. Again, he started off the business as a partnership, this time with a Simon Lai and putting in HK$1.75M for his 50% stake. Carson sold this business to Lai in March 1996 for about HK$3M. Carson told the court during his trial that this salon was less successful than his other ventures, and he only made around HK$1M a year from it before he sold his share. The last salon Carson opened was also called Vanity, and was situated in the New World hotel in Tsim Sha Tsui. He opened the business using profits from his other salons in June 1995.

Carson wasn't just your run-of-the-mill barber. Ng Loi Ping, a Kazakhstan-based businessman and friend of Carson, recounted during his trial that he had to book a day in advance to make an appointment with Carson and would pay HK$500 (about £40) for the privilege of a haircut in the company of high society and movie stars.[12]

It wasn't just in his salons that Carson coiffed and styled hair. With a growing reputation in hairdressing circles, he was called to film sets and TV studios both in Hong Kong and on the mainland. He styled the hair of the rich and famous, including actor Jackie Chan and Taiwanese actress Brigitte Lin. Carson was seen as a man with a burgeoning talent – a far cry from the slightly insulting "barber" moniker he was saddled with in his later career as President of Birmingham City.

Carson's earnings in his hairdressing days were hotly disputed by the prosecution in his money laundering trial. Judge Douglas Yau Tak-hong found in his judgement that Carson had exaggerated his income and that he had lied about the huge sums of money he claimed to have earned styling hair in his salons.[13]

12. *Ibid para 157*
13. *Ibid para 567*

As his wealth grew, Carson's interests diversified. He moved into property investment, opening a company called Richfield (Asia Pacific) Limited with a partner, which engaged in property investment in Malaysia and Thailand amongst other countries. He acted as a sales agent introducing potential purchasers to property developers in both countries, who in turn paid Richfield commission. Carson also bought a small apartment and parking lot complex in the New Territories town of Fanling, transforming it with his "Wealthy Villa" project and selling it on, netting him a purported HK$15M in 1997. However during cross-examination in his court case his evidence revealed that he had been forced to take on mortgages to pay the developer on the original purchase and sold three units at a loss, eventually defaulting on one mortgage in 2001.

In addition to all this commercial activity, Carson had become most interested in the stock market. He began trading shares as an eighteen year old, even though at that time he had a monthly income of just HK$10,000. It seems incredible that Carson managed to open an account to trade shares at that time – in 1978 Carson would still have been a minor and ineligible to do so as the minimum age to trade shares in Hong Kong was 21[14] until 1990. Any contract involving a minor would have been legally unenforceable but Carson was adamant in court that he had bought and sold stocks at that time, confessing he had lost all the money he had earned as a trainee hairdresser in the crash of 1978.

Carson started off investing relatively modest sums of HK$100,000 to HK$200,000 (around £7,500 to £15,000) when he first started trading,[15] gradually expanding his portfolio with Sun Hung Kai Securities after the 1978 crash to a level of HK$1-3M worth of shares. Carson's strategy was to sell his shares once he had hit a profit margin of 15%, trading tips with his father who was also playing the market.

14. *Ibid para 258*
15. *Ibid para 259*

In his examination-in-chief in court, Carson testified that his portfolio was worth around HK$30M (around £2.4M) by 1998[16] when the stock market crashed once more and he lost about 70% (approximately HK$20M) of its value. One may think that having made and lost fortunes twice in the stock market, Carson would have felt his fingers had been burnt a little too much and taken his losses and avoided further risk; however, that was far from the case. The loss was on paper only as Carson didn't sell his shares; he admitted in court that some stockbrokers chased him for money after the crash but not all of them did. He managed to weather the storm, and started to build again.

There has always been a fascination in trading shares amongst the ordinary working folk in Hong Kong because apart from horse racing – the only legal gambling activity – speculating on stocks satisfies the ancient Chinese tradition of gambling, which continues to play an important role in contemporary Chinese culture. Carson first became involved in buying penny stocks in 1998 with his friends through a stockbroker called Taiwan Securities. Share trading with his crew of mates was like a game – who could make the most profit that month, who could pick the biggest winner and who would be able to dodge the biggest loser. Carson and his buddies would discuss tips and market gossip over drinks and food in one of the multitude of restaurants or teahouses in Hong Kong as they dreamed of making their fortunes in the stock market recovery.

In 1999 his status had changed. All of a sudden, Carson appeared to have elevated himself to a different league having made huge profits on his stock trading and he was flashing it around with impunity. Somehow everything he touched appeared to turn into gold; he would pick a stock to speculate on, its price would soar and he would make a killing on it – but when asked how he kept doing it, Carson would smile, pour another beer and have a laugh with his friends. Carson was on a streak. It was a lucky streak that would continue well into the middle of the next decade and turn Carson from another stock market wannabe into a true high roller. There is great importance attached to luck in Chinese business and Carson evidently had it. Now everyone wanted to know him.

16. *Ibid para 264*

Although by this point in 1999 he had opened five salons he no longer cut hair. Instead he spent his time hunched over a stock trading terminal with a phone clamped to his ear, studying profit and loss and balance sheet reports trying to pinpoint where he could make his next killing in the market. Part of it he attributed to his own research company, "Bull and Bear"[17], which analysed trends in the stock market and gave him his investment insights. Bull and Bear employed around eight staff and Carson himself participated in the research, which was snapped up by a client list that included various listed companies. Something clearly worked for him as he earned HK$90M in two years, multiplying his personal wealth by ten times as he built a huge stock portfolio over a multitude of margin accounts. In his evidence in court, he testified that his portfolio was worth around HK$30M in 1998 before it lost 70% of its value in the stock market collapse of that year, HK$100M in 2000[18]and HK$200M[19] in 2001. The speed at which his wealth accumulated was incredible. Was he blessed with amazing good fortune or was something more sinister afoot?

Carson wasn't interested in any old stock. Turning his nose up at the more conventional blue chip stocks as being too boring, Carson concentrated on the so-called "red chip" market, which was much more volatile but offered better chances to make profits quickly. Working his share transactions both on-and off- market, ("off-market" meaning a deal with an individual buyer or seller not offered through the stock exchange), Carson would look for opportunities to pick up shares as cheaply as possible – often utilising a steadily growing network of friends for tips – holding his shares for a short period before trading them for a quick buck. He tracked companies that were trying to diversify and grow and there were plenty of IPO offerings in which new companies would be launched on the market hungry for money to expand.

One such example of his share dealings emerged in the court hearings in 2013 and concerned a company called Gold Wo International Holdings. Gold Wo was to be listed in April 2001, and Carson was asked by his contact Ben Cheung at Taiwan Securities if he wanted shares in the IPO.

17. Ibid para 266
18. Ibid para 272
19. Ibid para 296

Carson declined, but a few months later after the listing – when asked again by Cheung if he was interested – he bought 28M shares "off-market" at a couple of cents discount from the market price of HK$0.43 in a transaction that cost him HK$11.2M[20]. After holding on to the shares for a couple of months he sold them on, again in an off-market transaction making a profit of approximately HK$22M[21] – nearly £2M at the time – not too bad for a couple of months work.

When asked in court why he had bought the shares "off-market", Carson replied that "it was more convenient for him"[22]. In his summing up, Judge Douglas Yau Tak-hong noted that it was more convenient for Carson because he could save on stamp duty payment, something that Carson appeared to confirm in his evidence saying, "if it was done off-market and then I further transfer to another party, because at that time we could not have known at what prices the shares would be sold later"[23]. The judge took this to mean that since the shares were bought off-market, and they were then sold on to another party, the ultimate transaction could be made between the original seller and the final purchaser and stamp duty would only be paid once by those parties, not by the middle man.

There is some doubt as to how much profit he truly made on the deal, with a confusing round robin of payments and movements of stock and involvement of third parties who shared in the spoils from the transaction. Carson testified in Court that he sold out for less than half the market price in the "confirmor" transaction, splitting his proceeds with a lady called Yu Xiao Mai. Carson's evidence under cross-examination concerning the transaction was difficult for even trained ears to follow and there has to be scepticism as to how much cash Carson actually made on the deal; this is impossible to work out without a full examination of the paper trail – much of which had been destroyed by the various brokers involved due to the lapse of time between the transaction and the criminal charges.

20. *Ibid paras 311-313*
21. *Ibid para 321*
22. *Ibid para 313*
23. *Ibid para 313*

Carson gave evidence that he had sold the shares to Ms Yu with her acting as "confirmor". Carson would receive HK$1.20 per share for the deal with Yu selling them on to a third party at the market price of HK$2.80 per share. The idea was that Yu would be able to fulfil a request from a contact of hers willing to pay the full market price for a significant holding and would share the profits with Carson as the price for introducing someone to him who would take the shares at the market value.

In his judgement on Carson's money laundering charges, Judge Douglas Yau criticised the transaction due to the lack of paperwork involved, concluding that he didn't know why the concealment of Ms Yu's involvement was necessary and that a reasonable person would have reasonable grounds to believe that the money involved was the proceeds of an indictable offence – in other words, it was laundered money[24].

Interestingly, Gold Wo was wound up in 2004[25] by the High Court of Hong Kong after it emerged that its IPO documentation included serious misrepresentations and the company had defrauded the HKSE in its application for its listing. Carson's connections to the company are unknown; however it does seem probable that he benefitted from a forced sale of shares when the HKSE noted that the public shareholding in the company or "spread" was too low and the shares had been concentrated in too few hands.

Another suspect deal highlighted in the court hearings involved a company called Kanstar Environmental Paper Products Limited. In 2007, Carson became interested in the petroleum business and wanted to buy into Kanstar as it had a venture it was developing in Brunei. Controversial former legislator Chim Pui-chung, who was convicted in 1998 for conspiracy to forge documents, gave evidence for Carson at his trial claiming that when approached by Carson about investing in Kanstar he considered it an advantage for the company's stock trading if a big speculator like Carson became involved.[26]

24. Ibid para 575
25. Companies Winding Up Proceedings 33 of 2003, (Kwan J)
26. HKSAR v Yeung Ka-Sing, Carson DCCC860 of 2011 (DJ Douglas Yau) Para 115

Carson bought 280M shares in an off-market transaction for just 10 cents a share – when the market price was then at a multiple of four times that – from chairman Jacky Chim, the second son of Chim Pui-chung who held the shares through a company called Siko Venture Limited. During his evidence, Chim Pui-chung was shown documentation from Lippo Securities that disclosed that 280M Kanstar shares were "delivered free" to Carson's account there on 8 July 2007. This means that the shares were bought without using the broker and were deposited into his account there without any commission paid to Lippo. The shares were then moved again to another broker – this time Kingston Securities – again with no commission paid on the following day.

Carson paid HK$28M for the shares to Chim Pui-chung through a casino in Macau two or three days later. When asked in cross-examination why he had sold the shares so cheaply, Chim Pui-chung told the court:

"There are 2 to 3 reasons. First, you people who earn high wages do not know the operation of the market. Secondly, because there was such large quantity, you cannot sell such a large quantity without a big speculator, it would not be able to sell. Third, the timing must be right. The current market price is no more than $0.005, half a cent. Not even 1/20 of the price that I sold to him for. The simple answer to you is it was a commercial decision."[27]

Chim couldn't recall how he was paid – it didn't matter to him if it was received as a cheque or casino chips, as long as he received it. When asked why he had received the money and not Jackie Chim, Chim Pui-chung told the court that his son owed him money and it didn't matter if the money went to him or his son, it was a matter for him and his son to settle. Chim Pui-chung also confirmed to the court that there was no receipt for the shares, telling the court, "he just received my shares and I received his money." Carson sold the shares off-market within a couple of months, this time netting a huge profit of HK$56M.[28]

27. *Ibid para 124*
28. *Ibid para 127*

Again, this transaction was later criticised by the judge in Carson's money laundering trial for its lack of documentation, the concealment of the involvement of Chim Pui-chung and the manner in which payment for the shares was made.[29]

In 2004[30], Carson fell foul of the authorities for the first time when he was convicted of fourteen breaches of the Securities (Disclosure of Interests) Ordinance in connection with the purchase of shares in a company called Cedar Base Electronics. Carson had repeatedly bought shares which took him over reportable thresholds without reporting his full beneficial shareholding to the HKSE; however, although he was fined HK$43,000, he wasn't in any great trouble – the SFC failed to make the main charge of stock market manipulation stick and Carson was free to continue investing. Had he been convicted of stock market manipulation, the punishment would have been a lot harsher and it's even possible it might have precluded him from buying a football club later in his life.

Carson has always been a larger than life personality. He is well known in England now for his appearance and particularly his clothes; tailored sombre suits in court contrasting with huge fur coats and sunglasses when Carson has been seen in Birmingham. He always liked the finer things in life; according to his close friends Carson is a whiskey drinker by choice, he liked nothing more than to drink a few glasses with lunch, have a massage and a nap in the afternoon before continuing his drinking in the evening, often to titanic excess. Carson liked to display his wealth with huge gala dinners, with lots of food, lots of alcohol and lots of singing. It's ironic that he became so hated by the majority of Birmingham City fans because in his personal life most of what he enjoyed would have been admired by stereotypical old-school football fans.

29. Ibid para 617
30. "SFC Prosecutes Yeung Ka Sing Carson for Breaching the Securities (Disclosure of Interests) Ordinance", Hong Kong Securities and Futures Commission Enforcement news, 27 September 2004

As he lived the high life in the glory days, he hosted huge gala dinners where rich and powerful business people from the mainland and Hong Kong gathered to sup champagne and toast their enigmatic host while he gloried in the triumph of the League Cup win in February 2011 and celebrated the birth of his daughter, Camilla, in that same year. In Birmingham, he would demand the largest private room in one of the biggest restaurants in the Chinese quarter whenever he came to eat – even if the room was fully booked or occupied – something that did not endear him to the staff. Flunkies would be dispatched to run errands for Carson as he sat with his friends enjoying the finer trappings of his life. It may sound demeaning but it's a measure of the hold he had – young men were willing to do his bidding in the hope that luck (or Carson himself) might take a shine to them and they too might end up at the top table with him eating fine foods.

Carson has always been quite the ladies man. Although he has only been married once, he has had two common-law partners following his divorce in 1997. He has always been accompanied by beautiful women whenever he has been seen in public, and has often been seen happily serenading members of the fairer sex as another gargantuan dinner wound down.

His first wife was Li Wing Sze, a Hong Konger who is the mother of his eldest son, Ryan (Tsz Tsung). Not much is known of their relationship other than they split when Ryan was relatively young and that Li has since remarried a Frenchman. The second lady in his life was a mainlander, Zhou Dan. Carson was involved in a relationship with her for almost a decade and a half, which started when they met at a Christmas party in 1997. It was through Ms Zhou that he was introduced to her sister, Zhou Xin, and her brother-in-law, Liu Xingcheng. Zhou Xin and Liu Xingcheng were to feature heavily in Carson's life and peripherally in that of Birmingham City Football Club.

Carson and Zhou Dan bought a very expensive house together in a gated community in the Kingston upon Thames area, where Carson lived when he was in the UK. After they split up when Carson met his new partner, he allegedly promised to give his half of the house to Zhou as a settlement to end their relationship. According to Ms Zhou, Carson reneged on the deal and one month after the house was transferred to her, served a writ in May 2013 to try and have the house transferred solely to him, which remains outstanding because Carson is now adamant that he promised Zhou nothing. Zhou and Carson had no children together; although Zhou has alleged that Carson caused her second miscarriage by pushing her down the stairs of her house in Guangzhou while he was drunk.[31]

His third (and current) partner is another mainlander, Joanna Wang Manli. Born in Dalian in the north-east of China, Joanna is the mother of their children Camilla (born 2011) and Alexander (born 2012) and is the most recognisable face to Birmingham City fans. She was the lady who generally accompanied Carson to football matches in the UK and was present the last time Carson was seen in public in Birmingham at the end-of-season awards dinner in May 2011. Ms Wang is a former beauty pageant winner, who joined the editorial team of the Hong Kong magazine SPLUX[32] in 2011. Her portrayal as a beauty queen has been questioned in some parts of the media with the event she claimed to have won - "Miss Globe International – China Final Best Talent Winner" – not traceable under that name; furthermore, the heat she did win only had four contestants. Since Carson's arrest, Joanna has moved across the border to Shenzhen with Carson's two young children.

In 2005, Carson showed his ostentatious side by purchasing a house on the hyper-exclusive Barker Road on The Peak for HK$146M, paying the full sum outright without recourse to a mortgage. The three-story apartment had commanding views of the harbour, and remained in Carson's hands until he defaulted in 2012 on a mortgage that was secured on the property from Wing Hang Bank in 2010.

It wasn't his only expensive purchase though; Carson had bought the house in Kingston upon Thames – this time just short of £5M – again paying the full price in one go. In his evidence at his trial Carson testified that he had bought the property with money paid to him as a return on an investment by suspected triad Cheung Chi-tai; the judge saw things differently and infers

31. *Next Media, 6 March 2014*
32. *Images.yule.tom.com, retrieved April 2011*

in his judgement that he agreed with Mark Pulvirenti, who gave evidence as an expert witness for Carson and in his original expert report said that the money from Cheung Chi-tai was used towards the purchase of Birmingham City.

Ms Wang, along with Carson's mother, Yung Sui-mai, issued a writ against Carson on 5 October 2012 claiming that the Barker Road property was also beneficially theirs and it wasn't Carson's to mortgage without their knowledge or authorisation. No doubt this was a tactical ploy to try and delay the bank's possession proceedings. Joanna joined the suit giving the name of Wang Lifei, the name which appears on her Hong Kong Identity Card, which apparently contradicts the name that appears on her PRC passport. Wang Lifei is said to be her sister's name and it is a mystery why Joanna has an ID card bearing this name in Hong Kong. In his judgement dated 31 January 2013[33], Registrar KW Lung found that while Carson was a director of Success Orient Investment Limited – the company that owned the Barker Road house – he could not prove that he actually owned the company and, accordingly, he had no capacity to grant a beneficial interest to anyone.

Company registry records don't help much. Carson Yeung isn't shown as a director of Success Orient until July 2010[34], when he took over from a mainlander by the name of Huang Jing Dong – and the company was owned by a mainland company by the name of Kindever Investments – based at the same Shenzhen address as Mr Huang. Unfortunately further digging has proved to be fruitless and like a lot of Carson's life remains a mystery. On this occasion, hiding his beneficial ownership certainly didn't do him any favours.

All these properties were in addition to the apartment he bought with his first wife Li Wing Sze in Hong Kong's Mid-Levels district for HK$5M+ in 1996 – not to mention the cars and the yachts he bought both in the UK and in Hong Kong as he enjoyed the full trappings of success.

33. *Wing Hang Bank v Success Orient Investment Ltd and others HCMP2457 of 2011 (R Lung KW)*
34. *Success Orient Investment Ltd Annual Return 2010, 2011 – retrieved December 2013*

When travelling to the St Andrew's stadium in Birmingham, Carson would always arrive in his monstrous Maybach that was purchased in 2005 and in June 2011 was valued at HK$2M.

Carson's first involvement in football was apparently in 2005, taking on the chairmanship of Hong Kong Rangers, a club based in Sham Shui Po – a role he only held for a year. His tenure was noted for his desire to interfere with team duties – something coach Tim Bredbury was definitely unhappy with[35] before he ended up being sacked. Contrary to press reports that emerged in the wake of his initial purchase of a stake in Birmingham City, Carson never owned a stake in Rangers or any other club.

35. James Nursey, "Blueprint for Glory", Daily Mirror, 16 July, 2007

2

GAMBLING LIKE IT'S A BUSINESS

Macau lies about thirty-seven miles – an hour's ride on a jetfoil – south west of Hong Kong, and is a former European colony like its neighbour. The tiny enclave was the oldest colony in eastern Asia, belonging to Portugal and was the last remaining colony in the Far East when in 1999 it became the second SAR (Special Administrative Region) of China after Hong Kong. Whereas Hong Kong is a major finance and banking centre and economic gateway to China, Macau's economy thrives on it being an exit for the People's Republic's cash based on another Chinese fascination – gambling.

Gambling is an immense business in Macau. There are currently thirty-five casinos in Macau, from the kitsch old fashioned Lisboa to the ultra-modern Venetian and Sands casinos. The latest casinos were opened by American corporations, who came in seeking new revenue streams once deregulation of the old monopoly dominated by Hong Kong business magnate Stanley Ho was dismantled. Their investment in Macau runs into the billions of American dollars, with the Venetian alone costing US$2.4BN utilising land reclaimed from the sea.

The casinos themselves have to be seen to be believed; thousands of Chinese men and women swarm around tables, crunching odds in their heads, trying to figure out how to increase their chances of winning and gambling like there is no tomorrow. The main game in Macau is the punto banco variation of baccarat - an absolute game of chance with no skill required. A few tables start off with cheap minimum bets at HK$500 (approximately £40) but those tables are rare and most tables start at HK$1000. The stakes can pile up very quickly and many fortunes have been lost in one night in Macau – certainly many more than the fortunes made. Riches are won and lost on the turn of a card.

As with many other rich Chinese, Carson enjoyed spending his time in Macau gambling on the baccarat tables. Macau's gambling turnover now easily exceeds that of the more famous Las Vegas and Atlantic City combined. The ground floors of the vast casinos are given over to tables and slot machines for the crowds of everyday punters from mainland China, while the upstairs rooms are reserved for VIP guests willing to gamble much, much more money. Carson testified at his trial that it was in those VIP rooms that he made a substantial part of his fortune.

He first started gambling in the casinos in Macau in 1997. At that time, he was like many other Hong Kong businessmen and women; he would jump on the ferry across the Pearl River delta for the sixty minute journey to Macau and spend his time in the casinos playing baccarat, winning and losing significant sums of money but most importantly having fun. Back then he wasn't what is called a high roller – spending HK$1M or so a night is a lot to the everyday Joe but in Chinese terms it was fairly small potatoes. This was a pattern that would continue for the next few years; as a hairstylist extraordinaire and then as a share trader, every few weeks Carson would go over to Macau and cut loose a little. It was certainly regarded as nothing out of the ordinary by his friends and compatriots.

From his own evidence at his trial, it wasn't until 2004[36] that Carson started gambling in the big leagues. By this time Carson had made a lot of money on the stock market in Hong Kong and was looking ever more the prosperous businessman. He had made many connections and one of these – another Hong Kong businessman, Au Yeung Kai Chor, who he had met two years previously – approached Carson and asked him if he fancied playing the tables in the VIP rooms for serious stakes rather than slumming it downstairs with the riff-raff. Carson jumped at the opportunity – this was his chance at the big time and entry into the exclusive ranks of the high rollers.

One thing it's important to bear in mind is how business works in China – a great deal of importance is placed not only on what you know and your own status but who you know and in turn who they know -"guangxi" meaning relationships. It must undoubtedly be fun to place huge bets and feel like James Bond at a baccarat table but – just as importantly – Carson would now be in a position to meet real movers and shakers in the VIP rooms on the upper floors. Carson's first venture to the "high rollers" world of gambling

---

36. *HKSAR v Yeung Ka-Sing, Carson DCCC860 of 2011 (DJ Douglas Yau) para 410*

was at the "Neptune" VIP room in the old Lisboa casino. He was given a credit line of HK$10M[37] (about £800,000), and would draw HK$2M-3M in "mud chips" to gamble each time. Mud chips can only be used for gambling, they cannot be cashed out and junket operators who sell the mud chips are paid a commission. If Carson won his bet, he would be paid out in "cash chips" which could then be cashed out or used to buy more mud chips to continue gambling. If he lost, he would have to replenish his casino account by transferring more funds into it.

In three weeks in December 2004 and January 2005, according to his evidence Carson had what must have been his luckiest streak ever playing baccarat. The prosecution produced evidence which showed that he had banked HK$62.5M (about £5M) in three weeks – all cash cheques issued by the casino operator SJM – and, according to Carson, all winnings from the tables.[38] When asked how he became such a successful gambler, Carson testified that he "gambled as if it was a business."[39] Never one to be daunted by volatility and high risk, Carson maintained that he had been staking pots of money on the baccarat tables and as he had in the stock market he had struck lucky, picking the right times to place his chips on the table.

Carson received this money in a series of cheques issued to him over a period of about three weeks. When asked in court why he had received four cheques issued to him by SJM on the same day – 22 December 2004 – Carson explained that it was possibly because at that time in his gambling he had been serviced by different junkets and he might have had cheques issued to him from different chip rollers – who were the individual people who sold the "mud chips" – in various rooms.[40] It was also pointed out to Carson by the prosecution that although he claimed to be an avid gambler, these were the only cheques issued to him by SJM that showed up in the 5 disputed accounts.

Carson then told the court he had won HK$20-30M[41] from 2004 to 2008, and he was paid by a process of "off-setting" where his winnings were

37. Ibid para 411
38. Ibid para 345
39. Aaron Tam, "Birmingham City owner Carson Yeung guilty of money laundering", AFP, 4 March, 2014
40. HKSAR v Yeung Ka-Sing, Carson DCCC860 of 2011 (DJ Douglas Yau) para 346
41. Ibid para 347

transferred to an investment account he held in Macau with the casinos.

There had been a change in the law in Macau that meant cash cheques could no longer be issued by the casinos and as personal cheques took as long as a week to clear it made sense to Carson to be paid in this way.

Carson's explanations were dissected and taken apart in District Court Judge Douglas Yau's judgement following the money laundering trial. The logic the judge employs – that having won such a large sum of money in one go would surely be a memorable event in Carson's life; Carson's evidence that he couldn't remember why he was paid four large cheques on the same day was simply unbelievable[42] – is hard to criticise. The judge went on to find that Carson was lying as to the deposits being his winnings, that he didn't know the real reason behind or the source for the deposits and he couldn't and needn't speculate in finding him guilty of the charges.

Carson also confirmed that HK$10M[43] issued to his father's account in 2006 by SJM was from his gambling winnings, and that he had asked for it to be paid into his father's account to repay a loan that he owed his father. Further cross-examination revealed that HK$6.9M of that sum was then transferred to Carson's account to cover a problem with his own account, with his father's consent.[44] Again, the truth of the evidence was discounted by the judge.

Another casino Carson had dealings with was called Greek Mythology, at the New Century Hotel in Macau. Hong Kong Cantonese-language magazine East Week [45] claimed that Carson partnered Ng Man-sun, also known as "Street Market Wai", in an investment in the casino in 2004 through the listed company Amax Holdings, boosting the stock price through speculating on the stock and earning Carson more than HK$100M. "Street Market Wai" had seen his casino riddled with bullets in 1997[46] by a gang led by the legendary triad gangster "Broken Tooth" Wan Kuok-koi.

42. Ibid para 577
43. Ibid para 428
44. Ibid paras 431-432
45. East Week Magazine, 11 March 2011
46. John Garnaut "Macau's seedy casino war turns to gold" Sydney Morning Herald, 22 September, 2009

As Carson won plenty of money playing in the VIP rooms, he came to the attention of the people who ran them. There is no doubt that he would have made quite an impression on his fellow gamblers with his extravagant clothes and his ostentatious style – but clearly he was a man riding his luck, and one prepared to take chances. Luck is a predominant theme in Chinese culture – lucky people are seen as the right business partners and will be sought out by those looking to maximise their luck by associating themselves with successful people. Carson's luck was not a cause of annoyance for the casino owners by taking their money from the house, rather he was liked and respected as a successful gambler. They made him a proposition - would he like the opportunity to make even more money than he had on the tables by crossing over and joining the house by investing in the business of the VIP rooms? Once again Carson jumped at the chance – it was time for Carson to join the ranks of the junket operator in the early part of 2005.

Macau attracts almost all of its custom from the mainland, as many forms of gambling are illegal in the People's Republic of China. Millions of tourists cross the border – up from 800,000 in 1999 when China resumed sovereignty over Macau to 17M in 2013[47] - each year to gamble their savings in the casinos trying to make it big; however, due to foreign exchange restrictions, punters can only take a small amount of money across the border to be spent in Macau. For rich people, this presented a problem: how do you live the life of the high roller if you can't take your cash with you to spend?

Enter the junket operator. With such restrictions in place, casinos are wholly reliant on junket operators for their business with the high rollers, to be able to extend credit, to deal with offshore receipts and payments from mainlanders who otherwise cannot transfer currency out of the country. Junket operators purchase chips from the casinos which they then sell on to the high-rolling mainlanders, also ensuring their travel arrangements are first class and their stay in Macau is as comfortable as possible in the best hotels and they are looked after at every turn; after all, a happy punter is a returning punter.

47. Jonathan Kaiman *"Macau is betting on a new kind of Chinese Tourism" The Guardian, 5 January 2014*

As gambling debts are unenforceable by law in the People's Republic, junket operators are forced to operate on the fringes of legitimate business. Like the old fashioned bookmakers in England, they have to exercise somewhat extra-judicial means to recover bad debts. The potential for high profits in a legal grey area and with the occasional need to be able to bring in muscle when necessary has made junket operations in Macau a target for organised crime. In China, organised crime is run by the triads – a collection of various "societies" organised on similar lines to the mafia or the yakuza; a hierarchy of gangsters with a boss at the top and a legion of foot-soldiers who are known as "followers". Competition between triad societies is fierce and often deadly; especially when such enormous profits are at stake. In 2012, Macau had gambling revenues of US$38BN and, according to testimony in June 2013 before a US Congressional Commission, 75% of that was from junket operators believed to have triad connections.[48]

In 2005, a colleague of Au Yeung's by the name of Cheung Chi-tai, who is also a suspected triad boss, approached Carson. Cheung Chi-tai was a major shareholder[49] in the junket operator the Neptune Group, a listed company in Hong Kong, which ran VIP rooms in the Sands and Venetian casinos in Macau amongst others and also operated gambling ships in international waters outside the jurisdictions of the PRC and Hong Kong. Carson was also introduced to one of Neptune's largest shareholders, a man by the name of Lin Cheuk-fung. Lin owned a large stake in the company but Carson claimed he needed someone with expertise like Carson to help him run it. For an investment of HK$26.4M, he offered Carson 20% in the junket operator and later that year 20% of his share in the Neptune VIP Club, in Macau's Casino Lisboa for HK$20M. Considering the way he ran the BIH business later in his career there is a certain irony that his expertise was so sought after at this time.

---

48. Christine Duhaime "Hong Kong – organised crime visits the film set of Transformers 4 for alleged extortion and other thoughts on triads and money laundering" Duhaime's Anti-Money Laundering Law in Canada, 24 October, 2013
49. Matt Isaacs and Reuters Staff "Special Report: High Rollers, triads, and a Las Vegas Giant" Reuters, 29 March 2010

Lin's brother Lin Cheuk-chiu, also known as Lian Zhuozhao was claimed by Chinese magazine Caijing[50] to be the real power behind Neptune. Lian was alleged by the magazine to have laundered large sums of money for high profile individuals on the mainland through "underground banks" in Macau, including a massive RMB800M (about £79M) for the chairman of GOME Group, Huang Guangyu. Huang, was once named the richest person in China by the Shanghai based Hurun Report with a personal fortune of US$6.3BN was jailed for fourteen years in 2010 for stock market manipulation, with the Beijing Court finding him guilty of "illegal business dealings" and insider trading as well as bribing or inciting others to bribe five government officials. Huang was also linked to the disgraced politician Bo Xilai whose wife was jailed for the murder of British businessman Neil Heywood, and who has alleged links to VIP gaming rooms which were operated by Lian in Macau – such as Neptune.[51]

Lian was implicated in 2001[52] in an anti-smuggling crackdown led by Zheng Shandong in Guangdong Province. Zheng had shot to fame in 1998 when he caught the kidnapper of billionaire Li Ka-shing's eldest son but during this investigation he was bribed by Lian according to the court in Xi'an, China. Zheng, who at the time was deputy head of the public security department of Guangdong assisted Lian to evade prosecution according to the court judgement. Some years later Zheng would become assistant to the security minister Zhou Yongkang, one of the most powerful men in China, who had also been implicated in the GOME Group investigation. It's not known if Lian was convicted or sentenced in 2001 and there is no indication whether he was investigated in the aftermath of the Carson court case either. With the chief investigating officer Gloria Yu confirming the source and location of much of the money involved in Carson's trial is still unknown, it would make sense if Lin Cheuk-fung, his brother, and the numerous other depositors to the five accounts were at least asked some probing questions.

50. Steven Stradbrooke "Junket Operator Neptune Group linked to Bo Xilai Corruption Allegations" calvinayre.com 27 February, 2013
51. Jason Dean and Jeffrey Ng "Ex Gome Chairman Sentenced to 14 years in prison", Wall Street Journal, 18 May, 2010
52. Shai Oster and Simon Lee "Jailed Birmingham City Owner Shows China Shadow Bank Link", Bloomberg, 7 March, 2014

It is rumoured that an arrest warrant was issued for Cheung Chi-tai along with seventeen other individuals shortly before Carson's conviction, which ensured he cannot return to Hong Kong for a while.

Zhou Yongkang also became implicated in corruption proceedings in the mainland in what was to be the highest profile arrest in the Communist Party since the Cultural Revolution. His connections to Carson will be considered later.

When Lin made Carson the offer, the former hairdresser jumped at the chance of investing in Neptune. Carson's evidence in court was that he sold his stake in another company called Prosper eVision[53] to finance the deal in early 2005. It wasn't picked up in court but the evidence given by Carson doesn't appear to stack up. Carson said that he made a deal to sell 15% of stock code 979 to a gentleman named Tam Kam Wing, a Dongguan businessman. Prosper eVision indeed was once listed on the HKSE with the number 979 but changed its name in June 2003 to China Nan Feng Group Limited.[54] Furthermore, there were no transactions disclosed to the stock exchange for this number of shares, which would have been clearly reportable because of the size of shareholding allegedly transferred.[55] The only entity connected with 979 at that time through any significant number of shares was Pollyanna Chu's Kingston Securities.

Carson also invested in Golden Resorts group, a junket operator in Macau and also the holding company of Kingston Securities. Carson owned more than 5% in the company in 2007[56] but sold the majority of his shareholding by the end of that year. Stock market filings suggest he retains a small stake in the company.

---

53. HKSAR v Yeung Ka-sing, Carson DCCC860 of 2011, (DJ Douglas Yau) para 440
54. Webb-site.com
55. HKSE filings
56. HKSE filings

Carson's testimony in court was that he moved the money needed for the investment in Neptune from the purported sale of his Prosper eVision shares via both Hong Kong and the mainland and got it transferred to Lin where he needed it in Hong Kong and mainland China.[57] Lin was to hold his shares in Neptune in trust so that Lin remained one of the largest shareholders and Carson's name would not be disclosed in stock market filings. It was a convoluted deal; Carson and his father invested money in the Neptune Group company as a stock market investment but also made loans to the informal syndicate "Neptune Club" to gain a share of its profit and interest.

On being pressed in cross-examination as to why his name didn't appear on the share register Carson explained to the Court that he was a "shareholder behind the scenes[58]"; it would appear from stock market filings that the largest shareholder was disgraced former legislator Chim Pui-chung. On being reminded of his right not to give answers that may incriminate him, Carson refused to answer further questions on this topic for fear of dropping himself in it further as a stock manipulator. In his judgement, Judge Yau said:

"Nevertheless it is my finding that the defendant, someone who had been trading in shares since he was eighteen years old and who had established a stock research company and participated in the analysis of stock investment in companies in Hong Kong, must have known that such behind the scene transactions without disclosure about his interest was inappropriate at best and illegal at worst.[59]"

The Neptune Club – which was not part of the listed company Neptune Group – was a syndicate that operated VIP rooms at the Lisboa. It was a syndicate of businessmen such as Cheung Chi-tai, Au Yeung and Lin with other investors like Carson adding liquidity for its credit facilities that it granted to the mainland punters. Around the time Carson was buying into the syndicate stock market filings made by China United International Holdings show that Eugene Chuang, whose name crops up several times in the judgement, was another potential investor, at one stage intending to

---

57. *HKSAR v Yeung Ka-Sing, Carson DCCC860 of 2011 (DJ Douglas Yau) para 450*
58. *Ibid para 451*
59. *Ibid para 585*

purchase an eighty percent stake in the syndicate for HK$250M[60] – which didn't come out in the trial as it appears he never completed the transaction. Chuang was also connected to a stockbroking firm called Chung Nam Securities via his brother Henry, who chaired its ultimate holding company. It was through Eugene's personal intervention in 2002 that Carson was apparently given leeway on a HK$2M margin call by Chung Nam Securities – a decision that, according to the prosecution in Carson's trial, saved the former hairdresser from bankruptcy.

In another connection to Carson, Chuang deposited four sums in a total of HK$2.69M into Carson's bank account from his own personal account. Carson claimed that the money related to the "matching or off-setting of the sums with respect of the shares[61]" that they might have made on share dealing together and they were personal investments. That evidence directly contradicted evidence given by one of Carson's expert witnesses, Ian Robinson, who said that it "was a loan arrangement between the defendant [Carson] and Eugene Chuang[62]". The judge found in his judgement that he believed Carson was lying in this regard.

The whole Neptune deal appears incredibly complex and inter-connected. As Carson described in court how he paid the money in and how the money came back to him during his evidence, it was difficult for onlookers to follow – apparently he had invested in three separate companies and was paid out loan repayments, dividends and interest by various members of the Casino staff, often from their private bank accounts and also from those of various "subsidiary companies". One thing that is certain is that Carson (and his father) were paid considerable sums of money from Macau from what – on the face of it – was a "small" investment which he claimed turned him from a prosperous man to a very wealthy one. In his ruling the judge emphasises that such transactions would give "the reasonable man" doubt about the origin of the money involved.[64]

60. *China United International Holdings Announcement, 15 March 2005*
61. *HKSAR v Yeung, Ka-Sing Carson DCCC860 of 2011 (DJ Douglas Yau) para 491*
62. *Ibid, para 492*
63. *Ibid para 628*
64. *Ibid, paras 596 and 599*

This is where the prima facie allegations of money laundering against Carson originated; he had no paperwork to document the track of the money or why he received the considerable sums he did; this lack of a paper trail was a constant theme in Carson's career. Having said that, the delay in prosecuting him and bringing the charges certainly resulted in the relevant banking and financial institutions destroying some supporting documents after seven years in the normal course of banking business. In the Neptune case this wasn't an issue – those events happened in 2005, only six years before Carson's arrest – something the judge noted in his reasons for judgement.

The Neptune deal would cause further problems for Carson down the line. Cheung Chi-tai wasn't just a successful businessman. He was known as "Tsung Pau" or "the Explosive Money Maker" in Hong Kong and Macau, and he was alleged to have been a leader of the Wo Hop To society of triads. In 2009, Cheung[65] was named in the High Court of Hong Kong as the mastermind behind a plot to beat up and potentially murder a chip dealer by the name of Wong Kam-ming, who had introduced Siu Yun-ping – the so called "Yuen Long God of Gambling" – to a VIP room run by Cheung Chi-tai. The beating came after Siu, a man who was described by his peers as an "inveterate gambler"[66] had vast wins at the Neptune VIP room and allegations of cheating were being made against him. Charges against Cheung Chi-tai were eventually dropped due to insufficient evidence, although other people involved in the plot were given prison sentences ranging from eight and a half to fourteen years. Cheung Chi-tai disappeared back to Macau and his name quietly disappeared from Neptune Group files. The Hong Kong listed company refused to acknowledge that Cheung had ever been connected with the company when various news organisations in the USA including Reuters picked up on the links after court transcripts from the attempted murder trial came to light.

65. Matt Isaacs and Reuters Staff "Special Report: High Rollers, triads and a Las Vegas Giant", Reuters, 29 March 2010
66. Evan Osnos "The God of Gamblers" New Yorker, 9 April, 2012

One of the principal transactions covered in those hearings was the purchase by Neptune of a company called Walden, which owned a gambling ship. The ship, a former Russian cruise liner, was to be refitted with casino accoutrements and would then head out into international waters where the punters could gamble without worrying about the legal ramifications. According to Next Media, the ship was previously owned by Ye Shou, who was alleged to be Cheung Chi-tai's boss in the Wo Hop To triad society and has known Chim Pui-chung for more than thirty years. Ye had been lying low during Carson's court case so as not to bring attention to himself and denied any connections to Carson. At a birthday party held in a restaurant at the Shun Tak centre near the Macau ferry terminal, he refused to be interviewed by reporters who wanted to talk to ask him about his connections to the ongoing corruption scandals surrounding Lian Zhuozhao and his brother, along with the rumours of the arrests of others surrounding Carson's case.

Back in 2005, this was all a long way ahead and Carson was happy at that time with his investment that was making big money. As revealed in court, various people would send Carson money as the "returns" on his investment to his various accounts in Hong Kong. Carson went from being prosperous to rich, with a big house on The Peak, cars, boats and a substantial house in an exclusive area of London.

Having heard Carson's evidence in court, the lack of documentation about his dealings in Macau does lead to the conclusion that there is much more to his story than he revealed. Nevertheless, it is up to the prosecution to prove its case; Carson should not have to prove his innocence, which we will explore in a later chapter. One thing is for sure though – Carson began his commercial career in Macau in 1997 as a fairly comfortable businessman; he finished it in 2008 extraordinarily rich – and according to him extraordinarily lucky.

3

THE FIRST BITE OF THE CHERRY

At the start of the 2007/08 season, the owners of Birmingham City were in a quandary. Although the club had managed to regain its Premier League status at the first time of asking, feelings within the boardroom were equivocal.

Relegation had been hard to take in 2006 after a decent outlay on players, and it had been a real grind to achieve promotion despite heavy backing in the transfer market and high wages having to be forked out. On the pitch, 2006/2007 had started off as a rough season. Still smarting after relegation and taking a 7-0 thumping at home from Liverpool in the FA Cup, Steve Bruce wasn't the most popular manager around at the time. Blues were expected to rebound to the top flight straight away but the football was more dour than entertaining, more gritty than glittering and relied on wins being ground out rather than beating teams at a canter with any panache.

The fans in the Tilton had seen enough by the middle of the campaign. For the first time there were audible murmurings of discontent on the terraces and they sung for Bruce's head after a particularly bad performance when losing 1-0 at home to Norwich City midway through the season. The local phone-ins after the match were inundated with fans fuming about the team under-performing and calling for a change in manager; indeed, there were already rumours within the club that Bruce was contemplating walking and that the board was preparing to give him the Spanish archer and bring in someone else.

A flukey win against Derby County in the next game saved Bruce; a goal from a shot that deflected off about three defenders was the difference between the sides and the team managed to fashion a run following that game to advance into the automatic promotion places and achieve promotion at the first attempt. It had been a tough season, a slog, but Bruce had delivered and the team were back in the top flight.

For David Sullivan, however, enough was enough. The relegation season had been a tough campaign for the Welsh supremo and when Blues eventually fell out of the division Sullivan and the rest of the board had to suffer the extra ignominy of club captain Kenny Cunningham's complaints to the press[67] about the way the club had been run, emotionally declaring that the soul had been ripped out of it. Cunningham predicted that Sullivan and the rest of the board wouldn't be missed when they eventually left the club – a comment that was echoed by some fans[68] who wrote to the local newspaper to agree with the Irish defender's outspoken opinion.

The truth was that there was an air of staleness around the club. The board were into their fifteenth year at the helm and although they were running the club on an even keel, with a tight rein, fans were decrying the board's lack of ambition. Promotion had been achieved – it was now not so much about getting there but more about staying there and pushing on in that division – which was predictably going to cost further investment that the current board weren't happy to sanction. It had been a monumental gamble to even get the club to that stage – had promotion not been achieved there is no doubt that Sullivan and his cohorts would have been forced to rein in their spending on wages, which would have had a detrimental effect on the composition and standard of the team and years of rebuilding in the Championship.

Steve Bruce was a man on borrowed time too; after five years at the helm, he was struggling to grow the team from a team of gritty battlers to one that could play with style and verve; the lack of excitement was turning people away from attending the games and apathy was slowly returning in the fewer numbers left on the terraces. Value for money was a big issue with the fans, as ticket prices were high in comparison to other clubs because the board looked to maximise income from gate receipts. Although Blues fans of old had been used to the club struggling in the lower echelons of the football league, the newer breed were used to a bit more – and to maintain the standard required to survive in the Premier League the club needed to hang on to every season ticket holder it could.

67. *BBC Sport 11 May 2006*
68. *L Wilkins, "Your Shout: Kenny Cunningham was right all along", Birmingham Mail, 28 July 2006*

The club had a triumvirate in its senior management with Sullivan along with the two Gold brothers David and Ralph; but it was the Welshman Sullivan who was the real driving force at the helm of the club and who made the key decisions. With his two young children to think of – Sullivan had infamously told the press he didn't want to "spend his children's inheritance"[69] – and openly dreading the drive up to Birmingham from his Theydon Bois mansion every week, Sullivan decided during the 2006/2007 season in the Championship that it was time for some discreet enquiries to be made to see if anyone would be interested in taking on the club.

It was only when promotion had been achieved that interest appeared in the form of Carson Yeung. Carson had been looking for an investment in English football, having made enquiries at Sheffield United and Reading without success. One of his business colleagues – William Chan Wai-keung, who was later to become a director of BIH – was friendly with the investment banker Keith Harris of Seymour Pierce. It just so happened that Harris knew of a sleeping giant for sale at a reasonable price. And so Carson met Sullivan in mid-2007 and immediately showed an interest in Birmingham City.

Another friend of Carson, Sammy Yu Wai-ying, had taken Carson to St Andrew's to watch a game discreetly, and Carson loved what he saw. Like Carson, Yu was a football nut but he had also played semi-professionally in Hong Kong as a young man. Yu knew how to sell the idea to Carson – here was a club with a decent-sized ground and a hard core of passionate fans crying out for investment; they would surely love a rich benefactor who would pump millions into buying players and give him the adoration he craved. A club with an untapped fanbase in the large Chinese community within close proximity. A deal was promptly hatched in June 2007.

Carson couldn't afford to buy the whole club straight away, so an interim offer was made to the Birmingham board – Carson (and his corporate vehicle Grandtop) would buy 29.9% of the club immediately at 61.331p[70]

69. Graham Hill "Blues in serious financial mess; exclusive: Sullivan bombshell",
   Sunday Mercury, 7 May 2006
70. Grandtop Announcement, 29 June 2007

a share (which represented a fair profit to Sullivan and co), take a month or two to get his feet under the table and finances sorted out in Hong Kong and then buy the remainder of the club before Christmas 2007. Sullivan would be able to bail out to a richer businessman – fulfilling a promise he had made the fans – and the deal would see him considerably better off than when he bought the club. It seemed win-win all the way around.

In order to make the purchase, Carson was to take control of a Hong Kong shell company called Grandtop International Holdings. Grandtop was an apparel manufacturer that had made its money by "renting out" its quota of textiles to be manufactured for export to the USA. It had fallen on hard times after quotas were scrapped and had no real business of note when Carson arrived. It was a "shell" that needed filling.

Grandtop had an eventful few months before Carson bought into the company. Stock graphs show that in the months immediately prior to purchasing the club the share price had jumped exponentially, rising from around HK$0.12 a share at the start of the year to a high of HK$1.84 per share on 17 July, 2007 – three days before Carson became a director of Grandtop.

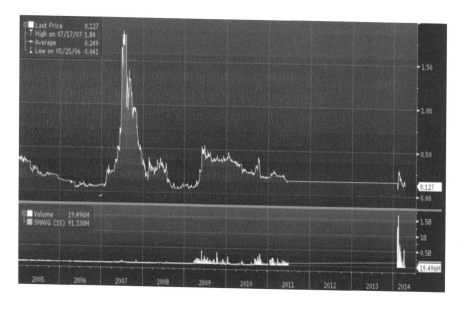

At that time, there were far fewer shares available – Vico Hui Ho-luek bought 64M and his wife Leung Choi Fan bought 12.65M shares on 6 February 2007 off-exchange for HK$0.121 per share, which equated to 16.67% and 3.29% of the company respectively – in four months those shares were worth fifteen times that. When Carson bought into the company on 20 June 2007, buying 115.2M shares via his Great Luck Management investment vehicle for HK$0.57 a share, he took a 16.67% stake that within a month would treble in value. With those sorts of jumps in prices, it's easy to understand why there were rumours of stock manipulation surrounding Grandtop at the time of their initial purchase into Birmingham City.

The idea to buy a football club was driven almost exclusively by Carson. The Grandtop board were unsure – was there money to be made in this deal? The original concept of taking over Grandtop was to own a publicly-listed vehicle in which they could tap the public for funds and make commercial investments in Hong Kong and China – the idea of owning a football club hadn't really occurred to them. Yu provided back-up and Carson pushed the idea of buying a club with the board of Grandtop, carefully explaining that if they could sell the idea of owning their own Premier League football club to the Hong Kong (and by extension Chinese) public, profits were bound to be made.

When questioned during his trial why he had invested in the club, Carson expanded further on this idea saying:

"I love to watch football a lot and I thought that Chinese football was not up to the standard yet. It was my intention to set up fifty football schools in China because Chinese parents can only have one child and every pair of parents give much care and concern to their child. Kids go to school and learn to play football. The Chinese market is enormous.

After kids have grown up they could be sent to Birmingham. That was my consideration and why I bought an English Premier League club."[71]

The Grandtop board agreed the deal would be done.

71. Thomas Chan "Carson Yeung planned mainland soccer empire, he tells money laundering trial" South China Morning Post, 22 October, 2013

Grandtop announced to the HKSE on 29 June 2007 that it would purchase 29.9% of Birmingham City PLC, the parent company of the football club. Grandtop came up with some of the money for the deal by selling 115M shares at HK$0.57[72] to Carson, giving him a 16.7% stake in Grandtop, raising HK$65.4M. From this day forward Carson's stake in Grandtop (which later changed its name to BIH) never crossed the magic 30% barrier which would have triggered a general offer. One may wonder how he would keep control of the holding company, as he didn't appear to have a controlling interest, but there is no doubt he was in complete control of Grandtop.

The rest of the funds required for this purchase came from Carson himself, who agreed to put up a bridging loan of HK$250M to Grandtop to ensure sufficient funds were available to complete the purchase of the stake in the club. He also undertook that should the shareholders of Grandtop reject the deal at a Special General Meeting, he would indemnify the company and fund the purchase of the shares in full himself. According to the company's announcement, funds to do the deal were to come from third party financing and internal resources of the company. Of course, the shareholders acquiesced, and Grandtop went through with the deal. It was revealed in November 2013[73] in court that Kingston Finance had made a personal loan to Carson which he had then passed on to Grandtop of HK$140M to complete the transaction.

Grandtop named longtime friend of Carson ex-Liverpool, Real Madrid and England star Steve McManaman[74] to the board on 3 July, along with ex-footballers Christian Karembeu[75] in August and Fan Zhiyi[76] in November.

Carson himself was finally named to the Grandtop board on the 20 July [77] – some three weeks after the initial offer to buy the club was put to

---

72. *HKSE Filings*
73. *Thomas Chan "Carson Yeung lost HK$15.4m in stocks: prosecution", South China Morning Post,*
    6 November, 2013
74. *Grandtop Announcement, 3 July, 2007*
75. *Grandtop Announcement, 7 August, 2007*
76. *Grandtop Announcement, 5 November, 2007*
77. *Grandtop Announcement, 20 July, 2007*

shareholders and four days after due diligence was completed. Carson had been careful not to show his cards too early, having installed his friend Lee Yiu Tung to the holding company board first in 2006 and not actually taking full management control of the company until the deal was well under way.

For the fans, it was all a bit of a whirlwind. Out of nowhere this "billionaire" Chinese businessman had waltzed in, whacked down a wad of cash and landed a deal to buy the club. Bored with Sullivan, and tired of the propaganda fed to the press by media-hungry board members who only cared about how many more column inches they could elicit than their colleagues, the fans in the main quickly warmed to the deal. They had already seen the money splashed around at Manchester City and other clubs and they wanted some of that; it was about time someone invested in the club and lavished it with attention rather than treating it as a cash cow business and the fans as just customers.

Not much was known about Carson at this point. Even in Hong Kong, he was a bit of an enigma: a report in the South China Morning Post (SCMP) around this time recalls that one person said the following after seeing Carson at a publicity event: "He looked like a shrewd businessman in his 50s, but strangely, he never gives out his business card."[78] Given Carson's appetite for making contacts (and indeed that is the culture in Hong Kong and China) and building relationships, it seems odd that he was reluctant to offer his contact details to anyone.

Deals that seem too good to be true usually are, and so it proved in this case. While suspicions were raised in Birmingham when Carson failed to complete the full buyout by Christmas, it wasn't until the court hearings nearly six years later that any light was shed on the process. There had long been talk of shadowy figures operating behind Carson's back but no one had any real idea who these figures could be; a lot of speculation pointed to Pollyanna Chu whose Kingston Securities vehicle was heavily linked to Carson and the purchase of Birmingham City.

---

78. Neil Gough and Ben Kwok "The man behind the Birmingham bid", South China Morning Post, 29 June, 2007

In his expert witness report admitted in evidence in the money laundering trial, expert accounting witness Mark Pulvirenti confirmed HK$36.422M transferred to a firm of solicitors in England called Prince Evans came from the accounts in question and was used towards the purchase of the club. Carson disputed this in his own evidence, saying that the money was used to buy his house in London. In his judgement, Judge Yau disagreed, and said this:

"One example is the use of the HK$36.422 million which was paid to Prince Evans Solicitors in the UK. Mr Pulvirenti stated in his report that the money was for the purchase of Birmingham City FC while the defendant said it was for the purchase of a property in London. The defendant's evidence was that he had never told Mr Pulvirenti about the use of the money. Given that one of the grounds put forward by the defence as to the unlikelihood that the defendant would be doing such a high profile purchase of an English premiere [sic] league football club if he was engaged in money laundering, the purchase of the football club must have been one of the main concern[s] of the defendant's expert and it is inconceivable that he did not ask the defendant about it. It is even more inconceivable that Mr Pulvirenti would make up the fact that the money to the solicitors was for the purchase of the football club without anyone instructing him that it was so."[79]

Evidence was led at the trial that the HK$36.422M transferred to Prince Evans was made up of a series of deposits made to Carson's accounts including HK$18M from the alleged triad Cheung Chi-tai, which Carson maintained was a repayment of a loan to him. The fact that a significant sum of money – around £1.5M - towards the purchase of the club was found to have originated from someone who is named as a triad boss in court has very worrying implications for Birmingham City fans.

There is further evidence that funds received by Carson for his other business projects were from questionable sources and then dealt with in a way that didn't seem to be above board. In a Market Misconduct Tribunal hearing

79. *HKSAR v Yeung Ka-Sing, Carson DCCC860 of 2011 (DJ Douglas Yau), para 625*

in 2011[80] concerning dealings in the shares of ABC Communications (Holdings) Limited between 31 March 2008 and 2 May 2008, it emerged that Carson had received HK$35M from Vico Hui – Chief Executive Officer of Grandtop/BIH – who had in turn been advanced the money by a company called China Water. China Water had transferred the money to Vico to invest in water projects on the mainland but it ended up in Carson's accounts and strangely in a casino account in Macau held on Carson's behalf. The money was repaid to China Water within a month – although it was repaid from Grandtop, not from Carson's accounts. Vico was paid a fraction short of HK$1M extra, supposedly for arranging the advance.

In these times of serious anti-money laundering laws in parallel with the exponential growth of foreign investment in English football clubs, it does seem strange that an absolute unknown could buy a major club in such an apparently unregulated manner. Fingers could be pointed at Seymour Pierce for not caring about the background of the potential owner before introducing him to Sullivan and the Gold brothers. Indeed, Keith Harris was equally careless five years later when introducing a potential new owner Laurence "Bankrupt Baz" Bassini to Birmingham City in 2012. In March 2013 Mr Bassini was banned from any involvement in football for three years as a result of his improper dealings at Watford in 2011/12.[81]

Prospective owners who wish to buy a club are required to complete a self-certified form for the Premier League/Football League if they are either to become a director or own more than 30% of a football club.[82] The prospective buyer has to self-certify that he/she has no criminal history with respect to financial dealings, is not under any sanction from another sporting body and has not been involved in any previous football club insolvencies. Of course, at this point Carson didn't fall foul of any of those conditions – he has never owned more than about 28% of Grandtop, or Birmingham International Holdings as it became known on 9 December 2009 - let alone its subsidiary the football club; additionally, even more pertinent at this point is that

80. *The report of the Market Misconduct Tribunal into dealings in the shares of ABC Communications (Holdings) Limited on and between 31 March 2008 and 2 May 2008*
81. David Conn *"Watford's former owner banned from football for three years"*, The Guardian, 18 March, 2013

Carson was still only an investor, as he had initially been refused a seat on the board of the football club for him or any of his nominees.[83]

A parallel case involving Massimo Cellino[84] in his now successful efforts to take over Leeds United shows the worthlessness of the test; having served a suspended sentence in his native Italy for a false accounting offence in 2001, a conviction that was considered spent under the Rehabilitation of Offenders Act 1974, and therefore disclosure was not even required on the form. This was further compounded when he was convicted of tax fraud in March 2014 – an offence Cellino claimed was not "an offence of dishonesty" which has been upheld by a Q.C. after the Football League initially found him not "fit and proper" pending a further judgement from the Italian courts.

The test defines a disqualifying condition as "having an unspent conviction (or where the Rehabilitation of Offenders Act 1974 does not apply for any reason, having a conviction within the period that would have rendered that conviction unspent had the provisions of that Act applied) for offences including dishonesty, corruption and perverting the course of justice."

As the deal stagnated after Carson's failure to complete by Christmas 2007, tempers started to rise against him. David Sullivan was scathing of Carson's attempt to buy the club, venting his feelings in the local newspaper as the fans' emotions were stretched from happiness at anticipating the prospective purchase to slowly growing more distrustful before reverting to outright disdain.[85] They were stuck with the status quo for the time being. Like an unhappy marriage where neither side could obtain the divorce they so crave, Blues fans were stuck with Sullivan and he was stuck with them.

Matters weren't helped on the pitch either. Sullivan was a shrewd operator and knew Bruce was still a manager in demand having ground his way to promotion. He thought that offering a new deal to the Geordie manager

82. *The Football League "Owners & Directors Test & Publication of Ownership" retrieved 3 February, 2014*
83. *Colin Tattum "Karren Brady spells it out for Carson Yeung", Birmingham Mail, 21 February, 2008*
84. *"Cellino argues convictions 'spent' as he attempts to take over Leeds", The Herald, 4 February, 2014*
85. *"Sullivan Raises Yeung Concerns", Metro, 27 October, 2007*

with an increased compensation clause would be smart business because – should another club want to come in for the manager – they would have to pay through the nose for him.

Out of professional courtesy, once the contract terms had been sorted out Sullivan offered it to Carson and Grandtop for their final approval – after all, they would be taking control of the club shortly (or so it was thought). Carson decided that he would much rather deal with new contract negotiations with Steve Bruce himself rather than approve something Sullivan had done, and vetoed it.

Bruce was not impressed at all by this development and, mirroring the manager's frustration, the team's form took a nosedive. In November 2007 Wigan Athletic owner Dave Whelan, who had long been an admirer of Bruce and instinctively knew that the poor form that the Blues were showing was temporary, saw the opportunity to take Bruce to Wigan's JJB Stadium. He knew Bruce was a good manager and would be the man to turn around Wigan's fortunes. Knowing things were fractious at St Andrew's, Whelan made a move to install his former manager in the Wigan hotseat, asking the Blues board how much compensation they wanted for losing the Geordie.

Sullivan didn't want to lose Bruce in the short term – he also knew that Bruce was a safe pair of hands and only going through a temporary glitch, with the team having won only three games in thirteen from the start of the 2007/08 season. He decided to give Whelan an exorbitant figure to put him off. Sullivan had miscalculated the value of the admiration Whelan had for Bruce and when the Welshman demanded £3M for his faithful manager believing that Whelan would baulk, he promptly found his bluff called.[86]

Some might think that the move was disappointing, but from a dispassionate stance it was a good one for the club. Bruce was unpopular with some fans and the truth was he couldn't take the club any further; the team had gone a

86. Matt Lawton, "Wigan's £3m tempts Birmingham to release Bruce", Daily Mail, retrieved 5 February, 2014

bit stale under his stewardship and a change had probably been needed for some time. Sullivan had in some ways pulled off a master-stroke – rather than sacking the manager, having to pay him off and take flak from a section of the fans, he'd received a wad of cash, and had a scapegoat in Carson to blame for losing the boss; therefore he could move forward with someone new. It was most definitely a win-win situation for the Welshman.

Even that deal wasn't as straightforward as it should have been. Bruce's original press conference in which he was to be unveiled as Wigan's manager was postponed[87] after an argument about the image rights due to the manager – Blues had paid the full amount due under his contract up front when he signed it and wanted a pro-rated refund of what was attributable to the balance of his contract. As that impasse was sorted out, Bruce's coaching staff were held to virtual ransom by Birmingham City until Dave Whelan ponied up more money to take them with Bruce to the Latics, ending the fiasco once and for all.

With Autumn 2007 slowly waning and no sign of money appearing to complete the takeover, the "Chinese" were viewed with more and more distrust by the incumbent board and when it came to appointing a new manager Sullivan et al decided simple courtesy was no longer necessary; they'd do what they wished and leave the Chinese with a fait accompli if and when they ever came up with the cash to buy the club.

Sullivan decided on Scotland manager Alex McLeish as Bruce's replacement, came to a financial agreement with the Scottish FA – one that cost him less than he had received for Bruce – and appointed his man.

Carson and his pals were told they were no longer allowed in the boardroom at matches and even when they were admitted to an away boardroom at Middlesbrough by accident the friction was apparent. Despite owning a large chunk of Birmingham City – Grandtop were the largest single shareholder at that point – they had no control of the club and had been declared persona non grata by the incumbent board. Carson was forced to

---

87. Peter Ferguson and Neil Moxley, "Steve Bruce's switch to Wigan from Birmingham turns farcical", *Daily Mail, retrieved 5 February, 2014*

buy tickets and sit with the ordinary fans if he wanted to watch the football club his company substantially owned. It was a studied, calculated insult from Sullivan who felt wronged by the extended time Carson was taking to complete the purchase of the club. The insult would not be forgotten and would be repaid when Sullivan came with his new team West Ham United to St Andrew's a few seasons later, when Sullivan was advised he was not welcome in the Birmingham City boardroom for the game.[88]

All in all, Carson's attempt to buy Birmingham City had come crashing to a halt. The deadline of 15 December 2007 came and went and with it the first opportunity for Carson to buy the controlling interest in Birmingham City. For the fans, there was lots of talk of what would happen next; not only did we have a board who didn't want to be at the club, but we now had an investor we knew nothing about who had a big piece of a football club he couldn't do anything with and who couldn't even enter the boardroom.

With Carson unable to complete the deal, it left Grandtop at an impasse. It owned nearly 30% of a Premier League football club but had no control over its asset whatsoever. There was no revenue stream from Birmingham City as the club wasn't in a position to pay dividends to its shareholders. For Grandtop to be a profitable investment vehicle for Carson and his friends, money had to be made from other sources.

As 2008 began nothing had changed. Sullivan and the Gold brothers very much remained in control at St Andrew's. After the fiasco surrounding the departure of Steve Bruce, the incumbent board refused to seek the sanction of the Chinese for anything and were carrying on as they always had. It was business as usual for them and nothing that Carson or his cohorts said was going to change that.

Grandtop Holdings announced to the HKSE on 2 August 2007 that they would buy a stake in a PRC company Guangzhou Music Factory (GMF)[89].

88. Mark Ryan "David Sullivan declares a truce with Carson Yeung after stormy return to St Andrew's", Daily Mail, 8 November, 2010
89. Grandtop Announcement, 2 August, 2007

The agreement was complex; they were looking to buy a stake in one company using a newly incorporated subsidiary in China, with the aim of launching a chain of cafés and bars on the mainland.

It looked like an overly-complicated way of conducting business; the target company was being bought from three shareholders by a man called Chung Tat Fun who would then sell half to Grandtop. He would then have Grandtop's help in running the company, requiring a lot of company restructuring within the target business. The apparent reasoning behind this methodology according to people connected to Grandtop at the time was that Chung wanted to do a deal with a listed company to reduce any personal financial risk and, should the deal be successful, it would allow him to perform new ventures in the future.

The concept was for the cafés and bars to be themed with football memorabilia and paraphernalia – specifically related to Birmingham City. Chung would run the cafés on Grandtop's behalf and the profit would be split between the two 51%/49% in Grandtop's favour. With its large stake in Birmingham City, the Grandtop board wished to diversify its income base and grow the Birmingham City brand name.

Whether the cafés would ever have been popular is another question. There is undoubtedly a growing culture of western-style restaurants in China but promoting the Birmingham brand name?

Birmingham City wasn't exactly the most high profile of teams and were struggling in the Premier League at the time. Would the Chinese understand relegation and accept it as a matter of course?

The deal rumbled on for twelve months before Grandtop announced to the HKSE on 19 September 2008 that the proposal was dead[90]; Chung had not been able to solve the regulatory and legal problems needed to get the deal done to the satisfaction of Grandtop, which terminated the negotiations.

---

90. *Grandtop Announcement, 19 September, 2007*

According to people who were inside the company at the time, the reason behind the termination was that Carson had got cold feet and had bailed on the idea[91]. Carson had shared doubts that the venture would work with his fellow board members and had decided to end Grandtop's interest in it.

Another business interest Carson did pursue to fulfilment was the newspaper industry, by making an investment into the ailing Sing Pao in April 2008. He made a loan to the company of HK$60M[92] through a BVI company vehicle Billion Wealth, taking the shares owned by the major shareholder Strategic Media International as collateral. Carson hadn't been able to invest in the newspaper in the usual way because its shares had been suspended from trading since 2005.

As time went on SMI Publishing was unable to pay Carson back, so he took up the shares that had secured his loan and became the biggest shareholder in the company. In doing so he was forced to fight off a claim by businessman Peter Ong, who claimed Carson owed him money for introducing him to Sing Pao[93]. Ong is the younger brother of solicitor and former actress Mary Jean Reimer who was once an assistant solicitor to Andrew Lam Ping-cheung, a close confidante of Carson. Reimer is also alleged to have been behind an attack on Lam (through her mother, an alleged senior triad member) that left a five-inch scar down the right side of Lam's face[94].

91. *Name withheld, Personal Interview, August 2013*
92. *SMI Publishing Group Announcement, 24 April, 2008*
93. *Natalie Wong, "The Final Whistle?" HK Standard, 8 July, 2011*
94. *Albert Wong "Sex, scars and soured affairs" HK Standard, 1 April, 2006*

THE FIRST BITE OF THE CHERRY

4

THE BUYOUT

On 12 August 2009[95], Grandtop International Holdings made an announcement to the HKSE. After two years of sitting on the sidelines with no board representation, the single largest shareholder in the club was finally intending to complete the deal to purchase Birmingham City Football Club.

Within the walls of the Grandtop boardroom in the Shun Tak Centre overlooking Victoria harbour, there had been much discussion about what to do with its dysfunctional stake in the football club. The directors sat around the boardroom table considered the deadlines they had consistently breached and argued about who was to blame. At the head of the table Carson was very firm in his opinion that BIH should still buy the club. Other directors questioned whether there was any money to be made in football but Carson was insistent – the time had come to return cap in hand and buy the remainder of the BCFC shares.

It wasn't a popular decision. The only person at Grandtop who cared about football was Carson. Former footballer Sammy Yu was a big influence on Carson but he wasn't a director. Chief Executive Vico Hui was unsure about the deal, he couldn't see how money could be made from the club and was anxious for Grandtop to diversify its interests, but Carson was top dog and Grandtop were destined to buy the club.

For the incumbent board, this was an unexpected development. Things had looked grim for the club in April 2009, with promotion to the Premier League by no means certain after what had been an incredibly dour season of football under the equally dour Alex McLeish. Players' wages at the club were overblown by Championship standards, with Sullivan and co gambling on bouncing back up at the first attempt and the consequences of possible failure to do so were already being discussed – a player clear-out and operating costs would have to be slashed, which would make them even more unpopular[96] than they already were in Birmingham and would put paid to any chance of promotion at the second attempt.

---

95. *Grandtop Announcment, 12 August, 2009*
96. *James Nursey "Blue Murder; Takeovers all change at the top for Birmingham City and Portsmouth",*
    The Mirror, 7 October, 2009

The board were still looking for an exit but with an intransigent estranged party owning nearly a third of the club any deal would have to meet with their approval, so any sale to a third party would be difficult. The perfect solution would be to sell to Carson and Grandtop and when they came calling the BCFC board would have been expected to snap their hands off. Not the Welshman Sullivan, still smarting from their previous failure to complete the purchase of the club and believing Grandtop to be untrustworthy and still short of cash he pitched the deal at a whopping £1 a share, which on any reasonable basis was twice, if not three times what the club was worth. Would the Chinese bite?

Initially, no, William Chan Wai-keung, a member of the Grandtop board in charge of negotiations, tried to strike a deal at 80p a share[97] – still a significant premium – which may have clinched the deal; however, this was overruled by Carson who decided he was going to go for it at the price Sullivan wanted: £1 a share. It was either an amazingly stupid act of bravura by Carson; or he had an ulterior motive in forcing through the deal quickly which made the inflated premium paid immaterial. His motive in paying over the odds has never been revealed and the deal he sealed valued the club at £81.5M. In comparison, Randy Lerner paid £62.6M[98] for Birmingham City's hated rivals Aston Villa in 2006, who were an established Premier League club at the time.

On 21 August 2009[99], the Grandtop board confirmed to the HKSE that an offer had been made for the incumbent owners' controlling shareholding in the football club, and – as that took Grandtop's holding over the magic 30% threshold – a general offer had to be made for the remainder of the outstanding shares. Grandtop were intending to purchase the club outright and to delist it from the UK Alternative Investment Market (AIM). With an offer of £1 a share, the premium on the share price was tempting even to the most ardent and loyal fans who held the small number of shares publicly available in Birmingham City PLC.

97. Name withheld, Personal interview, October 2013
98. Chris Noon "Aston Villa Approves Billionaire's takeover", Forbes, 14 August, 2006
99. Grandtop Announcement, 21 August, 2009

David Sullivan openly bragged about how he had delivered incredible value for shareholders, many of whom had bought their shares at 25p or less and stood to make a handsome profit.

It was indeed an incredible coup for the Welshman and in some ways it demonstrates his shrewdness and luck. Many (rightly) criticised Sullivan at Birmingham for being a bit brusque in his media appearances and for not showing the ambition at Birmingham City that the club deserved (and which he has subsequently demonstrated at West Ham United), but there is no denying that Sullivan knew how to make a quid. He'd done well in liquidating many assets before the global financial crisis in 2008 and now he had sold an asset (whose value to anyone else apart from Carson would have been significantly lower as a result of the overhanging Grandtop shares) to the only possible bidder who would pay his grossly inflated price. Love him or loathe him, you cannot argue with his result and you have to admire his patience – especially in driving to Birmingham every week from his Essex mansion.

Within the next few weeks, offer documents were sent out and shareholding fans were able to accept what was an unexpected windfall. Sentimentality went out of the window; it was an offer the vast majority couldn't refuse. What was once almost a worthless bit of paper – the shares were trading at around 17p in the months prior to the sale – was now worth real money that could be used towards season tickets, the family holiday, a new car, or a fur coat.

There was a lot of talk among Blues fans who felt almost treacherous in accepting the offer. A few fans couldn't bear to be parted with the shares they owned and declined the deal, hoping that when the delisting came and the shares could be forcibly taken from them the Chinese would relent. As it turned out, the incoming board did indeed decide it wasn't worth the candle to force out the few remaining shareholders who wanted to keep their stake in the club and quietly left them to it. You should never look a gift horse in the mouth.

In the Chinese community of Birmingham it wasn't such an unexpected windfall; rumours had long been doing the rounds in the Chinese Quarter in the summer of 2009 that BIH were returning to complete the purchase of the club. Various members of the community had been given the nod that an offer was going to be made at a massive premium to the then current share price and anyone in the know was snapping up Birmingham City shares confident in the knowledge of a guaranteed profit.

Sullivan was no mug. He knew that the deal had been scuppered on the previous occasion by Carson's lack of cash, so it was money up front this time. He didn't care how Grandtop raised it; that was their problem. He wanted the readies in his bank account before he would do the business. No problem, said Carson.

A rights issue was launched by Grandtop to fund the deal and Carson went about taking up his allocation ensuring that his own stake wasn't diluted. It was repeatedly published that Kingston Securities[100] had financed a bridging loan of £57M – Vico Hui referred to it directly when interviewed by The Telegraph – to allow Grandtop to complete the deal before the rights issue was completed but this wasn't strictly accurate. The loan came from a company called Best China Ltd[101], which was owned by Pollyanna Chu, controlling shareholder of Kingston but not from Kingston Securities itself.

At this stage Carson owned less than 16% of the total issued shares of Grandtop but he still retained sufficient support from the other significant shareholders to remain chairman of the company. Other investors bought into the new shares under the rights issue, as the lure of owning a club in the richest league in the world seemed an attractive money making proposition to some: investors included a venture capital firm named Shenzhen Capital (Hong Kong) Ltd that bought a 2.5% stake[102] and Vico Hui, who purchased just over 5% through his British Virgin Islands investment vehicle Premier Rise Investments as the rights issue was fully subscribed.

100. Malcolm Moore "Carson Yeung's team hoping to unlock lucrative Chinese market for Birmingham City"
       Daily Telegraph, 26 August, 2009
101. Grandtop Announcement, 21 August, 2009
102. HKSE filings

This was to be a constant theme throughout Carson's tenure as Chairman of Grandtop/BIH. He never held a stake over the magic 30% barrier that would trigger a general offer but he exerted complete control over the company as if he owned it outright. One would have to assume that he was held in the utmost confidence by at least some of the more significant minority shareholders (including those who held less than 5%, which would otherwise require disclosures to be made to the HKSE) and it begs the question how many shares he really controlled.

Excitement was rising in Birmingham at the offer price for the club and Sullivan told the local press it was proof that Carson was going "to throw money at the club"[103]. Sullivan noted how Carson planned to bring in a football expert to help run the playing side of the club once he had taken over and was negotiating various sponsorship deals with Asian businesses in selling the deal as beneficial to the club and supporters. Whether he believed the rhetoric or not is another question; had he been blinded by the £ signs and deafened by the boos wanting him out, or did he truly believe Carson was as rich as he had made him out to be in the press?

Undeterred by his earlier failure to purchase the club, some fans were guardedly enthusiastic about Carson. The price of the club was hotly debated – after all, the offer rated Blues as more valuable than their local rivals Aston Villa, which – although ego-boosting for the fans – didn't make commercial sense. It was widely presumed Carson had paid possibly triple what the club was worth as the price for not completing the deal the first time around.

Some fans saw the premium as proof that Carson was indeed minted and that good times were just around the corner; others believed that Carson was being ripped off and was a bad businessman – or worse, that there was some nefarious reason for paying too much for the club. It is worth noting that one of the badges of money laundering is to pay too high a price for a seemingly legitimate purchase, although no one has yet been able to prove that the club itself was purchased with dodgy cash. After the previous experience, it seemed sensible not to believe in the sale until Carson was allowed back into the boardroom, having completed the deal.

103. Colin Tattum "Birmingham City; Carson Yeung tipped to start throwing money at Blues", Birmingham Mail, 19 September, 2009

Predictably, Sullivan et al couldn't leave without some sort of grand gesture and billboards[104] appeared around the city proclaiming their farewells after seventeen years at the club, although – with their classic commercial cynicism – their message was complimented by an advert for tickets for the next game. It seemed like a grandiose "well, we did what we could and now we're going – we know you will miss us soon enough"; the advert for the tickets just meant that the club paid for them to be thanked.

David Gold initially wanted to stay on to work with the new regime in some sort of board capacity[105] but the Chinese quickly decided (much to Gold's consternation) that they wanted to bring their own man in; Michael Dunford was appointed Chief Executive immediately[106]. He might not have believed it at the time, but it was probably better for him and the club that Gold walked away – there was a need for a clean break from the old regime and had he stayed there would inevitably have been a hangover of cynicism towards him from the start.

On 23 September 2009[107], Grandtop announced to the HKSE they had gained sufficient acceptances to guarantee the takeover of the club once the offer expired. Two days later an announcement was made confirming that Carson and Vico Hui had passed the "fit and proper person test" and would be sanctioned by the Premier League to become directors of the football club[108]. This was the first confirmation the deal would be ratified by the footballing authorities.

As discussed, the fit and proper person test administered by the Premier League was a self-certification form in which an applicant needs to confirm along with other personal information that he/she has no criminal convictions relating to financial affairs; that he/she hadn't been a party to a football club going into administration twice in a three year period and that he/she had no bans from any other sports organisation worldwide.

104. Colin Tattum "Cheerio, Cheerio, Cheerio", Birmingham Mail, 17 September, 2009
105. "Birmingham chairman David Gold wants St Andrew's stay but no deal with Carson Yeung finalised",
     Daily Mail, 30 September, 2009
106. Colin Tattum "Birmingham City: Why Michael Dunford was chosen as CEO", Birmingham Mail, 13 October, 2009
107. Grandtop Announcement, 23 September, 2009
108. Grandtop Announcement, 25 September, 2009

The flaw in the test is that while it should ensure no one who has been found guilty of a previous offence can repeat it at a football club, as they will not be "fit and proper", it does not provide for any outstanding investigations – in Carson's case, the investigation into his alleged money laundering activities had already begun in 2008, as confirmed by his Senior Counsel Graham "The Edwardian Gentleman" Harris in his application for a permanent stay of the proceedings on the opening day of his trial[109].

All seemed well at the time; the money was evidently there, no new debt had been assumed by the club; it was not a leveraged buyout landing the club with massive debt like Manchester United and the authorities were happy. What could possibly go wrong?

A minor bump in the road occurred in October, when Grandtop confirmed it had been served with a writ from Seymour Pierce that claimed a fee associated with the successful purchase of the club[110]. Keith Harris of Seymour Pierce had initially introduced Carson to the football club as a potential bidder and Carson had signed a contract that confirmed he would be paid a success fee should Carson be able to purchase a club. Carson dropped Seymour Pierce as advisors not long after the initial takeover attempt but crucially didn't cancel or settle the contract and so Harris and Seymour Pierce quite rightly believed that they were owed the fees even though they did nothing further to facilitate the sale.

The fees due amounted to £2.2M and Seymour Pierce obtained a charging order over the shares Grandtop had purchased to secure its fees and ensure they would eventually be paid. After some arguments between the two parties, Grandtop eventually settled the payment in full in April 2010[111].

On 6 October 2009[112] Grandtop confirmed to the HKSE that it had received enough acceptances to formally delist the football club from the Alternative

109. "Carson Yeung's lawyer asks for case to be thrown out" ITV, 29 April, 2013
110. "Twelve O'Clock High: Court Upholds 'tail-gunner' clause and awards success fee to former financial advisor", Norton Rose Fulbright, June 2010
111. "Carson Yeung regains control at Birmingham after settling £2.2million debt with Seymour Pierce", Daily Mail, 27 April, 2010
112. Grandtop Announcement, 6 October, 2009

Investment Market (AIM) and it completed payment to those accepting the offer for their shares a week later. The club was now formally owned by Grandtop, which promptly changed its name to Birmingham International Holdings to reflect the connection with its shiny new purchase. The football club was delisted from AIM on 11 November. There were still around 4% of the shares outstanding that could be forcibly purchased by the holding company if it so desired, but the board of the newly named BIH believed it would be better public relations if they left them with their obviously loyal owners.

On 15 October 2009, Carson finally had the pleasure of walking into St Andrew's as the head honcho. Surrounded by his acolytes – Vico Hui, Sammy Yu and Peter Pannu – he gave a press conference to local and national media where he boasted about how he was going to pump money into the club, and make as much as £40M available in transfer fees and wages in the January 2010 transfer window, with the same sum potentially available again in the summer of that year[113].

As the flashbulbs popped Carson was all smiles; champagne was drunk and Vico exhorted the fans "to buy the tickets"[114] as Sammy Yu told assembled reporters that the club would become like a family again after a long period of estrangement between the board and the fans – the irony of that statement came to pass as more and more of Carson's family and close friends joined the board of BIH and Birmingham City and took up share placements. Carson had achieved his dream of owning a Premier League football club and, as he was introduced to various luminaries, it was clear to all that this was a momentous day for him.

The board were no less magnanimous with the players. Manager Alex McLeish took the players to meet the board in November 2009 at a reception at the China Court restaurant in Birmingham. Vico Hui famously challenged six foot five Irish goalkeeper Colin Doyle to a drinking contest, predictably losing as the Dubliner downed his pint in 2.5 seconds[115].

---

113. "Carson Yeung to splash out £40million on Birmingham City", Metro, 15 October, 2009
114. "Birmingham City is for the people", Birmingham Mail, 13 October, 2009
115. Colin Tattum "Colin Doyle downs Birmingham City chairman Vico Hui in pint contest", Birmingham Mail, 16 January, 2010

The story continues that an unnamed player refused a second bet, which was to drink a bottle of Tabasco sauce for £10,000 but no one has owned up to that yet.

Carson's generosity knew no bounds as shown by an incident in 2009. In the city of Linyi, Shandong province, Carson donated HK$920,000[116] (approximately £71,000) to a secondary school for a new building, which was named after him. Carson attended the opening ceremony along with Hu Jinxing, Chairman of the Shanghai More Love Foundation and cousin of Hu Jintao, the former President of the People's Republic of China. At the time, Hu Jinxing was also managing a company called Kai Yuan in Hong Kong with his son Hu Yishi and both were implicated in the Rio Tinto bribery scandal in 2010[117].

Behind the scenes in Birmingham it was a different story. The club's managing director Karren Brady had left the ground with a £1M golden goodbye and the Porsche Cayenne 4x4 she regularly drove; David Sullivan, David Gold and Ralph Gold had charged the club £420,000[118] each in advance management fees. Carson was livid to find a club Sullivan had repeatedly said was debt-free actually had liabilities of £11M that had not been picked up in his due diligence investigation before parting with his hard-earned cash.

Caveat emptor applied but the Chinese were insistent they had been ripped off. As part of the conditions of the sale, Sullivan had demanded that money be placed in an escrow account to show Carson had the funds necessary to complete the deal – hence the need for a bridging loan – and had not allowed Grandtop and their accountants much more than a cursory look at the books. Carson had been warned by both his auditors BDO and his lawyers Robertsons that there may be risks in buying the club blind but he felt the risks were worth taking and went full steam ahead. It wasn't just the books either; there is an apocryphal story of computer equipment being left in pieces prior to Carson's arrival ensuring its data was no longer accessible.

116. East Week, 9 March, 2011
117. Naomi Rovnick and Daniel Ren "Kai Yuan strikes it rich but lands in steel war",
    South China Morning Post, 2 April, 2010
118. Stuart James, "David Gold and David Sullivan to sue new Birmingham City owners",
    The Guardian, 8 April, 2010

Carson found this behaviour completely unacceptable and instructed his right hand man Peter Pannu, a former Hong Kong police officer and barrister who had been practising up until the month before the take-over to institute legal proceedings to recover £7M from the previous board. Karren Brady's car was found to belong to the club and was returned to the ground. David Sullivan made a peace offering of £500,000 and some jewellery – a blue and white brooch and cuff-links – that he had designed and made when he was in charge of the club to try and smooth over the waters. This was viewed as an unmitigated insult by Carson and his team, who roundly rejected the offer and summarily returned the jewellery to Sullivan's Essex mansion.

The case was eventually settled out of court, with Sullivan and the Golds returning £3.1M of the money claimed, of which ten percent was controversially handed to Peter Pannu as a fee for achieving the settlement[119]. Pannu claimed that he had an agreement with Carson dating from June 2010, which entitled him to 10% of "whatever I bring into the club by way of earnings and profits"[120]. Naturally, the finance officer at Birmingham City requested further details of this agreement, to which he was told Pannu had agreed this commission structure in the presence of BIH director Steve McManaman – something the former Liverpool and England winger vehemently denied to the press. Pannu then told the perplexed finance officer via email when asked for authorisation that he would "get something in writing" and "this is not theft, ok"[121].

Carson and BIH now owned Birmingham City. A new era had begun at St Andrew's. Legend has it that there is an old Chinese curse heaped on enemies that roughly translates to "may you live in interesting times" – this was most certainly to be the case for Carson in the next five years.

119. David Conn "Birmingham City face questions as emails show Pannu's demands for cash", The Guardian, 27 March, 2013
120. ibid
121. ibid

5

THE SIDEKICK

When Carson finally took control of the football club in 2009, he brought along with him a new right-hand man replacing William Chan as his go-to guy - Peter Lakbir Singh Pannu. His story might not be quite as colourful as Carson's but is one that needs to be told.

Pannu, who was born in Hong Kong from an Indian Sikh family, joined the Hong Kong police force at the age of 21 in February 1985 where he rose to the rank of Senior Inspector. He came from a family with a tradition in the force: his great grandfather was a Hong Kong policeman and many of his relatives held civil service positions, including his father who was President and Chairman of the Khalsa Diwan Sikh Temple Board. There is a great tradition of Indians holding positions within the police force in Hong Kong, which dates back to the days of the British Empire when the colonial leaders employed them after they realised that the local Chinese were reluctant to bust their compatriots. Pannu was unlucky not to win the highly prestigious "Baton of Honour" at police training school for the best recruit and came top of his class in detective training school.

He first came to public prominence as a policeman when he was sensationally arrested on 7 January 1993 after a joint investigation between the OCTB (Organised Crime and Triad Bureau) and the ICAC (Independent Commission Against Corruption). He was then serving in the anti-triad force in Kowloon and was charged with two counts of assault, one count of intimidating a witness and one of perverting the course of justice. All of those charges were eventually dismissed but at that time he was immediately suspended from his duties.

Pannu was arrested along with his co-accused David Khosa by Detective Superintendent Bob Youill and Chief Inspector David "Digger" Fernyhough at the Tonnochy nightclub[122], Wanchai. Pannu and Khosa were earlier observed at the nearby Fisherman's Pier restaurant talking to triad boss Andely Chan Yiu-hing – known as the "Tiger of Wanchai" and his Tsim Sha Tsui counterpart To Luen-shun during a stakeout after the ICAC had been tipped off that both police officers were being bribed.

122. *Mark Hughes "Court victory raises hope for reinstatement", South China Morning Post, 23 February, 1994*

When he was arrested, Pannu had a large amount of cash on him – understood to be around HK$10,000 – which had placed him under suspicion because he was seen to be spending money that did not match his wages as a police officer. Pannu and Khosa were based at that time in the anti-triad squad at Yau Tsim District Police HQ on Austin Road, Tsim Sha Tsui. That part of town was full of clubs and bars and was described by a senior police source as "a hotbed of triad activity".

Pannu was cleared by the ICAC after their initial investigations but the OCTB continued to make its own enquiries and he remained suspended from the force. Local media reported at the time that the ICAC had found HK$99,000 in his desk when they searched Pannu's office but accepted his explanation that it had come from a legitimate source[123].

The first case that came to court following Pannu's arrest was the charge of criminally intimidating staff at Rick's Cafe in Tsim Sha Tsui. The prosecution claimed that Pannu had tried to obtain entry into the establishment without paying the entrance fee, threatening the assistant manager Mark Woods in the process. Pannu denied the charge claiming that he had a VIP membership of the club that entitled him to free entrance on Fridays and Saturdays.

That case was thrown out in January 1995 after the prosecution offered no evidence. However, the prosecutor Wayne Moultrie confirmed to the Court[124] that Pannu would remain suspended from the force as "enquiries were continuing".

The assault charges were dismissed when it emerged that neither the alleged victim Tong Ching-hei nor the alleged witnesses had reported the incident until two years later when it was discovered as part of an internal investigation by the police force into another incident. The evidence given by Tong and others in court was found to be conflicting and contradictory.

123. ibid
124. Charlotte Parsons, "Witness Blow Frees Pannu", South China Morning Post, 8 February, 1996

The most serious charge – that of perverting the course of justice – foundered after triad boss Andely Chan Yiu-hing was shot dead during the 1993 Macau Grand Prix weekend and the chief witness Lin Chun-yip went into hiding and avoided being summonsed for the court case. The law enforcement agencies found themselves heavily criticised for the money spent in attempting to bring the cases to trial when it had become obvious that the trials would collapse.

David Fernyhough told the SCMP at that time that the police investigations into Pannu stemmed from a wider probe into the Sun Yee On triad society's stranglehold over the entertainment industry in Tsim Sha Tsui in the early 1990s. Fernyhough, in his role as Detective Chief Inspector with the Organised Crime and Triad Bureau headed the probe, which was known as "Operation Furcate".

Fernyhough is quoted in the SCMP as saying: "We were looking at a totality of Sun Yee On controlled crime across the film and entertainment industry, from actors being pressured right down to extortion of nightclubs and rackets involving car-parking jockeys." He went on to say "The money involved was enormous."

"We started discovering a few police officers were allegedly accepting free entertainment from suspected triad figures.

"Some witnesses disappeared, others retracted statements and when they did testify we were relying on witnesses with dubious backgrounds of their own to testify against serving police officers.

"We could never put the full picture before the courts. But that is the way the system works and I have no quarrel with the outcome.[125]"

Pannu had filed a formal internal complaint against Fernyhough following his suspension, who he unhappily shared an office with at one point, claiming that "Digger" was employing unethical methods. There is no record of any action being taken against Fernyhough.

A senior police source involved in the case confirmed that Pannu had come under suspicion because of the lavish lifestyle he was leading. In his role with the anti-triad squad it was expected that Pannu would have to infiltrate triad societies and socialise with them but there were procedures in place to seek authorisation and report on the triad activities. There was increasing concern as to just how much he was socialising with them when he was seen in hangouts like Club Volvo and China City – both known Sun Yee On hotspots. Club Volvo[126] was known for its opulence and extravagance, with patrons being driven to their private booths in golf carts kitted out to look like Rolls Royces. Those clubs have since closed.

Another name potentially linked to the Sun Yee On triads was that of Carson Yeung. At this time Carson was still styling hair in the salons of Tsim Sha Tsui but it has been confirmed by a well-placed senior police source that his name "came up" in connection with the Sun Yee On triads. Although there were no charges filed against him and no clear link has been made between Carson and the triads or, for that matter, between Peter Pannu and Carson at that time – Pannu later claimed in 2009 to have known Carson for "two decades"[127].

Pannu claimed he was the victim of a vendetta based on race and jealousy[128]. During his time with the force Pannu received thirty commendations for his work on the thin blue line. He had been seen once as the "Golden Boy" of the police force, rising from the rank inspector to senior inspector in just three years. Judge Gould wondered aloud during Pannu's trial for assault in 1995 if there was a hidden agenda behind his prosecution. Pannu was accused of beating Wong Ching-hei outside Yee Do Po Karaoke lounge in Tsim Sha Tsui in February 1992. David Khosa then intervened, allegedly persuading Wong not to press charges. Three of the five witnesses in the trial had police connections.

125. Barclay Crawford and Greg Torode, "Cleared officer takes post at UK soccer club" South China Morning Post, 8 October, 2009
126. Vaudine England "Hong Kong's lavish nightclubs lose their appeal", The Guardian, 12 December, 2012
127. Colin Tattum "Full Interview: Birmingham City chief Peter Pannu tells of triad battles", Birmingham Mail, 9 October, 2009
128. Charlotte Parsons "Trials of force's Golden Boy", South China Morning Post, February 8 1996

Pannu always protested his innocence and claimed he would reveal his side of the story once the trial of his co-defendant David Khosa was concluded.

He told the Birmingham Mail on his appointment at Birmingham City that "When you are dealing with very, very vicious people, you have to enshrine yourself among them to bring them down.[129]"

Pannu has been characterised by those who dealt with him during his time in the police force as a show-off. A barrister in Hong Kong recalled a time when Pannu removed his jacket in a meeting room openly displaying the pistol he was carrying and left the room ostensibly to look for something. The barrister called him back and told him not to show his firearm in his chambers. This show of arrogance back-fired on Pannu, as he was subsequently rebuffed when he requested if he could spend his barrister's pupillage with the same barrister.

Pannu spent three years suspended from the Hong Kong police force on full pay as a result of the OCTB/ICAC investigations. During his time out he studied a LLM (Master of Laws) degree from the University of London as an external candidate. Although he was never removed from his position within the police force and the charges were dropped, it seems it was impossible for him to remain in the force; he probably accepted that he would never receive another promotion and it made more sense for him and Khosa to leave the force now they were both well on the way to becoming qualified lawyers.

Pannu was called to the bar in Hong Kong in 1997, having been accepted as a pupil under senior barrister Jack McNamara. He then worked as a barrister from his own Chambers on Connaught Road West, Sheung Wan, mainly representing criminal legal aid clients and working closely with the solicitors from KB Chau, who included amongst their partners Anthony Cheung Kwai-nang, who would later become an executive director of BIH.

129. Colin Tattum "Blues chief: My triad battles; INTERVIEW EXCLUSIVE: Dealings in a danger zone", Birmingham Mail, 9 October, 2009

By the time Carson rocked up to St Andrew's as owner, Pannu was still very much a junior barrister with little reputation in legal circles. Indeed, it is rumoured that he only actually ever won one case – but this is not unusual in Hong Kong as we shall see. Soon after moving to England, Pannu gave up his practising certificate to concentrate fully on his job as Vice-Chairman at Birmingham City.

Pannu was a close friend and trusted confidante of Carson and quickly assumed effective control at Birmingham City – in the first place in Machiavellian style by squeezing out Chief Executive Michael Dunford. Pannu settled into his role of "Vice Chairman: Football" but seemed to have eyes on the job of Chief Executive. Sources close to the board say he proceeded to put pressure on Dunford to conduct business his way, unsettling him and ultimately forcing the former Everton man to resign at the end of April 2010. His association with Carson is one shrouded in mystery; some connected to Carson's inner circle have confirmed that Pannu has known Carson for a couple of decades but cannot or will not clarify the exact circumstance of their acquaintance. There is also a rumour that Carson and Pannu only became acquainted in 2008 after Carson required some help with a problem with a businessman who had taken a particular dislike to him; however, like so much in Pannu's life, it's difficult to verify.

Pannu spent a year at the University of London studying an MA in the Management and Business of Football as a demonstration that he could effectively do the job of chief executive of a Premier League football club. He was a recognisable face in the directors' area particularly when Carson couldn't be present – his eyes and ears if you will but it wasn't until Carson's arrest that Pannu's influence was truly felt around St Andrew's.

With no other BIH personnel in the UK to challenge him, Pannu became the domineering influence at the club. He moved up from "Vice-Chairman: Football" to "Acting Chairman" in the autumn of 2010; although he didn't become a registered director of the football club until July 2011.

By that time his control over the club appeared absolute because apart from him there were two other directors of the club: Vico Hui, who was based in Asia looking after BIH in his role as CEO there and therefore never made it to Birmingham, and Carson's then seventeen-year-old student son Ryan Yeung Tsz-tsung, who was the youngest football club director in the country and didn't have any experience. Long time Blues fan and board member Michael Wiseman had been shunted into a largely ceremonial role as an "Honorary Vice President" on the appointment of Pannu and Ryan Yeung as directors of the club, which ensured that Pannu had complete control of the board and all information emanating from the club at board level.

Pannu also had the advantage in that he was the only person of any authority within the club who could speak to Carson in Cantonese; due to Carson's poor spoken English, this made it easy for Pannu to act as the essential cog in the wheel and he could carefully control the flow of information from Birmingham to Hong Kong and vice versa. If anyone at the club wanted to speak to Carson, they had to go through Pannu and if Carson wanted to know what was going on at the club, he would have to phone his right hand man. It was an extraordinarily powerful position for the former policeman and barrister.

THE SIDEKICK

DODGY DEALINGS

BIH was just one of several HKSE listed companies Carson was involved in. Many of his dealings on the stock market have been the subject of controversy but they have only seen him in the dock twice before his money-laundering charges: the first time when he was fined in 2004 for 14 breaches of the Securities (Disclosure of Interests) Ordinance for his various failures to disclose his dealings in Cedar Base and the second time in 2010 when he was also fined for not disclosing his shareholding in BIH in a timely manner.

In his money laundering trial, Carson admitted on more than one occasion to behaviour that would have more than likely seen him similarly censured if detected by the authorities. He gave evidence in Court that his investment in Massive Resources International Corporation, stock code 070 (which would later become Neptune Group) in 2005 was funded by selling a 15% stake in Prosper eVision, stock code 979[130]. Even taking into consideration that Prosper eVision had changed its name in 2003 to China Nan Feng Group Limited which makes his claim suspicious, it would have been a discloseable transaction to buy or sell that percentage of shares – and there was no such disclosure made to the HKSE[131].

Carson also gave evidence that he and his father Yeung Chung had bought a 20% stake in Massive Resources for HK$26.4M[132] in early 2005 from Lin Cheuk-fung after being invited to do so by Lin and Cheung Chi-tai[133]. Carson testified that the purchase was neither on- or off-market but by way of a "private transaction"[134]. When it was put to Carson that buying the shares would have reduced Lin's stake below that of the majority shareholder, Carson said that as far as the HKSE were concerned, Lin was still the majority shareholder; Carson would be the "shareholder behind the scenes"[135]. Given his previous convictions, he must have known this would be admitting a clear breach of the Securities (Disclosure of Interests) Ordinance.

130. HKSAR v Yeung Ka-Sing, Carson DCCC860 of 2011, (DJ Douglas Yau) para 440
131. HKSE filings
132. HKSAR v Yeung Ka-Sing, Carson DCCC860 of 2011, (DJ Douglas Yau), para 450
133. Ibid, para 364
134. Ibid, para 444
135. Ibid, para 451

What is more confusing is that Lin Cheuk-fung didn't own 20% of Massive Resources to sell to Carson. Carson gave evidence that he bought the shares in early 2005; however, HKSE announcements and filings confirm that Lin Cheuk-fung didn't own a single share in the company until 7 June 2005[136] when Massive Resources managed to complete the acquisition of a company called Walden[137], which owned a gambling ship. It's also worth noting that Chim Pui-chung owned a stake of 20.04% in the company at the beginning of 2005 but lent out a shade over 1.8BN shares (16.6% of the company) on 24 January 2005[138] before receiving them back again two weeks later on 7 February[139]. All very mysterious.

Carson's evidence in court was contradictory; he explained that his investment was not to become a shareholder, "but to chip in money to do a deposit for interest". The prosecuting counsel John Reading SC didn't understand that and asked Carson for clarification, to which Carson replied "I became a shareholder with them in another business". When asked what business that was, Carson said "At that time, they had acquired code 070 company, Lin Cheuk-fung and Cheung Chi-tai invited me at the same time to buy the shares of 070, that's what I meant by joining to become a shareholder."[140] Whether he initially meant that he was assisting in the purchase of the gambling ship and then changed his mind and explanation is unknown; as it stands his evidence makes no sense when tested against the announcements and disclosures made to the HKSE. If the prosecution had gone through the public documentation they could have destroyed his testimony. Perhaps because of the draconian nature of the money laundering law, the prosecution didn't feel they needed to dig very deep.

When asked for any documentation to show his ownership of the shares in Massive Resources, Carson said it had gone missing.

136. HKSE filings
137. Massive Resources Announcement, 21 January, 2005
138. HKSE filings
139. HKSE filings
140. HKSAR v Yeung Ka-Sing, Carson DCCC860 of 2011, (DJ Douglas Yau) para 442

In his judgement, the judge points out that this investment occurred less than seven years from Carson's arrest – his complaint of records being destroyed by institutions in the ordinary course because of the lapse of time does not hold up in this instance[141].

One feature of all these deals-Cedar Base,Prosper eVision and Massive Resources is the non-disclosure of shareholdings above the threshold 5% which should have been disclosed to the HKSE. In addition, in the case of Massive Resources, Carson admitted using a nominee arrangement. There appears to be a distinct pattern in his concealment of his true shareholdings from the regulatory authorities. This alone shows how easy it would be to circumvent the threshold in The Owners and Directors Test that the footballing authorities employ.

The sums of money involved in the Massive Resources transaction pale in comparison to an allegation made against Carson by his former partner Zhou Dan. We have not been able to verify these claims from any other source. Zhou alleges Carson was involved in an enormous oil deal in a remote part of China without disclosure to the HKSE. It's quite a long story.

On 4 February 2009[142], a company called China Energy Development Holdings (stock code 0228) announced to the HKSE it had agreed a deal to buy a group called China Era Energy from a company called Total Build Investments, owned by a mainlander Wang Guoju. The deal, which was worth between HK$2BN and HK$10BN would see China Energy obtain the rights to the North Kashi Block gasfield, in the Tarim Basin of Xinjiang province, in remote western China near the borders with Kyrgyzstan and Tajikistan.

The deal to buy the rights to the gasfield was complex and took nearly two years to complete, with no less than six supplemental agreements to the deal made to smooth over issues as they arose. Before the deal came about, China Energy's business was only operating Chinese restaurants in Hong Kong, having disposed of a Macau-based liquid natural gas business in December 2008.

141. Ibid, para 446
142. China Energy Announcement, 4 February, 2009

The company was hungry to get back into the oil and gas market and the deal Wang put forward would open the door in a big way.

To pay for the deal, China Energy had agreed a convertible bond which provided for the issue of up to 58BN shares to Wang at HK$0.168 per share (depending on the eventual valuation of the gasfield), with the bond maturing after thirty years. Under the terms of the deal Wang wouldn't be able to convert all of the bond to shares at once; he wasn't allowed to own over the magic 30% barrier which would trigger a general offer. Instead, he would have to sell some of his converted shares before converting more, meaning it was in Wang's best interest that the share price remained above the price he had negotiated in the conversion bond. It was the normal way of financing a deal in Hong Kong and no eyebrows were raised.

China Energy paid a refundable deposit of HK$185M on 23 January 2009 to secure the deal and after two announcements confirming more time was needed to gain the approvals required from the PRC Government, China Energy had to extend the deadline[143] to complete the deal from 30 July 2009 to 31 December 2009. To do so, they had to offer up a second refundable deposit of HK$260M in cash by 30 November 2009. China Energy needed to raise the cash to be able to pay this and so on 21 September 2009[144] agreed a "best effort" placing using Kingston Securities to place 604.78M shares, raising HK$235.9M, which they completed by 8 October 2009[145].

More time was needed to finalise the deal and so another extension of the deadline was agreed[146], with a further HK$400M having to be paid up as a refundable deposit – this time by 30 April 2010 – which once again would be funded by a placing of new shares, using Kingston Securities. This time 725M shares were to be placed by a "best effort" placing on 28 January 2010[147], which raised HK$326.3M. Once again, the shares were placed successfully, with the placing completed on 22 February 2010[148].

143. *China Energy Announcement, 30 July, 2009*
144. *China Energy Announcement, 21 September, 2009*
145. *China Energy Announcement, 8 October, 2009*
146. *China Energy Announcement, 31 December, 2009*
147. *China Energy Announcement, 28 January, 2010*
148. *China Energy Announcement, 22 February, 2010*

It would appear from the filings that under neither placing had any shareholder become a substantial shareholder in the company owning more than 5%.

The deadline to complete the deal was pushed back again to 30 September 2010[149], with the second refundable deposit deadline also pushed back to 31 July 2010. On 13 July[150], China Energy varied the deal again, splitting the acquisition into two parts, and whilst offering to cover a loan Wang had made to keep the target company going, China Energy also reduced the convertible bond it would offer to make the purchase by the deposits already paid and to cover just the first part of the proposed deal. The first part of the deal encompassed the Akemomu Gas field, a small portion of the original gas field planned for acquisition.

It made what had been an enormous deal into something more manageable – it might be asked why the company hadn't started off small and then expanded. Was there another reason to announce a huge deal that would be this difficult to pull off? Share prices had jumped from HK$0.168 to HK0.255 when the deal was announced and had pushed as high as HK$0.87 in April 2009; some speculators had evidently made a lot from the deal and there lies the obvious question whether the share price was being manipulated.

The deal was delayed again in August 2010, and then in September[151] China Energy finally confirmed the total value of the deal would be HK$2.558BN, plus the loans that Wang had made to keep the company going – minus, of course, the deposits paid. They also wangled terms to extend the time to pay the additional HK$400M deposit, and an amount to be paid back by Wang should there be issues with the purchase at a later date.

It took until 3 December 2010[152] for an EGM to be called to ratify the deal, and on 3 January 2011 China Energy finally completed it, paying a sum of HK$2.558BN with HK$1.279BN held in escrow to be repaid if there were unresolved issues, plus HK$106M to cover loans to the company made by

149. *China Energy Announcement, 30 April, 2010*
150. *China Energy Announcement, 13 July, 2010*
151. *China Energy Announcement, 28 September, 2010*
152. *China Energy Announcement, 3 December, 2010*

Wang in addition to the HK$800M deposit.

For eighteen months, nothing happened. There was exploratory work at the site but no money was made from it; China Energy announced to shareholders in their annual accounts that it was awaiting government approval and until then there would be no profit made on gas exploration. The convertible notes issued to cover the acquisition were slowly converted to shares and then sold off, making a steady stream of money for UK Prolific Petroleum (as Total Build Investments now seemed to be called) a company now wholly controlled by Wang Hanning, son of Wang Guoju. In the meantime no income was forthcoming from the site for the long-suffering shareholders of China Energy.

On 16 September 2013[153], China Energy made an announcement to the HKSE noting that the share price had decreased and volume increased and also noting that Wang Hanning and Wang Guoju were involved in an "investigation" in China. Whether that investigation is linked to the huge controversy surrounding former oil magnate and Minister for Public Security of China Zhou Yongkang remains to be seen but Zhou Dan insists that it is.

It is intriguing that China forced a publication called "21st Century Business Herald" to remove an article which discussed the deal between Wang and China Energy way back in March 2010[154] – someone in China did not want the deal and those involved to become public knowledge there. At this point Zhou Yongkang, a former chief executive of China National Petroleum Corporation (who were working with China Energy on this gasfield) was responsible for China's courts, police, paramilitary and various state security and spying agencies[155]. It's no leap of the imagination to wonder if he was involved in suppressing in China a report of a public announcement made in Hong Kong.

153. *China Energy Announcement, 16 September, 2013*
154. *"IFJ Report lists China's Secret Bans on Media Reporting", International Federation of Journalists, 31 January, 2010*
155. *James Anderlini "Bo fallout threatens China's security chief", Financial Times, 20 April, 2012*

The connection to Carson according to Zhou Dan lies in the convertible notes, and a document she has a copy of which states Wang promised to give the convertible shares to Carson as a gift. Of course, Wang was entitled to do what he wants with his money and shares, if he wanted to give away a huge sum of money it would be up to him. If the transaction was valid, then Carson would have had to announce to the HKSE that he was interested in such a large percentage of a company, which of course he did not - unless of course he was using Wang as a nominee. Zhou Dan alleges that Carson made an undeclared HK$1BN on the deal – not bad considering China Energy is still yet to see any return on its investment and now may be implicated in a growing corruption scandal on the mainland.

Without seeing the further documentation that Zhou Dan claims to have showing the full extent of the deal[156], it is impossible to verify just how much Carson allegedly made out of the deal; however, if true, it shows once again how Carson operated – behind the scenes and beyond the eyes of the regulatory authorities. We should make the point that there is no love lost between Zhou Dan and Carson – after all, this was the man who ditched their fourteen-year-long relationship to take up with a younger woman, with the first news Zhou Dan hearing about this new relationship being when she heard of the birth of Carson's second child by his new lady, Joanna Wang Manli.

It's also worth noting the links between China Energy and BIH; William Chan Wai-keung[157], a long time friend of Carson was at various points Executive Director and Chief Executive of China Energy between 2006 and 2009; Chang Kin-man[158] was also an Independent Non-Executive Director there for six years between 2003 and 2009, which runs partly concurrently with his Independent Non-Executive Directorship status at BIH.

Another company with a myriad of interconnecting links with BIH and China Energy was iMerchants, stock code 8009 (which perhaps unsurprisingly now trades from 2012 as Chinese Energy Holdings Limited).

156. *Zhou Dan, personal interview, 22 February, 2014*
157. *webb-site.com*
158. *webb-site.com*

The aforementioned William Chan was Chief Executive of iMerchants from October 2010 to August 2011; Chang Kin-man was an Independent Non-Executive Director from March 2008 to September 2011. Raymond Yau Yan-ming[159] was Chairman and Chief Executive Officer at various points between June 2008 and February 2013 and is still an Executive Director there; he was an Independent Non-Executive Director at BIH from October 2007 until May 2013. Carson Wong Ka-chun[160] (not Carson Yeung) was Financial Director at iMerchants from August 2008 to February 2013 and has been an Independent Non-Executive Director at BIH since June 2012.

Other executives at iMerchants have links to Carson too; Jackie Pan Chik[161] who gave evidence at Carson's trial was an Independent Non-Executive Director there from March 2008 to November 2009 and Carson's cousin Yang Bin[162] was an Executive Director from March 2008 to September 2011.

On 8 February 2014, Carson Yeung issued a writ[163] against a mainlander called Chen Lixue claiming title to the shares of two companies named Even Glory Holdings Limited and Will Success Holdings Limited both incorporated in the British Virgin Islands with a nominal value of US$51. The writ claims that Chen failed to transfer the companies to Carson as he was contracted to do on 8 April 2011 and that Chen had subsequently sold the companies on to another third party. Interestingly, the address given for Chen Lixue in Guangzhou doesn't look accurate, and the address given for Carson – 86th floor International Commerce Centre – is out of date, as BIH moved out of there on 27 April 2012[164]. On the face of it the writ looked nonsensical, as the companies were worth virtually nothing; however, what it didn't mention was that Even Glory and Will Success at one stage both held highly valuable convertible notes issued by iMerchants from another deal that turned sour.

159. *webb-site.com*
160. *webb-site.com*
161. *webb-site.com*
162. *webb-site.com*
163. *Yeung Ka Sing Carson v Chen Lixue HCA221 of 2014*
164. *Birmingham International Holdings Announcement, 27 April, 2012*

On 5 May 2009, iMerchants announced to the HKSE[165] that it had agreed that one of its own subsidiaries would buy a company called Rightshine Holdings from its joint owners Even Glory and Will Success, for HK$900M. Even Glory was owned on a 50/50 basis by mainlanders Chen Lixue and Wang Hongjun whereas Will Success was owned solely by Chen Lixue.

Chen Lixue was Carson's family doctor and was looking after Carson's father Yeung Chung who was suffering from bladder cancer when he eventually died. Chen is also the brother-in-law of Yang Bin, who is Carson's cousin (their fathers are brothers) although Yang referred to Carson as "uncle" as Yang is thirteen years younger. Wang is a businessman and a partner of Carson and – if Carson's ex-partner Zhou Dan is to be believed – Wang also had an affair with Carson's current partner Joanna Wang Manli[166].

The deal with iMerchants was to purchase a company which provided management services to a PRC company called Shenzhen Careall Capital Investment company, of which Wang Hongjun was also a Director and Chairman. The deal was that iMerchants would receive through its subsidiary 70% of the net profits of Careall Capital with a guaranteed net profit of RMB100M in the first year, RMB150M in the second year and RMB200M in the third. Careall Capital is a venture capital firm investing in new IPOs in Shenzhen and Southern China. According to iMerchants, the strict rules in relation to cross border investment meant that the only way they could join in this venture capital business with Careall Capital was to enter into this management agreement.

On 31 August 2009, iMerchants sent out a circular to shareholders notifying them of an EGM[167] to gain their approval for the deal on 17 September[168], when all resolutions were passed unanimously. The deal was completed on 23 October[169] and bonds for the issue of 2,938,477,840 conversion shares were issued to Chen Lixue and Wang Hongjun through their BVI

165. iMerchants Announcement, 5 May, 2009
166. Zhou Dan, Personal Interview, 22 February 2014
167. iMerchants Announcement,31 August, 2009
168. iMerchants Announcement, 17 September, 2009
169. iMerchants Announcement, 23 October, 2009

companies to pay for the acquisition. iMerchants then held a further EGM to arrange a subdivision of its shares which saw the 2.9BN shares split into five resulting in the conversion bond being changed to nearly 15BN shares[170].

A similar outcome to the China Energy deal was the result for the poor shareholders. Guaranteed profits turned out to be not so guaranteed, with just RMB78M paid in the first year and RMB40M coming in the second year. Interestingly, in 2012 iMerchants were also chasing payment of an outstanding debt of HK$10M which was revealed by stock market filings as owed by BIH when China Water (who were the parent company of iMerchants at that time) were forced to make an announcement[171]. China Water were also chasing HK$43.2M owed to them directly by BIH.

Again, the stock price graph makes interesting reading. When the deal was initially announced in August 2009 iMerchants shares were at HK$0.178 – by November its share prices had nearly doubled to HK$0.26 but as the deal progressed the share price dropped to HK$0.013 in July 2011. Was the price being manipulated upwards for the benefit of the convertible bonds and was the deal a good deal for shareholders or just those in on the share speculation?

As the judge stated in his reasons for sentence, Carson had "considerable skills in share dealings". Had the prosecution not had such an easy ride at Carson's trial – for reasons discussed in a later chapter – the investigation would no doubt have required a deeper analysis of his financial dealings which could have had a massive impact on how the footballing authorities viewed his running of the club. Perhaps for Birmingham City fans, ignorance in this case may truly be bliss? So far the club has avoided the financial meltdown suffered by that other former Hong Kong-owned club Portsmouth.

170. iMerchants Announcement, 18 November, 2009
171. China Water Announcement, 3 August, 2012

7

THE GLORY YEARS

The first year and a half of Carson's reign witnessed scenes of extraordinary success at Birmingham City. Having completed his takeover in October 2009, the Blues experienced an almost immediate change in fortunes. They did lose their first game of Carson's reign 3-1 to Arsenal away at the Emirates stadium but they wouldn't lose another game in the top flight until they lost to Chelsea away at Stamford Bridge some 105 days and twelve Premier League games later.

It was an incredible time to be a Birmingham City fan. Blues won an unprecedented (for them) five matches on the spin in the Premier League and used the same eleven starting players in consecutive games in what became known as the "unbeatables" run of ten games without defeat. The team went on to set an incredible record of twelve consecutive games without changing the starting line up[172] when it took to the field on 7 February 2010 against Wolverhampton Wanderers, a game won 2-1 thanks to a brace from substitute Kevin Phillips to come back from a goal down late on.

It wasn't the prettiest of football at times, but McLeish's men seemed to be able to grind out the results. Roger Johnson and Scott Dann in defence had grown in stature from players with potential to consistent performers; Barry Ferguson and Lee Bowyer in the midfield were showing bite and resilience as the ill-fated Christian "Chucho" Benitez (who tragically died in July 2013 aged 27 from a heart attack whilst playing in Qatar) and Cameron Jerome were willing runners up front, chasing everything and tiring out defences. The team was described by local reporters as a "band of brothers"[173], a team of players who would put everything on the line for each other; this resonated strongly with a fanbase that put a high value on effort and tenacity. It was the very definition of the whole being greater than the sum of its parts.

It's fair to say that none of the team achieving this unprecedented success had been bought by Carson – he hadn't been allowed to chip in with money

172. Colin Tattum, "Colin Tattum reflects on Birmingham City's remarkable 2009-10 Premier League Season", *Birmingham Mail*, 11 May 2010
173. Colin Tattum "Birmingham City 1, West Ham 0: Colin Tattum's Big Match Verdict", *Birmingham Mail*, 14 December 2009

in the transfer window after offering to lend the club £5M to buy Tuncay Sanli[174] from Middlesbrough under stock market rules – but it would be unfair to say that he had nothing to do with the success of the club in this honeymoon period. Stale feelings left by the former board had been washed away and the team were enjoying themselves before a crowd that sensed that something exciting was happening at St Andrew's. The crowd were sparked by the tigerish attitude of the team, which in turn took confidence from the raucous noise from the fans cheering the team to "Keep Right On", with each spurring the other on in a virtuous circle. Birmingham City legend Trevor Francis agreed, saying that he hoped "the change in the mood will continue because it can only be good for the club.[175]"

It might be claimed that Birmingham City had a lot of luck with injuries and suspensions but it also has to be said that winning teams don't tend to suffer as many injuries; when the team is on a roll, players will want to play and will play through pain and play far above their normal standards to remain part of that success. Success breeds success and as Birmingham City kept winning it became a habit – the team believed they could get something from every game and that confidence invariably produced a result. This was typified in creditable draws against vastly superior opposition in Liverpool, Manchester City and Manchester United, and a 3-2 win against Wigan Athletic after going 2-1 down.

The good times had really started to roll at St Andrew's; one of the first signs of the new order was the reduction in ticket prices, which drew larger crowds and fostered goodwill with the fans, although it was roundly criticised by former director David Gold, who said when referring to Carson that "if he keeps doing it [reducing ticket prices] individually, he will get relegated. Fans will love him but he will get relegated because the model doesn't work.[176]"

---

174. "Birmingham forced to abandon Tuncay Sanli signing", The Telegraph, 27 August, 2009
175. Colin Tattum "Mood has changed at Birmingham City – Trevor Francis", Birmingham Mail, 3 November, 2009
176. "Birmingham face relegation if Carson Yeung reduces ticket prices, claims ex-Blues chairman David Gold", Daily Mail, 14 October, 2009

Cheaper seats filled with happier fans after the apathetic years of the previous board produced an amazing atmosphere at home and Birmingham City became a force to be reckoned with. With its fans happily singing the praises of the team who were looking invincible it was a great time to be a Birmingham City fan.

Behind the scenes, the staff at the club were more relaxed. Under the previous board there had been a culture of micromanagement, of trying to save every penny possible and squeeze every potential drop of income from every conceivable source. Michael Dunford, who had been brought in as chief executive by Carson in October 2009 realised swiftly that the staff knew what they were doing and just needed support from management to maximise their potential. Previously staff had been prevented from working together across the segregated departments, now cooperation was encouraged and lines of demarcation blurred to ensure a happy team off the pitch as well as on it.

Fans who had been fobbed off when trying to ask questions of the club or when they had suggested improvements under the previous regime were welcomed to air their views once more. Sammy Yu's declaration of "we are family"[177] at the press conference convened to announce Carson's arrival were not just words; subsequently, the club threw open its doors like a mother bringing her prodigal sons back into her clutches. Unpopular decisions made by the old board were reversed quickly and ideas were listened to, fostering a better atmosphere within the ground and a feeling that the fans would once again be treated as supporters and not just customers. At the first fans' forum shortly after taking over the club, Sammy Yu could be seen outside the gates of the ground handing out free tickets to encourage people to attend the game.

Football clubs are a business, but fans aren't like customers whose custom can be bought by price wars or with gimmicky special offers; the intangible feeling that the club is "theirs" has to be understood by the owners or else

177. Colin Tattum "Sammy Yu opens his heart on his shock exit from Birmingham City", Birmingham Mail, 26 September, 2010

those fans who are alienated will just walk away from the game. Carson's team seemed anxious not to make this mistake.

Carson, meanwhile, was enjoying the life of a football supremo. Although he lived primarily in Hong Kong he made the 6000-mile plus trip regularly to see the team play. He cut a slightly bizarre figure in the directors' area, wearing what looked like a bearskin coat, celebrating every goal wildly and lapping up the atmosphere of St Andrew's. His every movement was faithfully reported by his newspaper in Hong Kong – Sing Pao – and gala dinners were held in his honour in Hong Kong and Shenzhen as he lived the lifestyle of the rich and famous. Carson was at the pinnacle of his success and with a reputation for being lucky he must have felt like all of his Christmases had come at once as he was showered with praise and attention in his homeland.

At his home in Kingston upon Thames, Carson liked to relax watching re-runs of the games or Sky Sports News – his passion for football seemed to know no bounds. BIH commissioned a video of him in this beautiful home, before he travelled to the Midlands in his Maybach to take in the game showing the shareholders that their man meant business – this was a guy on the rise. Carson hammed up to the camera, playing with his dogs in the back garden, before taking the crew on a tour of the bedrooms and what looked like a barely used office where he struggled to turn on the computer before finally retiring to the kitchen for a sandwich made by his maid.

As a televisual spectacle, it was akin to "MTV Cribs" – but it served a purpose. The concept of "face" and reputation in Chinese business and society is dominant and the video demonstrated Carson's new found standing as a serious player on the football stage. Showing off the cars on the drive, the expensive furniture, and the clothes in his wardrobe didn't reek of class, but then again Birmingham City fans were familiar with this nouveau riche behaviour having seen David Sullivan flaunt his Theydon Bois pad in the local newspaper, complete with newly decorated "Blue" games room.

The riches promised at the October press conference[178] didn't quite materialise in the January transfer window – but Blues did make a couple of additions and the squad was coming together. Midfielder Michel[179] had been signed after a protracted chase from Spanish side Sporting de Gijon and local lad Craig Gardner made the decision to cross the Aston Expressway from Aston Villa to join his boyhood club for £3M[180]. Even the failure to sign Roman Pavlyuchenko[181] from Tottenham Hotspur due to problems agreeing a transfer fee and personal terms hadn't really dampened fans' enthusiasm and it felt like the sleeping giant was coming around at last. Gardner in particular settled in quickly and the team looked like one that could push on from a Championship and Premier League yo-yo side into one that could push for the top half of the table, maybe even on to European football.

Birmingham City eventually finished the 2009/10 season in ninth position[182] – its highest place in fifty years. Although it was in the shadow of its more famous claret and blue neighbours in the league standings, there was a growing feeling that the hierarchy was changing. The club could have finished even higher up the league but for a slight faltering in the final months of the season, slightly disappointing the fans who had been singing "we're all going on a European Tour" to the tune of Yellow Submarine at the prospect of the club entering the Europa League, which would have come with a top six finish.

The signs of improvement grew with the expensive acquisitions of Ben Foster from Manchester United (a reported £6M)[183], Nikola Zigic from Valencia (also a reported £6M)[184] and Jean Beausejour from Mexican outfit Club America (a reported £3.5M)[185] in the summer of 2010 along with the

178. "Carson Yeung to splash out £40million on Birmingham City", Metro, 15 October 2009
179. "Birmingham City sign Michel from Sporting Gijon", The Guardian, 11 January, 2010
180. Sandy Macaskill, "Birmingham seal £3 million move for Aston Villa defender Craig Gardner", Daily Telegraph, 26 January 2010
181. Colin Tattum "Birmingham City remain in talks for Tottenham Hotspur star Roman Pavlyuchenko" Birmingham Mail, 28 January, 2010
182. EPLMatches.com "EPL Table 2009-10"
183. "Ben Foster challenged to make a name for himself after clinching £6m move from Manchester United to Birmingham City", Daily Mail, 19 May, 2010
184. "Birmingham complete £6m deal for Serbia striker Nikola Zigic", The Guardian, 26 May, 2010
185. "Birmingham recruit Hleb, Jiranek and Beausejour", BBC, 31 August, 2010

"Bosman" free transfer of Martin Jiranek and the loan captures of former Arsenal midfielder Alexander Hleb from Spartak Moscow and Spanish giants FC Barcelona respectively, as Carson opened his chequebook.

These were just the deals that came off – behind the scenes Carson was happy to spend as much as he could, with deals for Bobby Zamora[186], Mauro Boselli[187] and Moussa Dembélé[188] amongst others just failing to materialise.

Alex McLeish told his staff he was concerned that some of the players were being forced on to him and there were tensions when he was told in no uncertain terms that failing to sign one of the players for "the boss" would result in him joining the dole queue. It didn't come to that, as Boselli went to Wigan Athletic and McLeish acquiesced in the signing of Zigic, keeping Carson happy and ensuring he retained footballing control of the club.

The team went on a pre-season tour of China and Hong Kong in July 2010, winning three exhibition matches against teams in Hong Kong, Beijing and Liaoning as Carson paraded his new acquisitions and sought to improve the Birmingham City brand. There was a conscious effort made by Carson's team to show off the club as a successful and valuable product to the Chinese people while at the same time media personnel from the local press in Birmingham embedded on the tour were shown the palatial riches of Carson's Peak home in Hong Kong to further demonstrate his wealth and success to the fans back home.

Big receptions were held in the days between the games where the players socialised with wealthy Chinese businessmen, prospective sponsors and investors and the games themselves were played in huge stadia – the Beijing friendly was in no less than the "Birds Nest" stadium built for the 2008 Olympics. However, there were a few cracks in the façade starting to appear, as some expenses weren't immediately paid and support staff were forced to use personal credit cards to pay off hotel bills. The Birds Nest Stadium,

---

186. *"Birmingham City urged not to sign Bobby Zamora", Birmingham Mail, 5 July, 2010*
187. *"Wigan lead race to sign Estudiantes £7m striker Mauro Boselli", Daily Mail, 31 May, 2010*
188. *"Birmingham close to £5m signing of Moussa Dembélé from AZ Alkmaar", The Guardian, 5August, 2010*

which had been barely used since it hosted the Olympics, was never suitable for a football match.

Although there were 70,000 fans in the ground, the pitch was described as "a dogs dinner"[189] and behind the scenes the club and media alike struggled with a lack of power points and internet capability. As much as BIH wanted to show off their shiny new Premier League team, the tour was considered a joke by the squad and the coaching staff who were spending too much time travelling instead of preparing the team for the season ahead.

In Birmingham, the belief grew stronger among the fans that the 2010/11 season would be even better – the team looked to have some real quality about it and there was a buzz about the city. Carson had shown the colour of his money – here was an owner who was ready to put his money where his mouth was and back his lofty ambitions for the club.

As a rule, Blues fans had become terrible cynics as a result of the numerous signings promised by the previous board in the press that then failed to come off – infamously including Diego Maradona in the early nineties. Many fans had reached the point where they only believed a player had signed when he was pictured holding a scarf in the Kop stand. Carson hadn't done business that way; of course there had been speculation linking the club to players, but the rumours hadn't come from the club directly and the quietly effective way the new board went about its business was something the fans then held in high regard.

The belief that success on the pitch was going to continue and even increase proved to be correct – at least for a day, on 27 February 2011. At Wembley Stadium, the Blues finally ended a drought of forty-eight years without a major trophy by winning the League Cup against Arsenal thanks to a late winner scored by Obafemi Martins after a mistake by Arsenal's keeper Wojciech Szczesny and his team mate Laurent Koscielny[190], which saw the Frenchman

189. Colin Tattum, "Match Report Beijing Guoan 0 Birmingham City 1" Birmingham Mail, 22 July 2010
190. "Carling Cup Final: Arsenal 1 Birmingham City 2 – Full Time Match Report", Birmingham Mail, 27 February 2011

crash into the Pole. It had been almost half a century since winning the League Cup in its infancy over two legs in 1963 and in modern terms the 2011 victory represented the first major trophy the club had ever won.

In front of a crowd of thirty thousand deliriously happy Birmingham City fans, Carson held the trophy aloft with his manager Alex McLeish, celebrating his fifty-first birthday in style. There is a rumour that Carson had made a bet with his fellow Hong Kong-based football club owner Balram Chainrai on the outcome of the match, so no doubt Carson was doubly pleased knowing he was going to trouser £250,000 and the bragging rights from one of his peers.

It followed a cup run you could have read in "Roy of the Rovers": a debut for sixteen-year-old local wunderkind Nathan Redmond[191] in the early rounds; a win on penalties against a lower league side when it looked like the game was lost[192]; a win against hated city rivals Aston Villa with the winner scored by the talismanic Zigic in front of a packed Tilton[193]; a two-legged comeback against West Ham, a team run by the former owners finished by the local boy (and boyhood fan) Craig Gardner also in front of the Tilton to complete the victory after being behind 3-1 on aggregate[194]. It's fair to say the early round draws favoured Birmingham City, and pulling Villa out of the hat in the quarter finals ensured McLeish had to take the game seriously; it was a massive achievement for the club all the same. None of it would have been possible without the investment Carson made in the club.

Judging by the floods of tears pouring down many grown men's faces at Wembley, the cup win had erased a lot of the pain of countless previous seasons. For so long Birmingham City had been the bridesmaid, the "nearly" team who had never quite done it; falling at the last hurdle as they had in the 2001 League Cup final against Liverpool or cruelly beaten at the FA

191. Colin Tattum, "Birmingham City 3, Rochdale 2: Colin Tattum's big match verdict and player ratings", Birmingham Mail, 27 August, 2010
192. Colin Tattum, "Birmingham City 1, Brentford 1 (aet, Blues win 4-3 on penalties): Colin Tattum's big verdict", Birmingham Mail, 27 October, 2010
193. Phil McNulty, "Birmingham 2 – 1 Aston Villa", BBC, 1 December, 2010
194. Phil McNulty, "Birmingham 3 – 1 West Ham (agg 4-3)", BBC, 26 January, 2010

Cup semi-final stage in 1975 against Fulham. Even the win against Arsenal looked like it would be another of those heroic failures after Lee Bowyer was wrongly flagged offside before being cynically brought down by Szczesny in the opening few minutes. But – for just once – it was Blues who benefited from a lucky happenstance when the Frenchman collided with the Pole and although he only made six appearances in a Blues shirt Martins made sure his name would be forever etched in Birmingham City folklore with the fans singing "Who put the ball in the Arsenal net – Obafemi Martins".

For Carson, it was the realisation of a dream. An obsessive football fan who had named his eldest son after Ryan Giggs[195], this moment was a long way from being chairman of a small Hong Kong football team – Hong Kong Rangers – and his picture was splashed in newspapers around the world. For Blues fans, at least it signalled the end of a lot of pain and the bragging rights in the second city for a short time. After being taunted by opposition fans with songs about the lack of silverware – "you've never won fuck all" – in the trophy cabinet at St Andrew's for so many years the feeling that this millstone had finally been lifted was incredible and, as an added bonus, Birmingham City would compete in European competition for the first time in fifty years and for the first time ever on merit.

The League Cup win also guaranteed Carson's elevation in the Hong Kong business world: his "face" was enormous and there was no better way to show that he was the big tamale than to be seen as the owner of a successful football team. Carson flaunted Birmingham City's success in the press - in Sing Pao in particular - for a good few weeks afterwards, holding gala dinners in Shenzhen celebrating the cup win combined with the "100 days" celebrations for his daughter Camilla and showing everyone he was the man.

195. Brendon McLoughlin "Birmingham City owner Carson Yeung gives 18-year-old son a seat on the club's board of directors", The Telegraph, 18 July, 2011

THE GLORY YEARS

THE SLIPPERY SLOPE

One could be forgiven for assuming that after winning its first major trophy for nearly half a century all would be well in the Birmingham City camp; that the euphoria would continue and that the blue skies that had been hiding for so long had returned. Nothing could be further from the truth. As the team collapsed towards relegation on the pitch, it was evident that things weren't right off it either.

Within a week of the glorious victory at Wembley, it was announced to the HKSE[196] that Carson had been forced to mortgage his own house on Barker Road to inject much-needed cash into the club. Football clubs tend to receive their income in lumps at certain times of the year – television rights, merit payments and season ticket receipts – but between times the pastures are fallow and cashflow is required to pay the bills. Under the previous board, Blues required injections from their owners every year or so but it had never been an issue because members of the previous board had been ready to lend the club money when required.

It's one thing to be able to claim ownership of a HK$146M apartment in Hong Kong, a £5M house in an exclusive gated community in Kingston upon Thames and a host of cars and other paraphernalia between the two – but the club needed cash to pay the bills. In previous years the directors would lend money from their other businesses to the club (at a moderate rate of interest of course), to be repaid when the next chunk of cash came in.

Carson's problem was that his other businesses, such as the Sing Pao newspaper, were also suffering cashflow problems; so much so that he was forced to mortgage his own property to Wing Hang Bank and use that to loan money to the club. The alarm bells were starting to ring as fans questioned why Carson would have to resort to such extreme measures to finance the club.

Unfortunately for the club, this was always likely to be the issue with the rich benefactor model of ownership. For the period the benefactor has liquid assets and the desire to support the club with funds, then all is well, money can be spent willy nilly and no one minds. Once the rich benefactor loses

196. *Birmingham International Holdings Announcement, 3 March, 2011*

the desire or the means, problems come to a head quickly. Footballers and football clubs are very well protected from creditors under the controversial "football creditor" rule[197] – even if a football club goes into administration they have to pay their players and any owed money to other clubs in full, first – even before the taxman, much to the consternation of HMRC who tried to have the rule repealed at a five day trial in November and December 2011 but were overruled by Mr Justice David Richards on 12 May 2012. Debts pile up very quickly and it doesn't take much for a situation to spiral out of control – Portsmouth's sufferings being a case in point.

A study by BDO in August 2013 confirmed this hypothesis[198]; with the tightening of financial fair play regulations and higher numbers of clubs suffering operating losses, 94% of those clubs that responded in the Championship confirmed that they required help from their principal shareholder to maintain the operation of their club. More worryingly, 36% of those clubs had owners who were looking to sell up because of the risks involved in running the club and the worsening returns on their investment. English football had become a fashionable accessory for multi-millionaires after the advent of the Premier League but now more and more owners are disenchanted.

Under the previous board, Birmingham City went from being a club on the verge of extinction to one capable of an extended stay in the Premier League; however, as fans demanded more and more success the patience of Sullivan and the Gold brothers had run out when they realised that they didn't want to take it any further and risk any more.

Carson still had the desire to run the club but without the means to continue to invest and prop up the club it was always going to be a rocky path, even if relegation had been avoided. Player wages were a massive proportion of turnover with nearly 95p in every £1 the club generated paid out to the players by the end of the 2010/11 season[199]. There was no possibility the business could be run for any length of time in this way without further

197. Bill Wilson, "Football repels taxman's bid to change creditor's ruling", BBC, 25 May, 2012
198. Nabil Hassan, "Financial Fair Play: A third of owners considering selling club", BBC, 13 August 2013
199. BCFC accounts, retrieved from Companies House

infusions of cash; consequently, the club was looking down the barrel even before that final fateful Premier League game against Tottenham Hotspur. Staying up may have allowed Carson to paper over the cracks; relegation would widen the chasm.

In an attempt to generate new funds, in October 2010[200] BIH launched a new share placement to sell as many as 1.5BN new shares at HK$0.20 – increasing the amount of issued shares in the company by 50%. Unfortunately, less than a third of those new shares were underwritten by Carson's brokers, Kingston Securities, making it harder to guarantee new investors and an influx of cash. The remainder of the shares (1.1BN) were to be placed by "best effort". All that meant was that the brokers would do what they could to sell the shares but they weren't prepared to underwrite them, giving absolutely no guarantee that they could or would be sold. It demonstrated the broker's opinion that it was unlikely the rights issue would be fully subscribed.

Even with Birmingham City winning the League Cup, it seemed investors in Hong Kong and China were no longer interested – if the new shares weren't sold, new investment would not be forthcoming precipitating cashflow problems for BIH and the club. In the interim accounts released on 22 February 2011[201], BIH confirmed that they were looking to the rights issue to secure new capital for the business but it appeared there was no "Plan B"[202].

Carson himself needed cash to make certain he was able to buy shares to maintain his stake and avoid it being diluted – that he remained the largest single shareholder, which of course was going to cost him even more money he didn't have. In the end he managed to acquire the 315M shares[203] owned by Zhou Xin[204], the sister of his ex-partner Zhou Dan. The share transaction was problematic to say the least and is alleged to be under investigation by the Hong Kong authorities after Ms Zhou alleged to the police that Carson forged documents to gain title to the shares and that she had received no money for the shares now in Carson's name.

200. *Birmingham International Holdings announcement, 24 October, 2010*
201. *Birmingham International Holdings announcement, 22 February, 2011*
202. Nick Harris *"Birmingham tempting fate with their financial plans", Daily Mail, 8 January, 2011*
203. *Birmingham International Holdings Announcement, 14 April, 2011*

The whole story is made more complex in that she claims she had only obtained the shares in October 2009 as repayment for a debt incurred by Carson from a failed land deal, making it difficult for her to prove title to the shares in the first place.

Having twice extended the deadline for the placement of the new shares, BIH finally announced on 4 May 2011[205] that it had managed to place 250M shares of the "best effort" section of the placing at a price of HK$0.20 each – raising around £4.2M in funds for the company. The placing was initially supposed to raise around £18M, leaving a shortfall of £14M and increasing the cashflow issues of BIH.

It was a worrying business model when every time the company required new money it reverted to selling more shares. It's like taking water from a well – there are only so many trips you can make before the water dries up. Here the new money bought penny shares with no chance of ever receiving a dividend and the only possible hope of any return on the investment would be a sale of the company or a future speculative ramp in its share price; this was hardly likely given the state of its finances. BIH had reached the point where new money had dried up and with the failure to expand the Birmingham City brand in China there was no diversification of its business to make certain the company could cope financially with the relegation of its only "performing" asset – the football club.

The club had been utterly reliant on the Sky TV money – it amounted to 74% of the club's turnover in the 2008/09 season[206]. With 95% of the holding company's revenue from the football club those TV rights were the bottom row of the house of cards BIH was built on and relegation from the top flight caused severe cracks to appear in those uncertain foundations and in the accounts of both companies.

204. HKSE filings
205. Birmingham International Holdings Announcement, 4 May, 2011
206. "Birmingham City Blues", The Swiss Ramble, 14 January, 2011

Carson had spent a fortune on the team – not just in transfer fees but in wages – and the wage bill was becoming a millstone around the club's neck. Relegation would result in a drop of approximately one third in the club's turnover and, although Carson was happy to give players what they wanted when they signed, he and his board had neglected to include relegation clauses in at least one contract – that of Nikola Zigic. With Zigic, who was signed in May 2010 and earning in excess of £50,000 per week, the failure to include a clause halving his salary upon relegation[207] (as was standard in other contracts for players at the club) proved to be a very costly mistake; the news that the contract was in fact incremental and his wages would increase by an unspecified percentage year on year just exacerbated the detrimental effect of this startling lack of business acumen.

As the team struggled to pick up points in the closing months of the season, the worries intensified within the club – sponsors and commercial partners had been signed up for the new season but caveats would allow them to break those contracts should the team be relegated. There was also talk at the time that, should the club avoid relegation, the wage bill would still have to be slashed because the realisation had eventually dawned on the board of BIH that football at Birmingham City wasn't the cash cow they had anticipated.

Investors in football clubs are obsessed by the blinding lights of the Premier League TV revenues and are drawn to them like moths; if players were robots and didn't age or depreciate in value as their bodies pass their sell-by date, there would be serious money to be made in professional football. However, unfortunately it's a business of depreciating assets, which requires clubs to spend money year on year to ensure that they stand still – a constant need for regeneration – a point that BIH and Carson failed to grasp.

Is it possible Carson thought the good times would never end and so he never planned for the storm ahead? There's a possibility that, as with other tall poppies, Carson assumed because of the success and luck he had enjoyed in the previous decade it would just keep on coming; however, if you get too

---

207. Colin Tattum, "Birmingham City Talking Point: Colin Tattum explains why Nikola Zigic deserves more credit" Birmingham Mail, 13 November, 2013

far ahead of yourself too quickly in Hong Kong then you will inevitably be taken down a peg or three. It was also speculated by fans in Birmingham that BIH hadn't even factored in the possibility of relegation[208], which seemed to be borne out by the lack of any financial forecast for the club should it fall through the relegation trap door.

If he thought the good times would keep rolling, Carson was certainly disabused of that notion on the pitch. Birmingham City went into freefall as the 2010/11 season came to a close; players' form deteriorated on the pitch and points became rare and precious commodities. Matters came to a head in the last home game of the season against Fulham, which Blues needed to win to give themselves a realistic chance of avoiding the drop. With Fulham being notoriously poor on the road and the Blues having a fairly decent home record, the fans expected their team had a good chance of saving itself.

What followed was one of the most gutless performances of the season and a 2-0 home defeat[209]. The angst was tangible on the terraces; fans walked out early and some of the younger ones were in tears as they saw relegation staring them in the face. Carson didn't take it well either, reportedly resorting to the comfort of a bottle or three of whiskey in the boardroom before having to be carried out to his waiting car later that evening.

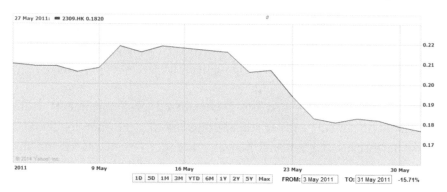

208. Nick Harris, "Birmingham tempting fate with their financial plans", Daily Mail, 8 January, 2011
209. Peter Scrivener, "Birmingham 0 – 2 Fulham", BBC, 15 May, 2011

Financially, it could have been much worse. Although the club were left to cover Zigic's near £3M annual wages in the Championship on an income reduced by a third; the failure to sign Mauro Boselli, Moussa Dembele and Roman Pavlyuchenko meant the wage bill was nowhere near as catastrophic as it could have been. Had Blues signed those players then would the club have found itself in the relegation zone? It's a moot point – the fact remained that with relegation came massive writedowns in financial goodwill and for shareholders as the BIH stock price nose-dived, falling from HK$0.219 to HK$0.1580 in two weeks.

Even so, when relegation arrived Birmingham City went into financial meltdown. Premier League TV rights and merit payments guaranteed at least £40M annual income for the club; on being relegated, the football club would receive "parachute payments" which were just £16M annually for two years and then £8M annually for a further two years. Commercial sales were expected to drop by around 40%; for example, the club lost out on a lucrative kit sponsor which had been lined up for the new season. Sponsoring the team in the Championship just did not appeal.

The only solution for the club was to release some of the older players who were coming to the end of their contracts and to sell off the more valuable players which would lower the wage bill and bring in some much needed capital to help pay the running costs. This was not an attractive scenario to the fanbase – in previous seasons following relegation under the previous board, the playing staff had been preserved to give the club the best possible chance of promotion back to the top flight at the earliest opportunity.

The situation wasn't helped by ill-considered pronouncements from players in the media either; Roger Johnson was the first to demand a transfer because he believed he was a Premier League player and the Championship was beneath him; Craig Gardner told the local radio station it was a "no-brainer"[210] for him to move on to Sunderland (although the

210. "Birmingham City: Craig Gardner joins Sunderland and describes moving as a 'no-brainer'", Birmingham Mail, 1 July, 2011

impression behind the scenes was that he didn't want to go). The fans saw it as rats leaving a sinking ship and it left a bitter taste in the mouth. It was nothing compared to what was to come.

ARRESTED DEVELOPMENT

On 29 June 2011, Carson's world fell apart. Hong Kong police arrived at his house in Barker Road to arrest him on suspicion of money laundering, and took him into custody overnight. He appeared next morning at Eastern Magistrates Court for his bail hearing[211]. Simultaneously, two offices in Kowloon and in Wanchai were raided and documents and computers were seized. Carson was charged under the Organised and Serious Crimes Ordinance (OSCO)[212] with five counts of knowing or having reason to believe that he had dealt with the proceeds of an indictable offence – otherwise known as money laundering.

He cut a forlorn figure as he was roughly marched into the back of a people carrier before being driven to the police station to be formally cautioned and questioned. Just a month before he had been the centre of attention at the club end of season dinner, looking dapper and happy with his beautiful partner, Joanna Wang Man li clinging to his arm. Now in stark contrast he looked older and tired, almost frail and apprehensive of what lay before him.

Although Carson was under arrest he was still surrounded by his flunkeys and when released on bail, the press couldn't get a quote out of him. This was to be a recurrent theme; following his arrest Carson didn't speak directly to the press for over two years until October 2013.

The news of Carson's arrest and charges spread quickly to the UK, with shock quickly giving way to outrage amongst the fans. There was disbelief to begin with – after all, the internet thrives on the rumour mill but as the pictures appeared the full thrust of the story took hold. Internet message boards and social media went into overdrive as fans debated what problems this could cause the club and decrying the shame brought upon it by Carson and his legal woes.

It had barely been one month since the club's defeat in the last game of the 2010/11 season by Tottenham Hotspur, which confirmed the relegation to the Championship; additionally, it had been barely a fortnight since the manager

211. *Sandy Macaskill "Birmingham City owner Carson Yeung arrested on suspicion of money laundering",*
    The Telegraph, 29 June, 2011
212. *OSCO*

Alex McLeish had tendered his resignation by email. It was a lot to take in in one go and, having seen the disaster at Portsmouth, a similarly Hong Kong-owned club – the doomsday scenarios were openly debated. Would Blues be dumped into administration? Would the club be docked points? Carson was deemed persona non grata by many fans as they immediately assumed he was guilty; the bigger and selfish worry in their minds was the future of their beloved Birmingham City rather than the fate of its beleaguered "President".

It was tough to take too; it had been a rough few months since the high of Birmingham City beating Aston Villa on their way to winning the League Cup. Relegation had restored bragging rights in the city to the Villa fans (or so they believed) and this latest reversal of fortune just made them even more confident in their taunts towards the Blue half of the city. Jokes were attempted that Blues would be drawn against "Rapid Exit" in the Europa League before heading "Inter Administration". Blues nearly went out of business in 1991 before being rescued at the eleventh hour by Sullivan and co; it cut to the core of Blues fans who now believed that a similar predicament awaited them so soon after their greatest triumph.

The older and more cynical fans pointed out that the situation was simply an extension of the type of owners Blues had been blessed with before; Sullivan and the Gold brothers had come into the club from their porn empires; the Kumar brothers had been implicated in an "insurance job" involving a fire at one of their outlets as their world collapsed in the BCCI scandal; Ken Wheldon had sold the training ground, tried to merge the club with Walsall and was notorious for being a skinflint, unscrewing the light bulbs in the floodlights after a match. All in all, Birmingham City owners have been a rum old bunch.

Even so, the insults were close to the bone. Carson seemingly had a knack for embarrassing people in China with his thoughtless actions: for example, he had apparently made a grandiose gesture of making a huge donation, RMB20M (nearly £2M), at a charity auction held during a banquet following Birmingham City's game in Beijing only to tell organisers afterwards he was only joking and had been trying to make the event fun[213]. Now he had embarrassed countless thousands of Birmingham City fans who felt tarnished by his association with their club and, although they had been through similar episodes before, it hurt more because of the joy the fans had so recently experienced.

It wasn't just the fans, either. BIH moved swiftly, requesting a suspension of trading[214] in its shares the morning after Carson's arrest, which was quickly followed by an announcement a week later that the charges against Carson were not connected to either BIH or Birmingham City. Carson had assured the board of BIH after his arrest that the charges didn't relate to the football club or the holding company and they were merely a temporary inconvenience. The board reflected those sentiments in their announcement to the HKSE.

The subsequent judgement after his trial casts considerable doubt on the veracity of this announcement, with the judge questioning Carson's recollection of payments to the English solicitors Prince Evans, which Carson had insisted in his evidence were to pay for the Kingston upon Thames property; as mentioned earlier, this contradicted one of his own expert witnesses, Mark Pulvirenti, whose report initially found that the money was destined for the purchase of the first tranche of Birmingham City shares in 2007. At the time, the announcement was accepted by some fans as proof positive that everything would be alright.

It was a stunning fall from grace for Carson, who just 122 days previously had been holding the League Cup trophy aloft at Wembley, smiling for the world's cameras with his manager and his right hand man Peter Pannu by his side. Even though he quickly made bail the conditions were strict: he had to report to the police three times a week and surrender his passport. Birmingham City had made it into Europe for the first time in fifty years but Carson wouldn't see the games for himself[215] at St Andrew's or be able to revel in the media spotlight those games generated. For Carson, the only chance he would have of watching his team over at least the next few years would be on television or on DVDs faithfully sent to him by the club.

213. *Name withheld, Personal Interview, August 2013*
214. *Birmingham International Holdings Announcement, 30 June. 2011*
215. *"Birmingham City owner Carson Yeung refused permission to attend Championship match against Coventry City", The Telegraph, 11 August, 2011*

Carson wasn't happy with the prospect of not seeing his football club for the foreseeable future – or for that matter being prohibited from leaving the fragrant harbour of Hong Kong, so he made an application for his bail conditions to be varied, which would allow him to take one business trip to the UK. The trip would have seen him visit the UK for four days, coinciding with the first game of the Europa League against Braga on 15 September 2011 and the Championship game against Millwall.

To the amazement of most interested parties both here in the UK and in Hong Kong, the application was granted in Carson's favour and he made immediate preparations to return to the UK. The big question of course for the prosecution was would Carson return to Hong Kong once his business trip was over?

The decision to extend bail to allow Carson to visit England was immediately appealed by the Department of Justice, who demonstrated to the High Court that should Carson be allowed to leave Hong Kong there was a real risk he would abscond and not return to stand trial; the approval for his trip was summarily revoked by Judge Peter Line[216]. For the fans and probably the players, this was a good thing. Birmingham City would be playing in the group stages of the Europa League, a significantly positive development for the club, and the arrival of their errant President would have deflected attention away from the team and been a distraction that the club simply didn't need.

What was a great and joyful night on the terraces would have been a very different experience had Carson arrived back in Birmingham. By this time he wasn't appreciated at all; there were regular songs proclaiming the fans' disdain for him and it would have been sad if what turned out to be a triumph for the club was undermined by the off-pitch shenanigans. It's not certain how aware Carson was of the antipathy towards him but had he been present he would have been left in little doubt.

BIH was left with a problem. With its Chairman and major shareholder arrested and on bail on charges of serious financial wrongdoing, there was

---

216. *"Birmingham owner Carson Yeung refused right to fly back for Braga game", The Guardian,*
    14 September, 2011

little prospect of the holding company having its suspension on the stock exchange lifted for the foreseeable future – in fact it took until February 2014. Vico Hui in his capacity as CEO of the company urged Carson to step down from his position as Chairman of the board, pointing out that it would make it incredibly difficult for the company to continue operations without its stock trading on the market and that in the long run it would make things easier for both the company and Carson in that he could take time out to fight the charges against him. Carson, ever the proud man, refused.

It says something about the ego of the man that in the face of everything going on around him, he refused to even temporarily walk away. Swamped by legal issues, vilified by the fans and with his flagship suspended he still couldn't let go. Carson had to be the man in control until the company could be prised from his grip; perhaps he thought he would win the trial; maybe he was advised the case against him was weak but what is just as likely is that he still believed his legendary luck hadn't quite run out.

With Carson stuck in Hong Kong, Peter Pannu emerged as the new face of BIH in Birmingham. Claiming to be a long-term friend of Carson, Pannu had already been promoted from "Vice-Chairman Football" to "Acting Chairman", running the club at the executive level while Carson had to deal with various legal cases involving BIH in Hong Kong and his own personal fight for freedom. Pannu was appointed to the board of Birmingham City FC within a month of Carson's arrest, along with seventeen-year-old Ryan Yeung Tsz-tsung, Carson's son from his first marriage to Li Wing-sze.

Ryan's appointment was seen in Birmingham as a cynical move. Carson could no longer travel to the UK to run things, so by installing Ryan on the board Carson could ensure that he had a proxy representing his interests in the UK. Poor Michael Wiseman, whose family had been connected to the club for three generations, had been dumped from the board assuming the purely ceremonial role of "Vice-President" as Carson's wagons formed a tight circle to fight off any potential attackers, causing the trickle of information flowing from the club to dry up to almost nothing.

Wiseman was joined on the sidelines by Vico Hui. Even though he had put up Carson's bail money, which allowed him to spend time at home rather than in a prison cell on remand, Vico and Carson had fallen out spectacularly over Carson's relationship with Peter Pannu. Vico was adamant that agreement to pay Peter Pannu money for his housing expenses was inappropriate and possibly created a needless tax issue; simultaneously, Pannu blamed Vico for the fallout over the Xtep kit deal.

Carson's arrest caused waves of trouble extending far beyond his personal lifestyle: his assets were frozen by the High Court in Hong Kong by a restraining order made in July 2011, which would cause trouble for the football club as it relied heavily on Carson for infusions of cash at the time. It is doubtful whether Carson had much cash for the club anyway; the restraining order made by the High Court indicated Carson's known Hong Kong assets were about[217] HK$3.4M (about £290,000) in cash along with his houses on The Peak and in the Mid-Levels, four boats, two cars and HK$70M (about £5.8M) in stocks and shares, in addition to the shares he held in BIH. Bearing in mind Carson had mortgaged his own property to ensure cashflow was maintained for the club during the period before his arrest, it is difficult to see how he could have continued to fund the club indefinitely without outside investment.

Businessman Peter Ong had already issued a writ against Carson in the previous year[218] claiming payment of success fees due to him relating to Carson's obtaining control of the newspaper Sing Pao, and in that process he was granted a charge against another property owned by Carson along with his former wife, Ms Li. With two charging orders against his houses in Hong Kong, a company suspended and desperate for funds, while also being denounced across Birmingham for his alleged crimes, a lesser man would have collapsed in a gibbering heap.

The only saving grace was the lack of any affirmative action from the Football League. Their rules require owners to be fit and proper persons – to be

217. *HCMP 1254 of 2011 (V.Bokhary J)*
218. *Natalie Wong "The Final Whistle?", HK Standard, 8 July, 2011*

free of criminal convictions, not involved in multiple insolvencies and not sanctioned by other sporting authorities. There was little or no movement from the footballing authorities in failing to request answers to questions about how the club was being run with its owner awaiting trial in Hong Kong on money laundering charges. The lack of any pronouncement from the Football League was a source of much consternation to the more vitriolic fans; the more reasonable ones accepted Carson's innocence until his guilt could be established and understood that the Football League couldn't act until that happened. Even so, it was widely held that Carson should at least take a step back from the Chairmanship of BIH, particularly as he could not travel to Birmingham.

Carson must have considered his time was running out as owner of Birmingham City FC, as BIH started to look for a buyer for the club. He was introduced to a Cantonese businessman who operated a real estate company in the mainland, Yang Yuezhou, who was looking for a listed shell company in Hong Kong to start a real estate business and BIH appeared to fit the bill. A deal was negotiated in August 2011[219] to sell Yang 14% of the company through convertible loan notes at a price of HK$79.5M (about £6.6M) which would ensure an immediate injection of funds into the cash-strapped company, and within a month[220] a further loan of HK$80M (about £6.7M) was set up for Yang to lend further money to BIH – albeit at a huge interest rate of 12%. As the shares remained suspended and likely to remain so, the deal was never completed and Yang quietly bailed without any money exchanging hands, buying a company called Computech instead in which to concentrate his investments; he didn't return until late 2013 to rekindle his interest in BIH.

In Birmingham, widespread anger was directed at Carson and by the start of the 2011/12 season fans were already signalling their displeasure towards him – singing at least once every game that they didn't care about Carson and that he didn't care about them.

219. *Birmingham International Holdings announcement, 3 August, 2011*
220. *Birmingham International Holdings announcement, 31 August, 2011*

There was talk of protests[221] against Carson's ownership, which fizzled out quickly as the majority of fans realised that the man and his issues were 6,000 miles away in Hong Kong and unlikely to pay much heed to them. Concerned fans formed a supporters trust as they sought to try and understand the situation and build a dialogue between themselves and the board to mend broken relationships.

There wasn't much that could be done. Until Carson stood trial he had no way of proving his innocence and until he was proven guilty the footballing authorities were not prepared to become involved. It would have made more sense for Carson to step back but he declined to do so and there was no way of forcing him into such a move; questions from the fans, the supporters trust and the press were met with a stony silence by the board as formal announcements became less and less frequent as time passed. The press and fans were frozen out – even the staff were alienated and reminded of their obligations of confidentiality. How could a football club continue to be run in such a manner?

---

221. Brett Gibbons, "Birmingham City: Fans plan protest before Everton clash", Birmingham Mail, 29 July, 2011

10

THE BOARDROOM BATTLE

The boardroom of BIH wasn't a convivial place in the summer of 2011. As Carson was forced to concentrate on his legal woes, his right hand man came to the fore. Peter Pannu – who only became a registered director of the football club after Carson's arrest – increasingly exerted his influence over BIH even though he had no official position there until September 2012.

When Pannu arrived at St Andrew's he was only "Vice-Chairman Football"; a management role but not a directorial function. He quickly developed a reputation as Carson's enforcer at the club and slowly edged people out who didn't fit his management style – for example Michael Dunford. By the time Carson was arrested, Pannu had manoeuvred himself into a position of almost total control and power over the club's affairs.

In Hong Kong, Carson's arrest had thrown BIH into turmoil. The stock had been suspended and an announcement was made to the HKSE in an attempt to calm worried shareholders and assure them that his arrest wouldn't affect the day to day running of the company. BIH's problems were further exacerbated by its failure to file accounts for the year ending 2011. Initially, the delivery of the accounts was postponed for three months until January 2012[222] but it wasn't until mid March 2013[223] that they were finally filed. The football club's accounts were also delayed by three months until June 2012, which caused a transfer embargo[224] to be imposed upon the club, with the knock on effect of further performance problems on the pitch and more grief for the fans who had to suffer the continuing taunts of rivals about the parlous financial situation at St Andrew's.

At first, fans speculated that the delays in publishing the club's accounts were a deliberate attempt to enable transfer receipts from the winter 2012 window to be included in the future cashflow forecasts, which would make them more palatable. It was well known that Blues had lost a large slice of its income on relegation to the Championship and it wouldn't defy logic that the board of BIH would try and put lipstick on the pig. As it turned out the

222. *Birmingham International Holdings announcement, 31 October, 2011*
223. *Birmingham International Holdings announcement, 17 March, 2013*
224. *"Birmingham City placed under transfer embargo", BBC, 2 March, 2012*

accounts were delayed again at the end of January[225], and yet again at the end of April[226], prompting questions in the press and angry rebuttals from Pannu in particular, who told the fans "We should all wait to see what comes out of the end of April accounts to see exactly what situation the club is in[227]." He went noticeably quieter when the accounts were delayed again in April.

Pannu's style was bombastic. When confronted with difficult questions, he tended to do one of two things – he would either bluster and bluff his way through answers in an attempt to confuse the questioner or retreat into sullen silence, refusing to offer any comments whatsoever. Neither tactic helped, as both antagonised the fans who were used to seeing their owners on TV pontificating about anything and everything football-related – particularly if there was an opportunity for a helicopter to sit in the background making them feel important.

Later, Pannu blamed the delay in delivering the accounts on a sponsorship agreement with Chinese leisure firm Xtep[228]. The ill-fated deal had resulted in the football club failing to receive a single penny in income from the Chinese kit manufacturers – all income from Xtep went to a British Virgin Islands registered subsidiary of BIH called Birmingham (Hong Kong) Limited. At the same time, BIH effectively had to pay the kit sponsors for one season because of the bizarre nature of the agreements[229]. When the deal was announced in January 2010[230] it was trumpeted as a major success, with payments of HK$90M due over five years to the club. What wasn't announced was the second counter agreement in which BIH would pay HK$50M back to Xtep over five years for "advertising and marketing purposes"[231]. No one ever explained at the time what possible benefit the club would ever accrue from the counter-deal and in the event, no benefit has ever accrued to the club.

225. *Birmingham International Holdings announcement, 31 January, 2012*
226. *Birmingham International Holdings announcement, 27 April, 2012*
227. *Brett Gibbons, "Birmingham City FC tell fans: 'Wait for accounts before judging'", Birmingham Mail,*
     6 March, 2012
228. *"A statement from Peter Pannu", BCFC.com, 6 May, 2013*
229. *Brett Gibbons "Blues paid more to Xtep than they received in kit supply deal", Birmingham Mail,*
     8 January, 2013
230. *Birmingham International Holdings announcement, 18 January, 2010*
231. *Brett Gibbons "Blues paid more to Xtep than they received in kit supply deal", Birmingham Mail,*
     8 January, 2013

What made the situation worse was that relegation from the top flight halved the yearly income to be received by BIH from Xtep, while the counter agreement wasn't affected – meaning that for the 2011/12 season BIH (through its aforementioned subsidiary) lost about HK$6M overall on the deal. In addition Birmingham (Hong Kong) apparently neglected to pay any licencing fee to the football club for the usage of its logo and image rights, as had been agreed. The fallout led to a lot of accusations and debate among the fans as to exactly where or to whom the money went – although the single point every interested fan was consistent on was that the beneficiary which was supposed to receive it – the club – didn't.

The Xtep deal was symptomatic of the poor running of BIH by the board. It could have been a win-win situation for both parties – a leading Chinese sports firm dipping its toe in a lucrative foreign market and the club (and its brand) making inroads into the enormous potential fanbase in mainland China. Xtep have around seven thousand retail outlets in the PRC and the deal should have resulted in Blues kit being sold everywhere from Shanghai to Beijing and all points in between. The business model as loosely defined by Carson – that BIH had purchased the club on the potential to market it in China building a revenue base there which would seriously underpin the financial welfare of the team – would now appear to be fanciful; however, at the time it was seen as revolutionary and eminently feasible.

In its execution the deal never worked to plan; Xtep sold merchandise that used a rip-off version[232] of the club badge without paying for the intellectual property rights and BIH made no real effort to build the real Birmingham brand within China. Various products to be associated with the brand – such as beer, light residential housing and training academies were projects worked on by BIH employees and presented to the board but Carson nixed them one by one, with the result that the club's growth within the Chinese market never had a chance to take off. The issue came to a head in June 2012 when Peter Pannu unilaterally made the decision to drop Xtep[233], triggering threats of lawsuits and countersuits as both parties scrambled to recoup lost money.

232. *"Xtep Gone" Often Partisan, 29 June, 2012*
233. *Colin Tattum "Birmingham City rip up kit contract with Xtep", Birmingham Mail, 29 June, 2012*

Pannu pinned the blame for the Xtep fiasco squarely on the shoulders of club Chairman and BIH Chief Executive Vico Hui[234]. Hui had been responsible for negotiating the original deal and the boss of the subsidiary that handled it; for his part, Hui vigorously denied that he was to blame for the issues and strongly protested against the inclusion of the statement in the accounts[235] which blamed him.

Hui blamed Pannu for the deteriorating relationship with Xtep, reasoning that the former policeman was too quick to try and sort out business disputes by threats of lawsuits when one of the real issues so far as he was concerned was a lack of communication between BCFC, BIH and Xtep. It was certainly the case that Xtep used an illegally altered Birmingham City badge to sell its products in China[236]. Hui contended that he had reached an agreement with Xtep to withdraw the disputed merchandise from sale only for logistical errors in the leisurewear company to emerge, which resulted in them leaving the disputed stock on the shelves longer than was intended.

It was also noted that although the BCFC trademark was registered in Europe, there was no such registration in China – a situation that has long plagued western companies who have found their products ripped off in the PRC. The deal had to be done quickly and it was eventually contracted to the BVI subsidiary of BIH so that the PRC trademark registration application could be made as quickly as possible. What the former club Chairman Hui couldn't confirm is why the trademark registration application was never made and why the club was never recompensed for licencing its intellectual property.

It was eventually revealed in April 2013[237] that Xtep wasn't the only issue that was causing concern to the auditors, BDO. Unknown to the board of BIH, Carson had signed a consultancy agreement with Peter Pannu to pay him a substantial fee for the former policeman's and barrister's assistance with ongoing legal issues. The agreement allegedly came into force for a

234. Jon Griffin "Birmingham City hit by boardroom split", Birmingham Mail, 27 June, 2012
235. BCFC Accounts year end 2012
236. Jon Griffin "Birmingham City hit by boardroom split", Birmingham Mail, 27 June, 2012
237. Jeanette Oldham, "Special Investigation: Birmingham City chief Peter Pannu's secret £1.5m pay deal", Birmingham Mail, 26 April, 2013

period of five years commencing on 22 September 2009 with Carson paying – on behalf of BIH – a fee of HK$310,000 per month to Peter Pannu via "Asia Rays", his Hong Kong-based corporate consultancy firm. A letter signed by Carson addressed to Mr Pannu dated 28 July 2011 upped the fee to a whopping £65,000 a month from July 2011 in light of the additional problems caused to the company by his arrest[238].

A further fee was payable to Pannu for his accommodation and for his time in Birmingham: £180,000 was paid into Pannu's BVI vehicle Amazing Top International Enterprises Limited, which would later become another bone of contention between Pannu and Hui. Pannu produced for the auditors BCFC board minutes signed by Carson, which confirmed that a board meeting had taken place on 1 October 2010 with only Pannu and Carson (albeit by telephone) present to approve the payment. It is worth remembering that Pannu was not a director of Birmingham City FC or Birmingham City PLC (the UK parent) until July 2011, some nine months after the meeting allegedly took place. Neither Mike Wiseman nor Vico Hui, who were both directors at that time, have any knowledge of that board meeting.

The fees had allegedly been paid by Carson directly; however, as Carson had no way of paying the fees due to the restraining order applied to his assets after his arrest, it had been agreed between Carson and Pannu that the money would be drawn against the £14M loan Carson had made to the club or the £7M loan by BIH to the club. The club wasn't losing any money on the deal but there were now unbudgeted payments to be made and it stretched the already precarious cashflow situation even further. With Pannu already receiving a pay packet – according to the accounts of the football club – of close to £700,000 per annum, when the further news broke of his additional consultancy agreement it provoked nothing but disbelief and anger among the fans.

Football is a sport with high wages for the top 1% to 2% of participants but most of the top wage earners are on the pitch. To many fans it was rubbing

238. *Document withheld*

salt into the wounds that a man as unpopular as Pannu – who had been seen by many to be doing a poor job at any rate because of the continued lack of investment in the club from Hong Kong and China – was being paid so much money. It seemed especially galling when Pannu had previously spoken of the need for the club to tighten its belt and had openly complained of the ludicrously high wages that some players like Nikola Zigic were earning.

The BIH board of directors (apart from Carson of course) were unaware of Pannu's consultancy agreement until the issue was raised by the auditors and it caused a huge split within the boardroom. On one side there were Carson and Pannu (who wasn't a director of BIH at this point) along with solicitor Anthony Cheung Kwai-nang, who had been appointed at the behest of the former police officer. On the other side were the "old school" directors led by Hui and Lee, who railed against Pannu for his personal greed and his lofty ambitions that belied his lack of experience and accused him of stuffing the board with his cronies to gain control of BIH.

The BIH board was split over the arrangement to pay Pannu's consultancy fees with Hui and Lee in particular complaining that they had no prior knowledge before the money started leaking out of the football club to pay it. The same directors contended that their approval should have been sought before Carson committed the funds to Pannu. Their objections were ignored and the payments continued.

The infighting within the boardroom and loss of trust between the sides caused a loss of direction and leadership in BIH – at the same time as the man at the top was struggling to come to terms with his own legal battles.

BDO, whose Birmingham office acted as auditors to the football club and whose Hong Kong office acted as auditors to BIH, lost faith with Pannu too. BDO accountant Tom Lawton was threatened by Pannu in an email dated 15 March 2012[239], with the former policeman telling him "I am not bothered with your BS any more. Once the audit is over I will deal with u

---

239. *Jeanette Oldham "Special Investigation: Blues Chief Peter Pannu in 'threat' to club's auditor", Birmingham Mail, 27 April, 2012*

personally (sic)". BDO UK also claimed that Pannu had made a series of remarks about Lawton's conduct of the audit that were "factually incorrect" and that Pannu had put "considerable pressure on the conduct of the audit process" at times during the 2011 audit, threatening the independence of the audit. BDO UK took a very dim view of Pannu's conduct and intimated to the football club and Pannu that they took such personal threats seriously and were minded to involve the police. This forced BIH to apologise for Pannu's words and BDO subsequently decided against police involvement. They did tell BIH they would continue to monitor the situation, before they eventually resigned.

At the same time, in Hong Kong BDO HK continued to try to clear up issues surrounding the consultancy agreement, with concerns over the tax and legal implications arising from the non-disclosure of the agreement and the board's failure to ratify it. Pannu supplied various opinions from tax consultants and lawyers that argued that the agreement was legal and above board but BDO HK did not accept the explanations provided, requesting further clarification on how the management agreement related to the payments made. BDO HK were forced into a situation where they had no choice but to resign as auditors – much as their UK office were following the issues with Tom Lawton. They couldn't accept the validity of the agreement without the prior knowledge and approval of the BIH board. Matters came to a head in a stormy board meeting held at the offices of BIH's solicitors Robertsons on 21 September 2012 where Pannu argued his position and once again affirmed to BDO HK that the accounts were ready to be signed off. Coincidentally, this was the first BIH board meeting chaired by (and indeed, attended by) Peter Pannu. BDO didn't agree, and after first drafting an announcement sacking BDO as auditors, BIH accepted their resignation in October 2012.

When the accounts were finally released having been audited by much smaller firms than BDO – Birmingham accountancy firm Edwards in the UK and JH CPA Alliance in Hong Kong - they came with extensive qualifications. Auditors from both firms gave disclaimers of their opinion on both sets of accounts, in which they stated that they had not received enough information to be sure that the accounts were true and correct and couldn't fully audit them, which caused further embarrassment to the football club and anxiety for the fans who were increasingly concerned with how these irregularities and the money laundering allegations against Carson were affecting their club. There were concerns that the Football League wouldn't accept the Birmingham City FC accounts as sufficiently stated to lift the transfer embargo against the club, but thanks to assurances and evidence given to the Football League by Birmingham City staff members at various meetings following the publication of the accounts, the Football League finally agreed to lift the embargo in July 2012.

Carson's court case rumbled on. The trial hearings were originally due to begin in November 2012 but having changed his legal team to one headed by Joseph Tse SC, which led to the prosecution noting that Carson had used no less than five senior counsel[240], with Clive Grossman SC among them. Carson requested and was granted a further adjournment until the end of April 2013, much to the consternation of Blues fans who wanted an end to the whole drama. At the same time Carson was fighting a long and eventually losing battle in court over a default on a mortgage over his Barker Road house, delaying the repossession of his multi-million home by Wing Hang Bank for months before finally succumbing in June 2013[241].

What originally was a shocking story affecting the owner now had serious implications for the club. The delays in the accounts and lack of investment in the football club forced the continued selling of players such as Jordon Mutch (a reported £3M to Cardiff City) and Ben Foster (a reported £4M to West Bromwich Albion) keeping the club in the black. Slowly but surely, the number of remaining playing assets that could be liquidated was dwindling.

---

240. Austin Chiu "Carson Yeung granted four months to prepare defence", South China Morning Post, 9 November, 2012
241. Wing Hang Bank v Success Orient Investment and others, HCMP2457 of 2011, (R Lung KW)

Inside the BIH offices at Harbour Centre, Wanchai, the atmosphere was becoming increasingly ugly in the boardroom. Directors including Lee Yiu-tung were disillusioned with the running of the company and started asking pointed questions of Carson's management. Carson responded by naming Peter Pannu as Executive Director, Managing Director and Chief Executive Officer in mid-September 2012[242], giving him the authority to put those who were causing Carson problems in their place. Directors' questions were met with stone-walled silence, board meetings were called and suspended with only hours notice – a tactic designed to make it as hard as possible for the dissenting directors to attend and consequently causing them to fall foul of attendance requirements, which resulted in disqualification from their positions[243].

The press were continually blanked too by BIH as they sought answers to their questions about potential takeovers of the club. Gianni Paladini, a Solihull-based Italian businessman and former Chairman of Queens Park Rangers, was a guest on local broadcaster Tom Ross's show in September 2012 in which he claimed that he "could complete the takeover of the club within 48 hours"[244]. However his remarks turned out to be pretentious bluster, as in the same interview Pannu disavowed any talk of negotiations with him over the sale of the club[245].

The only information fans had to go on were the increasingly sporadic announcements to the HKSE, as BIH released information regarding board members leaving, new board members joining and abstract vague remarks concerning the potential sale of the club.

One director, Lee Yiu-tung, was disqualified from his role as executive director in January 2013 on the pretext that he had not attended a board meeting in the last six months. Lee was incandescent with rage over the slight against his character, claiming he had documentary proof that he had

---

242. *Birmingham International Holdings announcement, 19 September, 2012*
243. *Birmingham International Holdings announcement, 11 January, 2013*
244. *Colin Tattum, "Birmingham City: It looks like we have no deal – Gianni Paladini", Birmingham Mail,*
    15 September 15 2012
245. *ibid*

attended every meeting he possibly could at that time. While Vico Hui had grumbled about being forced out – and being owed money which had been recorded in the BIH accounts – no director before Lee appeared prepared to take on Carson and Pannu in the Courts. Lee was in a different category; money was one thing but his reputation was important to him and he made complaints to various regulatory authorities and instituted proceedings against BIH for wrongful dismissal. Had Pannu finally met his match?

Pannu was also struggling to keep all the balls in the air. He had reassured the BIH board he could sell a player (in all probability Jack Butland) for up to £8M having rejected a slightly lower offer from Southampton in the summer. Unfortunately, he had neglected to take into account that other football clubs now knew that Birmingham City were struggling financially and would test their resolve by making incredibly lowball offers knowing that the Blues were unlikely to be in a position to resist them for much longer. In the end, Pannu had to settle for just £3.5M for Butland over two instalments from Stoke City. It left Pannu and the club with a significant problem – he needed more money to pay the bills for the remainder of the season.

Pannu had three choices. The most obvious one was administration, which was unthinkable. Not only would it result in the certain relegation of the club, it would precipitate his own removal from running the company and the end of his hefty pay cheque. The second option was to keep selling enough players to make up the remainder of the cash required – which would alienate the fans even more and was still likely to lead to relegation – reducing the club's value and continuing the vicious circle that the club would have even less money to function in the new season. The final option was to "factor" a parachute payment. Birmingham City were due the third parachute payment of £8M in the 2013/14 season from the Premier League having been relegated to the Championship in 2011. Factoring this – meaning borrowing from a lender on the security of the forthcoming payment – would allow the bills to be paid, the club could keep its remaining squad of players together – and in the event of a miracle of achieving promotion it would be easy to sort out the next shortfall with the new TV revenue. If the club failed to attain promotion, the financial mess would have to be sorted in the summer.

The deal was done – Pannu managed to get £5M for the £8M payment, losing 37.5% of its value. It was confirmation of how desperate things were; taking a loan on at an interest rate of 12% as BIH had done from Yang Yuezhou in August 2011 was incredible, but to have to lose 37.5% of a non-recurring source of future income to keep the club afloat was almost farcical. Pannu would no doubt say it did the job – Blues stayed comfortably up in the Championship and it kept the club going until the summer of 2013 when season ticket money would come in.

As news of his consultancy fee broke in April 2013, Pannu was forced to go on the defensive. He had already been pressurised to explain his vast pay packet once to the local press during the previous summer – this time he was asked to explain why he was receiving a consultancy fee on top of that (along with a wage from BIH for being an Executive Director from September 2012). Legal threats were made prior to publication of the issues by the Birmingham Mail[246] but the newspaper held firm and Pannu was forced to climb down, abandoning his threat of a legal action and instead meeting the accusations with a statement blaming the situation on perceived leaks within BIH and attacking the reputations of those who disagreed with him, such as Lee, further in an attempt to deflect criticism[247].

Pannu won the next round of the boardroom battle at the BIH AGM in May 2013. The week before a potential shareholder revolt had looked possible after the second largest shareholder Liu Xingcheng gave a newspaper interview[248], in which he confirmed he would be voting against the re-election of Pannu to the board of directors and urging fellow BIH shareholders to do the same. Unfortunately, Liu's vote against all resolutions was rejected by BIH

246. Jeanette Oldham, "Special Investigation: Birmingham City chief Peter Pannu's secret £1.5m pay deal", Birmingham Mail, 26 April, 2013
247. "A statement from Peter Pannu", BCFC.com, 6 May 2013
248. Daniel Ivery "Birmingham City shareholder launching bid to force Carson Yeung and Peter Pannu out", Birmingham Mail, 2 May, 2013
249. "BIH AGM News – Liu Xingcheng Vote Denied?", Often Partisan, 10 May, 2013

due to procedural irregularities."[249] .This allowed Pannu to be convincingly re-elected to the board along with his acolytes, like Anthony Cheung Kwai-nang, and all motions were carried without further fuss[250]. Pannu then proceeded to make sure that the last vestiges of opposition were culled with Pauline Wong Po-ling pushed into stepping down at the meeting and Raymond Yau Yan-ming following[251] three days later having only narrowly been re-elected, which allowed Pannu and Carson to take absolute control of the boardroom.

Taking this setback in his stride, Lee continued with his labour tribunal case against his disqualification as a director and obtained an order that his case be transferred to the High Court[252]. This was bad news for Pannu, as it would allow Lee to give evidence of the questions he had raised at the BIH board meetings and information relating to Pannu's consultancy fees in open court – and which the press could report freely without fear of reprisal and could be potentially enormously embarrassing for Pannu, Carson and BIH. The battle was in full cry now and with attempts at a confidential settlement failing, the wheels were set in motion for another legal skirmish.

The HKSE were also applying pressure. With BIH shares then suspended for over two years, they wrote once again to BIH's head office requesting details of a resumption proposal, and asking pertinent questions: chief amongst them being the role of Carson within the company. Irrespective of his legal woes, Carson remained absolutely still the top dog at BIH; his word was the law and together with Pannu he controlled the boardroom. The HKSE were concerned whether Carson could properly discharge his duties fully as Chairman with money laundering charges hanging over him. Carson had no choice – he had to give ground and provide an assurance that he would walk away.

250. *Birmingham International Holdings announcement, 10 May, 2013*
251. *Birmingham International Holdings announcement, 13 May, 2013*
252. *"BIH Embroiled In New Court Battle", Often Partisan, 5 June, 2013*
253. *Birmingham International Holdings announcement, 19 August, 2013*

In the announcement BIH made to the HKSE in late August 2013[253], Carson made sure his departure would be on his own terms and in his own time. The announcement confirmed he would step down voluntarily from his management duties "before or on resumption of trading of shares". His compromise reached with the HKSE meant there was certainty that he would step down, but not until the HKSE allowed the suspension in trading of the shares to be lifted. He would remain in control with the semblance of having acquiesced to their demands. The announcement went on to say that once Carson had relinquished his directorial duties on the resumption of trading, he would remain on the sidelines until his case was concluded in his favour. The word he didn't want to use was "convicted".

The announcement dated 19 August 2013 also confirmed what the fans already knew; that BIH was strapped for cash and the club would have to be sold. For the first time, BIH confirmed it was in serious negotiations – albeit preliminary ones – and interested parties had completed due diligence examination of its books. In the interim BIH was forced to borrow more money – HK$15M[254] from a company called U-Continent (which later turned out to be owned by Yang Yuezhou) – to address its continuing liquidity issues. Having already borrowed HK$20M from U-Continent on 1 August[255], it did not augur well for the future.

254. *Birmingham International Holdings announcement, 19 November, 2013*
255. *Birmingham International Holdings announcement, 1 August, 2013*

11

UP IN COURT

It took nearly two years from Carson's arrest for his case to come up in the District Court, Wanchai Hong Kong on 29 April 2013. For the fans in Birmingham it was a long wait; many wanted to see justice done summarily and were frustrated by the delay.

After his arrest in June 2011, Carson appeared in Court a couple of times during August and September of that year when he made futile attempts to have his bail conditions varied to allow him to travel to the United Kingdom. It wasn't until his pre-trial review in December 2011 that those fans who remained interested keenly anticipated his trial dates being fixed. When the judge confirmed that the trial hearings would commence eleven months later on 29 November 2012 the news was met with dismay, like the mother-in-law staying for Christmas.

Results on the pitch had gone well with four straight league wins in October 2011, over Nottingham Forest, Leicester City, Bristol City and Leeds United; the club was unlucky not to qualify from their Europa League qualifying group during the same period, winning away in Belgium against Club Brugge and in Slovenia against NK Maribor. The new Birmingham City manager Chris Hughton, who was appointed in July 2011, had become a popular figure on the terraces having encouraged an attractive attacking brand of football at St Andrew's. Loanee striker Chris Wood from West Bromwich Albion had gone through a purple patch pushing his goals tally into double figures before the end of October – the first time a Birmingham City striker had managed that achievement since the late seventies.

Many hoped for a swift resolution to their owner's legal troubles as the club attempted to bounce back to the Premier League at the first attempt. Rightly or wrongly, delays in the court case were linked to the fans' natural assumption that any sale of the Club would also be pushed back as Carson clung on to the club he loved – this didn't appeal to the vast majority of fans, as it became clear that further misfortune awaited them as the club's limited resources slowly dwindled.

It was perhaps a measure of how much the prosecution authorities wanted to make Carson's life difficult, or simply how little they trusted him, that when he requested for a sympathetic variation in his bail terms to travel just across the border from Hong Kong to Shenzhen to attend his father's funeral at the end of July 2012 they objected. Although he offered to travel with policemen on both sides of the border and Peter Pannu tendered his HK$10M apartment in Sha Tin as an additional surety, Mr Justice Macrae refused to vary Carson's bail[256].

As much as anyone dislikes or suspects an individual of wrongdoing, he was after all still an innocent man; and it has to be said that the decision to refuse him the opportunity to pay his last respects to his father was inhumane. The Chinese set great store by the Confucian philosophy of filial piety, which is reflected in the way they deal with the death of an ancestor or a family member; it must have been an enormous blow to Carson, his father's eldest son by his second wife, the most important person in the family hierarchy in Chinese culture as a result of the estrangement of Yeung Chung's sons by his first marriage, to be forbidden from attending his father's funeral.

In many ways it laid down a marker for how the authorities pursued the case. Pressurised by the Hong Kong Government to crack down on corruption and money laundering and seeking a high profile suspect Carson fitted the bill perfectly; the prosecution believed that he would struggle to beat Hong Kong's draconian anti-money laundering laws without unexpected evidence turning up and no little good fortune. As one learned member of the bar was heard to remark in a social club in Hong Kong it was a case of "the tall poppy syndrome" – Carson had grown too high too fast and was being cut down to size.

The trial date approached with keen anticipation in England and a feeling that this was the start of the endgame. Persistent rumours abounded of the club being sold – after Gianni Paladini had begun talking up his chances of taking over the club, many thought the trial would be the final chapter in the saga before the club changed hands.

256. Candy Chan "Yeung Funeral Request Denied", The Standard, 31 July, 2012

Such notions were quickly dashed. Carson had changed his leading counsel from Clive Grossman SC to Joseph Tse SC and his new counsel told the judge he needed more time to prepare his client's case. To much consternation in England, Judge Yau acceded to his request for more time and adjourned the trial for a further five months, prolonging the agony for the fans who continued to link Carson's fate with the sale of the Club.

It wasn't until 29 April 2013[257] that Carson finally appeared in the dock on the first day of his trial. Media interest was high, with most Hong Kong newspapers represented in the press seats, along with international agencies like Bloomberg and Reuters. The BBC sent their Chinese correspondent down from Beijing. The sole representatives from the UK were two Birmingham City fans who with some help had made the 6,000 mile trip together to Hong Kong – one of those being your own Daniel Ivery who was covering the trial on a freelance basis for the Birmingham Mail[258].

Carson cut a disconsolate figure in the dock. He'd been seen walking around the countryside in the New Territories in the week before his trial and he had looked stressed and haggard. The pressure of losing his home on Barker Road in January 2013 and the strains in his personal life with his wife and children living over the border in Shenzhen out of his reach was telling. The lines on his face spoke of a man who was witnessing his world collapsing around him. He tried to remain calm on the first day of the hearings but Carson notably did a double take when he spotted two English "gweilos" in the public gallery, one wearing a Birmingham City scarf. It was possibly a moment of clarity in seeing how great an impact his trial was having, not just on his personal life, but also on others in his wider world.

He took his place in the dock and listened intently to the charges as they were read to him. He swayed gently as the interpreter spoke quietly in Cantonese, only breaking his silence with a quiet plea of "not guilty" as each charge was put to him. It was a charged moment – the culmination of the lengthy

---

257. *"VIDEO: Carson Yeung Trial – Birmingham City owner denies money-laundering", Birmingham Mail,*
  29 April, 2013
258. *Daniel Ivery "Haggard and under scrutiny from the press", Birmingham Mail, 30 April, 2013*

investigation and legal process of the last five years were now distilled down to these words – the next few weeks of the trial would decide his fate which was inextricably linked to the future of his beloved football club.

Carson was charged with five counts of money laundering under OSCO – specifically, knowing ("the first limb") or having reasonable grounds to believe ("the second limb") that the funds he dealt with were the proceeds of an indictable offence. The Hong Kong money laundering laws are draconian in that under the second limb of the offence the prosecution do not have to even prove the money in question was the proceeds of an indictable crime; merely that a reasonable man (in this case a District Court Judge) would have reasonable grounds to believe that the money originated from the proceeds of crime. Under this interpretation of the law, which we will discuss in more detail later, it is almost impossible to see how "the reasonable man" under the second limb in a case where hundreds of millions of unexplained dollars flows through personal accounts can come to anything other than a guilty verdict in the absence of an explanation from the defendant. The onus of proof is essentially shifted to the defendant; as Graham Harris SC later eloquently put it during the trial the "tactical burden" was shifted to Carson to explain the source and movement of the funds. Carson was accused of having laundered around HK$721M (about £57M) that flowed through five accounts he controlled – three in his own name and two in his father's – over a six year period.

As the prosecution only had to prove that the "reasonable man" would have reason to believe that the funds in the accounts represented the proceeds of an indictable offence, no attempt was even made to prove that the money had actually resulted from substantive indictable offences, for example drug-trafficking or prostitution.

It is no defence under Hong Kong law to say that you know and trust the person sending you the money. In HKSAR v Pang Hung Fai[259], in a judgement handed down by the Hong Kong Court of Appeal a money laundering conviction was upheld even though the accused could show he had known

---

259. *HKSAR v Pang Hung Fai CACC34 of 2012 (Hon Stock VP, Lunn JA and McWalters J)*

the man who had transferred money to his account for thirty years, that he had no reason to believe that he should not be trusted or to question the malice of his motives irrespective of the large sum of money involved. The law is certain; no matter who transferred the funds, no matter how long you had known them or how wealthy they were, you were obligated to question the provenance of the money and satisfy yourself it was legitimate; you could not just turn a "Nelson's blind eye" or make a cursory "nod and wink" examination, but you must conduct a proper enquiry that the "reasonable man" would expect. The final appeal in this case will now be heard in the Court of Final Appeal in the autumn of 2014, with one of the foremost advocates in the Common Law world Clare Montgomery QC rumoured to be appearing for the appellant.

The first day of Carson's trial was given over to his defence counsel's attempt to have the case thrown out. Carson was represented by Graham Harris SC, an eloquent and popular Englishman with an engaging and expansive manner, and a range of extravagantly coloured socks often described by his colleagues as "The Edwardian" or in such terms as "The Edwardian has been treading the boards". His words kept the courtroom rapt in the face of the often obscure legal points he made, as he set out his client's case for a permanent stay of the proceedings. Harris was adamant Carson couldn't receive a fair trial; financial firms were only obliged to retain documents for a period of seven years and Harris argued that – as a result of the unacceptable delays in the investigation – crucial evidence Carson would require to support his case was no longer in existence. Harris complained that the police had hindered Carson's defence by dragging their feet in investigating the case, taking three years to arrest Carson from the time the investigation began.

In contrast, the prosecution counsel, John Reading SC, formerly a Government prosecutor in the Department of Justice but now at the private bar, was much less flamboyant, and had to apologise to the Court for arriving late. The Australian prosecutor did not impress the judge with his tardiness and as Harris made his eloquent submission the enraptured public benches began to believe that the highly improbable had become possible and that Carson could be granted a permanent stay. Harris' arguments were persuasive and you could almost detect a feeling of sympathy for Carson in the courtroom. How could he receive a fair trial if the documentation he required for his own defence from impeccable financial institutions was no longer available to him, as the whole legal process had taken over four years and the banks and brokers had legitimately destroyed their records beyond their seven year requirement for safe keeping? The argument appeared compelling.

The key moment came late in the day when Judge Yau requested the defence counsel to explain the cash transactions in the accounts. Harris took instructions from Carson through his solicitor "Gorgeous" George Tung and informed the court that there were indeed cash transactions through the accounts in the tens of millions of Hong Kong dollars – maybe even a hundred million – but that there was no documentary evidence available to answer the judge's inquiries. It was at this moment one could sense from the faces in the public gallery that Carson's application for a permanent stay was doomed; in one sentence from his own mouth he had given the judge a good reason to reject the application.

It appeared Carson had effectively admitted in court that he wouldn't be able to provide paperwork to explain where the huge sums of cash had originated that had been deposited in and finally transferred out of his accounts. Large cash transactions are considered by financial investigators to be a key indicator of money laundering being in their nature anonymous and transitory. To suggest in court that you couldn't give an explanation of the origin of huge sums of cash because documentation was not available from third parties, while at the same time failing to remember the transactions yourself because you neglected to keep your own records, was a telling blow. Whether there was a breakdown in communication between Harris, Carson and Gorgeous George in the way Harris so freely – and in the end disastrously – expanded on the issue of cash in the accounts is a question only they can answer.

As expected, after a few days adjournment to consider the parties' respective

260. *"Birmingham City's Carson Yeung loses bid to stop trial"*, BBC, 3 May 2013

submissions, the judge threw out[260] the application for the permanent stay and the trial commenced with the opening prosecution arguments. The judge noted that although the finance companies hadn't kept their records, he would expect a reasonable person to have kept their own records. This was apparently something Carson had either failed to do or was unwilling to disclose at this stage.

Reading had obviously noted how Harris had won over the press by handing out copies of his application on the first day and made an effort to make sure the press received his written opening submissions, which he then proceeded to read out in court – making it easier for them to be reported in full by all news outlets present.

The first headline allegations were made immediately – names were disclosed of those who had remitted huge sums of money into Carson's accounts for no apparent reason. Cheung Chi-tai[261], who was suspected to be a major triad boss and had avoided trial for conspiracy to murder due to a lack of evidence was one of these individuals, as was movie mogul Abba Chan Tat-chee, who had previously been imprisoned for embezzlement[262].

The amounts were in the tens of millions of Hong Kong Dollars – millions of pounds – much of it in "cash", although this term was shown during the trial to be misleading because bank transfers are often labelled "cash" as are deposits or withdrawals from, for example, stock broking accounts. The question remained: why would people transfer so much money into Carson's accounts and for no apparent reason? Carson was going to have his work cut out answering those key questions.

Reading also maintained in his opening arguments that the money laundered through the bank accounts in question had been used to part-fund Carson's original share purchase in Birmingham City FC. This was the first time in public that the prosecution linked the charges of money laundering to the

---

261. Matt Isaacs and Reuters Staff "Special Report: High Rollers, triads and a Las Vegas Giant" Reuters, 29 March, 2010
262. Diana Lee, "Showstopper as 'Uncle Ba' gets 3 years", The Standard, 12 July, 2011

purchase of the club – something BIH had vigorously denied at the time of Carson's arrest. At the time of his original attempt to buy the club Carson had underwritten the initial share purchase in full, putting up HK$250M in security. Reading submitted that HK$84M was remitted at that time to a solicitor's account in England as part of the funding for the purchase of the club. It later emerged the sum in fact remitted to Prince Evans Lloyd was HK$36.422M and Carson disputed his own expert witness Mark Pulvirenti's evidence that the money had been used to buy Birmingham City, maintaining he had used that money to buy his property in London.

After the first couple of days of revelations, the case quickly settled down into a slower rhythm. The prosecution called a procession of witnesses from various stock broking firms, asking them to confirm the trades Carson had undertaken, how he had financed those trades and the sources of other shares and assets demanded from Carson as collateral for the debts or "margin" he ran up. Often the focus of questions was to enquire why Carson had been granted such huge credit lines at the same time as he claimed he had no income to the taxman and no readily visible means in which to repay the huge borrowings.

The difficult questions came quickly – why had Kingston Securities loaned BIH money as a company and Carson over £11M personally[263] to buy Birmingham City when they already knew he was under investigation in 2009? Why had Eugene Chuang's firm Chung Nam Securities allowed Carson such a huge credit line and then not chased it when Carson started bouncing cheques as he struggled to pay back the money he had borrowed on margin, having already written off 80% of the debt?[264] Time and again the same questions were raised – why was Carson allowed to run up such huge debts with their companies? Where had the money deposited into his accounts originated – and to whom was it transferred?

The questions continually examined the security and collateral that Carson had put up to cover the credit lines he had been given by these stock broking

---

263. Thomas Chan, "Carson Yeung's margin account traded more than HK$500m", South China Morning Post, 16 May, 2013
264. Thomas Chan "Soccer Boss Carson Yeung had money woes since 2002: prosecution", South China Morning Post, 29 October, 2013

firms. According to his tax returns, he had made no income from a regular job, so the prosecution aimed to prove that the credit extended to Carson was as a result of the securities firms knowing Carson had other sources of funds he was not disclosing to the tax authorities. There is no tax on personal stock trading profits or gambling profits in Hong Kong but extending a huge line of credit to Carson because he regularly got lucky on the baccarat tables in Macau wouldn't make much business sense – unless the institution concerned had reason to believe that the loan was secured from elsewhere. The insinuation was clear, although the torturous nature of the presentation of the prosecution evidence often seemed to cloud its own case.

Convincing answers were not emerging and even through the dour nature of the evidence, a prima facie case was building against Carson. There was no doubt huge sums of money had flowed through the five accounts in question; there was no doubt that Carson had declared little or no income to the taxman; the onus was very much on Carson to explain how he had come into the money and how he had formed a reasonable belief that the money wasn't "dark" to use the local parlance.

For all his eloquence and charm, the substance underlying the defence case Harris started to put forward seemed a little shaky. In a "normal" case the defendant would give evidence first, before his other witnesses, in order that he could not be said to benefit from hearing the evidence when presenting his own testimony; Harris successfully applied to the court for Carson to reserve his right to give evidence after his own witnesses had been called, although the judge ruled he would have to take into account that Carson had received the benefit of hearing his own defence witnesses first.

The big question was whether Carson would risk giving evidence at all. After the apparent mishap in the stay application, it's possible he thought twice about standing in the dock to answer what he knew would be difficult questions; by delaying the question of if and when he would give evidence he bought himself some more time – a regular theme in this story.

Harris called witnesses to testify that Carson was legitimately rich; that he had made money on the baccarat tables in the casinos of Macau and that he had been a great success in the hairdressing game. The lack of any paper trail to substantiate these claims seriously undermined the defence; familial links with Carson were pointed out for bias and past convictions and legal issues were mentioned to discredit witnesses. Former legislator Chim Pui-chung was reminded of his own spell behind bars when he gave evidence[265]; Kassi Yeung Tak-wai was noted to be Carson's niece and Yang Wu Jun his cousin before they gave evidence and Jackie Pan Chik was reminded[266] that he had given contradictory evidence in Court in 2002 about Carson's control of his father's account.

It was all too much for former legislator Chim Pui-chung, who verbally tangled with Judge Yau in the courtroom after being reminded not to raise his voice. The so-called "angry man from Chiu Chow" didn't appreciate being reminded by the prosecution of his own prison sentence for conspiring to forge documents. He gave evidence that he knew Carson well, that Carson was a rich man and confirmed to the court why he had not required paper documentation in connection to a specific transaction involving them both. Chim had to be reminded by the judge that it was he who was in charge of proceedings and not the former LegCo member after Chim told the judge off for raising his voice to him.

Carson wasn't helped by the quality of the evidence of his expert witnesses, which was based on their reports. Ian Robinson had to rely on internet research to back up his opinions noted in his evidence owing to the lack of information provided to him by Carson and his solicitors. Mark Pulvirenti was similarly handicapped – he would no doubt say that the findings in his report were directly linked to the quality of his instructions. No documents were available for Carson to present to the expert witnesses as proof of money earned from his hairdressing and share trading before 2001, and the judge would have to take that into consideration when he considered the evidence.

---

265. Thomas Chan, "Former lawmaker Chim Pui-chung chastises judge", South China Morning Post, 27 June, 2013

266. Thomas Chan, "Carson Yeung's access to his father's account disputed in court", South China Morning Post, 20 June, 2013

As Harris had pointed out on the first day, no records were available for many of the early transactions because, as he had explained, financial records only have to be retained for seven years and by the time some of them had been requested by the defence team such time had elapsed for the records to have been destroyed. This was a considerable advantage for the prosecution in showing that the money with no apparent provenance had flowed through the accounts in question; but for Carson it made explaining where the money originated a lot harder. The defence did not continue to make an issue of it when it was their turn to present their case, presumably keeping their powder dry for an appeal.

As the case dragged on, the big question was would Carson take the witness stand himself? The trial, which was originally scheduled to last twenty-five days, stretched into the thirties and was edging towards the forties when the last defence witnesses were called. The patience of the courtroom was wearing thin and Judge Yau appeared increasingly unhappy with the extended time the court case was taking. His impatience was mirrored in Birmingham, as anger gave way to incredulity and then to apathy as the case dragged on and on. Fans openly remarked in social media that they just wanted an end to the whole soap opera so that the club could move on.

The evidence in Carson's defence up to this point was termed "second tier" – it had come from third parties and could never carry as much weight as evidence from the protagonist himself, which would be "first tier". Carson had the dilemma of whether he would have a better chance of beating the charges by taking the stand and convincing the judge of his explanation; or, conversely, if he did so would he drop himself and others in it further?

By the end of the thirty-seventh day of the trial, in mid July 2013, the time had finally come for Carson to make his decision – take the stand and have a go or not take the stand, keep quiet but almost certainly be convicted given his unexplained receipts of and dealings in millions and millions of Hong Kong dollars through his accounts. Faced with possibly the most difficult decision in his life, Carson came up with another option – he didn't turn up to court[267]. Harris told the judge that Carson was in some discomfort from a cardiac condition and needed hospital treatment. In the face of a request from the judge that Carson must appear in court that afternoon, he still didn't show as Harris claimed he required a full medical check-up.

The judge wasn't impressed, and in no uncertain terms lectured Carson's legal team that unless he was dead or dying he would have to appear in court the next day – even if he returned to hospital that night. Carson did make it to the court room the next day having checked out of the exclusive Canossa Hospital early in the morning but overnight his decision had been made – he would not take the stand. Nevertheless, the present extended allocation of time allotted for the trial had expired and scheduling conflicts arose with other cases (Harris in particular was starting a big case in the next week) and Judge Yau, who was already annoyed at the time the case had so far taken up was forced to adjourn the trial for a further four months. Carson returned to hospital the next day for a colonoscopy and gastroscopy, but clearly wasn't in too much discomfort as he was seen in the Foreign Correspondents' Club in the next few weeks, chatting to his old friend Andrew Lam Ping-cheung, a high profile solicitor.

Lam is a celebrity solicitor in Hong Kong, not just recognised on the legal circuit but often appearing in the tabloids. Feared by the ICAC together with his favourite barrister Kevin Egan for their robust representation in successfully defending their clients, both had run into their own spot of bother and been charged on 3 March 2005[268] with conspiring to pervert the course of justice. They were alleged to have conspired to spring a witness from the witness protection programme and, in Egan's case, there was an additional charge of disclosing the name of that witness to the press. Egan was acquitted of the witness tampering charge in the District Court on 12 June 2006[269] but found guilty of disclosing the name of the witness in the witness protection programme. Lam was found guilty of conspiring to

267. Thomas Chan, "Carson Yeung shuttles between hospital and trial", South China Morning Post, 13 July, 2013
268. ICAC Press Release, 3 March, 2005
269, ICAC Press Release, 12 June, 2006

pervert the course of justice. In the Court of Appeal, Egan's conviction was overturned[270] but the prosecution appealed to the Court of Final Appeal against his acquittal. Lam lost his appeal against the witness tampering conviction in the Court of Appeal by a majority of two to one[271]. However, they were both entirely vindicated in the Court of Final Appeal on 28 June 2010[272] after a lengthy appeal process which, if anything, simply enhanced their reputations as a fearless team.

Carson was worried he was going to be convicted and was looking at a lengthy jail term. His old friend Lam could assist him on that score, having spent about six months in jail at various stages during his legal battle while he obtained bail pending his various appeals in his own case. Egan too had spent many weeks in custody, during which time he lost a considerable amount of weight and emerged positively glowing with health.

Having taken Lam's informal advice, Carson made the decision to ask Egan for a written legal opinion; to draft a document he could hand to the judge justifying his need to give evidence even though the defence had closed its case. The argument would be that Carson could not receive a fair trial unless he was allowed to do so. It was always possible Judge Yau could refuse an application to reopen the defence case but it was considered unlikely given it would make a good ground of appeal should Carson be subsequently found guilty. Having already lasted thirty-eight days, the trial was destined to last considerably longer. The Basic Law in Hong Kong is clear; every man has the right to give evidence in his own defence. The time had come for Carson.

270. HKSAR v Kevin Barry Egan CACC140/2007
271. HKSAR v Kanjanpas Chong Kwong Derek and Others CACC 248/2006
272. HKSAR v Kevin Barry Egan FACC 3 of 2009, Mandy Chui v HKSAR FACC 4 of 2009, Andrew Lam v HKSAR FACC 5 of 2009

UP IN COURT

12

CARSON TAKES THE STAND

Carson's problem was clear – the arguments in his defence case appeared to be weak even compared to the somewhat complacent presentation by the prosecution who had elected to pursue Carson solely under the "second limb" - that he had reasonable grounds to believe that the funds in the five accounts represented proceeds of an indictable offence or offences and then dealt with those funds – rather than seeking to prove that Carson actually knew those facts.

After the mid-July adjournment, it seemed likely the case was heading only one way, which was towards a guilty verdict and lengthy jail term. One of Carson's closest confidantes, Andrew Lam had detected the way the wind was blowing and suggested to his friend the only possible way to turn the situation around.

Having the defence case reopened so Carson could take the stand was the relatively easy part; it cost a bit to hire a new barrister – Kevin Egan – but it was money well spent as Egan wrote a persuasive advice that was disclosed to the judge in support of Carson's application to have the case reopened. The other pressing problem was sorting out Carson's legal team. Rejigging his strategy meant putting some noses out of joint by making a couple of late substitutions in his defence team.

Lam was not prepared to go on the record himself. He could provide personal support and guidance in the background, but did not wish to expose the case to an even greater press spotlight than it was already attracting. Carson's solicitor who had been dealing with the case since November 2012, "Gorgeous" George Tung, was a victim of the change in direction. Tung had shown up in court with a magnificent mane of hair – whether it was coiffed by Carson himself remains a mystery – but his contribution to the defence efforts had not stood up so well. This was the third time Carson had changed solicitors; his new solicitors were the relative unknown Bough and Co, whose representative appeared to take no active part in proceedings, arriving at court every day with a briefcase that remained unopened.

Harris would remain, as it would be difficult to maintain credibility in the defence by removing "the leader" at this key point; however, there is no doubt that he was the subject of a few sniggers in legal circles because everyone knew the legal opinion and the new direction was being driven by Egan. Harris retained his "face" in court as he would lead Carson's examination-in-chief and re-examination rather than Egan. Indeed, it was Harris rather than Egan who presented Egan's legal opinion to the Court in a mention hearing, on 26 September 2013[273] with no sign of embarrassment as the defence sought to have the case reopened. Privately, though, Harris was unhappy, blaming Egan for being forced to work under more stress than was necessary. The case was a nice little earner for him having extended well beyond its original time estimate but Harris's personal circumstances in maintaining seven or eight children (depending on who you ask) by several wives and partners requires him to keep a lot of balls in the air, so to speak, by taking on a heavy workload that he consistently undertakes with remarkably good humour and eloquence.

As expected, when Egan's opinion was presented to the Court, the judge allowed Carson to take the stand without hesitation. Under the Basic Law every man is entitled to present their own defence, give evidence and have their day in court; whether that man had messed everyone around, or been poorly advised was open to question but without a doubt Carson had avoided the prospect for as long as humanly possible. However, Judge Yau was firm; the case would restart on time on 15 October 2013 and continue to its conclusion. No further applications for adjournments would be entertained and any other Counsels' commitments would have to be moved around to accommodate the new dates. This put enormous pressure on Carson's team to have everything ready for the Blues supremo to present his evidence-in-chief and more importantly be ready for the stiff cross-examination to come.

When the news broke in Birmingham it was met with derision by most fans; surely this was a ploy by Carson to delay things even further? Having already decided on his guilt, people openly declared it was time for Carson

---

273. *Thomas Chan "Carson Yeung will take the stand at his money laundering trial after u-turn", South China Morning Post, 27 September, 2013*

to take his punishment; however, as the fury died down the more reasonable commentators picked up on how important this was – not just for Carson but also for Birmingham City. With the prosecution originally linking the purchase of Birmingham City to the laundered funds in the opening arguments how much further would the club get dragged into it? Would we learn why Carson paid so much for the club?

Anxiety was displayed by some fans who debated just who Carson might "drop in it" if he took the stand. If he said the wrong thing about the source of his funds, the club could potentially be in trouble. In Hong Kong other characters were also getting twitchy at the prospect of Carson opening his month. A cryptic text message was left on one of his adviser's phones – "Now see what you've done?" – after Carson was granted the opportunity to take the stand. Carson could be guided in the direction they wanted him to go when being questioned by his own defence team but once the prosecution began cross-examining him he would be entirely on his own. October promised to be a very interesting month.

The likely nature of his evidence and the perceived risks from third parties who might be implicated by it resulted in Carson being moved from his usual abode in Barker Road (from where he was still fighting his final eviction by Wing Hang Bank) to a secret location known only to his legal team and the prosecution to ensure his safety.

Carson took the stand for the first time on Tuesday 15 October 2013[274] and started off by giving evidence about his early life and his hairdressing days. Unlike the previous evidence given second hand by expert witnesses, Carson was able to give much more detailed information about where he worked and how much money he earned, as evidence the court was shown photographs of Carson styling various celebrities' hair. The atmosphere in the courtroom crackled as pictures of Carson with Jackie Chan, amongst others, were held up for the judge to examine. Carson was able to reel off a list of prices for various types of haircuts and styles – it was as though he'd never left the salon.

274. Thomas Chan, "Carson Yeung says styling and stocks made his fortune", South China Morning Post, 15 October 2013

It finally dawned on his defence team that they had done little previously to dispel the doubts surrounding the origin of Carson's wealth. They had spent their time preparing his evidence by which he could attempt to prove to the court he was a legitimately wealthy man throughout the period covered by the charges. The defence wanted to show not just how much money he had earned but also his prodigious spending; the picture of a rich playboy who had worked hard and played hard started to emerge. The defence argument reinforced that, although Carson lost large sums of money in stock market crashes, he had suffered no such problems since 1998 and that the money passing through his accounts between 2001 and 2007 was money that he had legitimately made or was for legitimate business purposes.

However, there were problems of interpretation between Carson and his Senior Counsel. Harris's courtroom manner was engaging and his demeanour pleasing on the eye and ear, but the unnecessary sophistication of some of his questions often resulted in Carson clarifying questions through the interpreter and taking more care than was necessary in giving what should have been straightforward answers. Frequently, Harris had to re-phrase a question as Carson searched for the meaning of what his barrister was actually asking him. From the public gallery there was a sense of unease – this was not helping Carson's case at all. If he were to prove his innocence he had to answer the right questions – it was as if Carson and his legal team were shooting themselves in their collective feet.

Although he gave his evidence through the court interpreter, to his credit Carson sounded confident and unemotional as he responded to Harris' questions (once he understood them) without hesitation and he was able to explain complex share dealings to the court using terminology and jargon that showed his considerable experience in the stock market. As they moved into the more complicated evidence of his share trading in Gold Wo and Kanstar Environmental, Carson was able to explain to the court how he had struggled to obtain the evidence he needed from various brokerage and securities firms. From a layman's point of view, it all sounded plausible.

The judge was careful too. An amazingly speedy typist, Judge Yau was able to keep up with typing what was said verbatim as he benefited from being bilingual and was translating Carson's answers in his own mind as the translator spoke, taking time more than once to correct the interpreter. Not only was he typing away, he had a separate pad of paper where he made notes to which he would revert to ask clarifying questions; there was definitely a sense that his patience and his thoughtfulness were not just an effort on his part to ensure a fair trial but also that justice was seen to be done; those watching in the press area benefited from his interventions, as answers that initially were difficult to understand were explained fully and could be reported correctly.

The thrust of Carson's evidence was that he had been legitimately playing the stock market and making considerable profits rather than trying to obfuscate his actions to conceal the real source of funds in his account. Carson explained that he operated so many accounts because it made sense to spread his portfolio around so as to not to tip off other players of his presence in the market; he also confirmed that he often made off-market trades by making the most of personal contacts and therefore obtaining better deals – such as the Gold Wo and Kanstar share transactions. He brushed off the questions as to why he concentrated on the somewhat maligned "red chip" penny stocks rather than the more respectable "blue chip" stocks by explaining that the volatility in penny stocks gave him the opportunity to make quicker profits rather than in longer term investments in the more placid blue chip market.

It was in the cross-examination that Carson inevitably struggled. As Reading picked holes in his defence Carson started hesitating, repeating and then contradicting himself. He denied reading his own expert witness' reports and testified that he didn't agree with some of their contents[275]. He confirmed that he had received money from potentially questionable sources without questioning its origin or if it was clean and repeated that he didn't have documentation such as accounts or ledgers to back up his evidence.

275. Thomas Chan, "The money I took was from my own investments: Carson Yeung" South China Morning Post, 31 October, 2013

When asked where the witnesses were who could help his defence, Carson could only answer that they had refused to do so.

His manner and demeanour changed. He seemed more agitated, more emotional and he started to resort to the tactic of requesting to see documentation as often as possible, therefore buying time in his efforts to give the correct answer. He was frequently reminded by the judge to speak up and to address the court and when a question looked particularly difficult to answer he would reply that he simply couldn't remember. The cross-examination became more of an interrogation by Reading, who had the manner and demeanour of a particularly strict boarding school maths teacher as he continued to bore down through his defence, demanding simple answers to his questions and refusing to accept what he saw as obfuscation.

The prospects were becoming bleaker. Carson denied knowing that Cheung Chi-tai was a suspected triad after both Harris and Egan were unable to block him being asked the question. As his answers started to hint at stock manipulation and fraud, the judge had to remind Carson of his right not to answer questions that could potentially incriminate him on other charges. By the end of the first week of cross-examination the writing appeared to be on the wall.

It appeared to the watching press and public that Carson was doomed. The prosecution had demonstrated the flow of money through the accounts and, although they didn't establish any kind of theory as to why Carson would be laundering money, they didn't need to; the prosecution were not required to prove where the money had come from – just that the "reasonable man" would have reason to believe it was the proceeds of an indictable offence. Links to Macau and a suspected triad was always going to make Carson's defence more difficult and his lack of personal paperwork or any witnesses of fact who were prepared to stand up for him spoke volumes.

The prosecution asked Carson why he hadn't called more people to explain the funds in his accounts and his answer that he had and they had refused carried the clear implication that they either didn't want to turn up to defend him or that they didn't want to answer difficult questions about the source of the funds that they had remitted to Carson. When Carson was reminded that he could have them summonsed to Court to give evidence on his behalf, he told the court that would not be helpful because he believed those witnesses would be uncooperative; this undermined his case even further.

As the cross-examination dragged on, Reading got bogged down in more and more technicalities as inaccuracies were dragged back up and contradictions noted. The mood in the courtroom (at least among the watching press and public) turned to one of frustration and apathy as the same questions were asked time and again in different ways and what had initially been scheduled as a two day hearing stretched on for more than a week. For those watching in the public gallery, the questions became increasingly convoluted and it became harder and harder to remain awake as the cross-examination became highly technical and Carson's answers progressively vague. The local press were struggling to keep up; often heads would be seen resting on the desk in the press gallery, eyes would be closed as the trial literally bored the reporters to sleep.

They were awoken with a start as the prosecution made a shocking admission. It emerged on 7 November, 2013 when the prosecution introduced new documentation in evidence which had been available to them all along and actually corroborated Carson's evidence about lending money to Abba Chan Tat-Chee to finance a movie. Although the evidence was more helpful to Carson than themselves, the prosecution had a duty to introduce it as it was within their power to obtain it from the people who held it – the ICAC. Furthermore, this important evidence had not been made available to the defence. Harris saw his chance and seized it. For a second time he applied for a permanent stay of the proceedings[276], once again making the point to the judge that Carson couldn't obtain a fair trial because the evidence he needed to establish his innocence was no longer available to him and going on to make the point that the prosecution hadn't proved or even alleged any predicate offence.

276. Julie Chu "Carson Yeung demands money laundering trial halt over unfair evidence", South China Morning Post, 9 November, 2013

Once again Judge Yau took his time in making his ruling[277], and once again he rejected Carson's application. It was clearly a victory of sorts for the defence if only as a solid ground of appeal should Carson lose the trial. It wasn't just that the documentation had been kept from Carson – there was proof that it had been available to the police who had not disclosed it and it happened to corroborate Carson's answers accurately. It may have only represented a small percentage of the total funds that flowed through the accounts but it raised a doubt in the minds of those watching – had Carson indeed been able to have a fair trial?

The defence rested at this point and a further adjournment was granted for both sides to prepare their final submissions, which were delivered to the judge on 12 December 2013[278]. The prosecution's case was simple – Carson Yeung had significant sums of money flowing through his accounts that he couldn't account for, the pattern of the movements of money was indicative of money laundering and he was consequently guilty under the second limb of the OSCO money laundering offence – in the eyes of the reasonable man he must have had reason to believe that the money represented the proceeds of an indictable offence.

The defence countered that Carson had explained as much as he possibly could as to where the money originated and, with no underlying predicate offence alleged, the prosecution had not proved an offence; essentially, the defence argued that the absence of proof of innocence was not sufficient to prove guilt. In addition, as Carson had not been able to gain access to documentation he needed to prove his innocence and in the absence of proof of guilt on the prosecution case, there was insufficient evidence to convict Carson.

Judge Yau indicated that he would deliver his verdict on 28 February 2014 – almost three years to the day from Carson's greatest triumph as Birmingham City owner; the famous victory over Arsenal in the League Cup final 2011, and the day after his fifty-fourth birthday. Would he be spending the start of his fifty-fifth year behind bars?

277. *Thomas Chan "Carson Yeung belittles talk of HK$248m takeover of Birmingham City FC", South China Morning Post, 13 November, 2013*
278. *Thomas Chan "Birmingham City chief Carson Yeung accused over "inconsistent evidence", South China Morning Post, 13 December, 2013*

13

THE TYRE KICKER

Tyre kicker (n.) A person who appears interested in buying your car, but on the day displays any of the following traits: does not show up; does not bring money; kicks the tyres and complains about even the most minor faults.

As the legal case was played out in Hong Kong, its financial effects were unravelling in England. Birmingham City was in the hole. Relegation from the Premier League had reduced the club's income by half and high wage earners remained on the books. With Carson on bail and his assets frozen he could not make any further personal financing available to the club and as a consequence the club started what many thought would be a downward spiral towards inevitable administration and oblivion.

To many fans, there was only one solution – the sale of the club to an independent party who could service the remaining debts, pay the players and invest money into the club, therefore giving it a chance of promotion. With no funding from Asia many fans believed that the sale of the club was inevitable, especially after its relegation. How wrong they were.

The fans had failed to grasp the juxtaposition between the situation the club found itself in and the personality involved. They believed a normal reaction from a person when confronted with the same issues Carson was facing, with the prospect of losing everything would be to cut his losses and walk away. The fans had not appreciated Carson's Chinese characteristic of patience and playing "the long game". In any event, with the restraining order over his assets Carson would not receive any funds from a sale regardless of how much he could get for his shares and while the club remained under his control there was always the possibility that he could eventually realise his investment or even hang on for a miracle promotion.

Of equal importance to his decision-making or – more accurately – his inactivity was Carson's gambling instinct. Gamblers who play for high stakes like him would anticipate an eventual change in their luck; in Carson's case he would succeed in his legal defence, retain his assets and remain in the game.

Former QPR Chairman Gianni Paladini was the first potential suitor to make a public pronouncement of his intention to buy the club, breaking the news in September 2012[279]. An Italian, Paladini had lived in the Birmingham area for more than forty years and had a cosy relationship with many of the press in the surrounding area. Although he had been derided by some for being a "waiter"[280], having previously worked in a restaurant, Paladini had spent many years as a football agent and "fixer" before his elevated role at Queens Park Rangers and he had a great many contacts within the footballing world. He felt an affinity with the Birmingham area and with the backing of an unnamed consortium from his homeland, which was rumoured to include Flavio Briatore, he desperately wanted to make a successful offer for the club.

What hamstrung Paladini was his fondness for self-promotion in the press. After the news broke of his intended bid in September 2012, Paladini was featured on local broadcaster Tom Ross's radio show, where he proudly boasted of his connections to the Birmingham City hooligan firm "the Zulus" and how he could complete a deal "within forty-eight hours"[281]. Understandably, a section of the fans were excited by the prospect of a new owner - albeit a waiter rather than a hairdresser.

The problem was Paladini took his hubris to the extreme in his statements to the press. As BIH is a publicly listed company on the HKSE, there were very well defined rules in place relating to the disposal of a subsidiary which made up 95% of the total turnover of the holding company. It wasn't simply a case of Peter Pannu agreeing a deal, taking Paladini's cheque and the job being done. Offers had to be put to the board, announcements made, Extraordinary General Meetings held and shareholder approval obtained – all significant details which would take time, money and effort. One question would be whether an offer acceptable to Carson would be enough for the minority shareholders, many of whom had seen massive paper losses in the plunging in price of the BIH shares since the heady days of Carson's quid a share offer for BCFC.

279. *"Gianni Paladini pledges to take Birmingham City back to the biggest stage", Birmingham Mail, 13 September, 2013*
280. *"QPR Report Friday: Gianni Paladini speaks", QPR Report, 18 November, 2011*
281. *Colin Tattum, "Birmingham City: It looks like we have no deal – Gianni Paladini", Birmingham Mail, 15 September, 2012*

Paladini had also made a crucial mistake in annoying Pannu. Pannu had been given responsibility for dealing with any potential sale of the club and he was explicit in his requirement to keep any pre-contract negotiations out of the press, as he was obliged to under HKSE listing rules. By involving the UK tabloid press at seemingly every turn, Paladini risked inciting Pannu's ire as well as endangering any chance he had of consummating the deal. Indeed, the former barrister quickly tired of the Italian.

Paladini told the press the deal was almost done in November 2012 – saying he was "hopeful that we can get something agreed within the next ten days". He then went on to add "We have spent a lot of money trying to get this completed and are looking through the books. We are keen to get it all sorted by the end of next week." This didn't go down at all well with Pannu, who released a statement of his own saying "There's been a complete misrepresentation that he's [Paladini] closing in on a purchase and it's totally without foundation[282]". Pannu went on to insinuate that Paladini didn't have the money to complete the deal, making the Italian look a bit of a fool in the process. Paladini was distinctly unimpressed when interviewed by the press over this development complaining that, "Mr Pannu has insulted me and our backers by saying we don't have the money." He threw the gauntlet down to Pannu, "Now, prove me wrong, Mr Pannu, by providing us exclusivity for two weeks to finalise the deal at the original price that was offered - and agreed." However much Paladini blustered in the press, he couldn't force Pannu to prove that the Italian "was a bullshitter"[283].

Caught in the middle were the fans. There had been some scepticism over the prospect of Paladini and potentially Briatore taking over the club after the Italians were heavily criticised in a documentary "The Four Year Plan" aired on British television, which highlighted their work at QPR and Paladini's regular pronouncements to the press had done little to dispel those concerns. There was also considerable antipathy towards Pannu; and

282. Colin Tattum, "Gianni Paladini throws down the gauntlet to Peter Pannu... again", Birmingham Mail, 26 November, 2012
283. Colin Tattum"Birmingham City Gianni Paladini deal to be struck 'within 10 days'", Birmingham Mail, 12 November, 2012

Paladini had been seen by many as the lesser of two evils. On the whole, both parties were roundly criticised by the fans who just wanted a deal to be done.

Paladini wasn't the only suitor interested in the club though. Staff at BIH had been trying to secure a sale to another Chinese party following Carson's arrest and had approached various firms in Hong Kong and Shanghai to take the club on or to make a significant investment in it.

One such firm was Shanghai Media and Entertainment Group but, although details of its interest were published in the local newspapers in Birmingham[284], it too fizzled out quickly as the finances of the football club weren't appealing to any company looking for a sensible investment at a reasonable price. Hong Kong property developers Nan Fung were also approached along with Chinese Super League sponsors Dalian Wanda but neither showed anything more than a passing interest in purchasing the club.

One of the principal hurdles impeding a sale was the personal loan of £15M that Carson had made directly to the Club, which he required be paid back in full on top of any sale price. There were also question marks over the origin of this loan and whether it had even come from Carson; there was a risk that down the line other creditors would emerge[285]. Potential purchasers of the club required warranties from Carson to make sure they were protected if claims were later made; however, none were offered. Enquiries concerning the accounts were met with out of date historic data supplied by BIH and these less-than-useful answers resulted in further searching questions until eventually the flow of information stopped. Carson had been in error in buying the football club without sufficient due diligence, finding the club £11M in debt when he had previously been told it was debt free – how could he expect someone else to fall into the same trap?

With a low price offered by Paladini for the club – rumoured to be no more than a £5M down-payment for the club with the balance contingent on

285. Colin Tattum "Pannu is ready to do business", Birmingham Mail, 19 December, 2012
285. Birmingham International Holdings Announcement, 21 October, 2013

performances on the pitch – there was some debate if the BIH shareholders would accept a deal in which Carson had his loan repaid while BIH made a massive loss on its £81M investment in the club back in August 2009. Carson's shareholding in BIH at this time was around 25% and, as he was a director of BCFC and a connected party, he wouldn't be allowed to vote in any EGM called to sanction the sale. It was a valid question whether he could even summon enough support to achieve a sale on terms he would accept.

In February 2013 a Birmingham-born businessman Darryl Eales got in touch with Pannu. Eales ran the venture capital arm of Lloyds TSB and as a Birmingham City fan he was horrified at the state of the club. Although he couldn't afford to purchase the club by himself he was prepared to put together a consortium to make an offer which would take the club back into local hands; he was confident he could run it as a viable business and put the club back on a firm financial footing. Eales, a naturally private and cautious man, visited Hong Kong to see Pannu and unlike Paladini found himself on the right side of the former barrister.

After discussions over drinks in Hong Kong went well, Eales's group put down a deposit in an escrow account and were formally allowed access to the club's books – the first consortium actually given the chance to conduct a proper due diligence process. What they saw scared them – the books didn't appear as healthy as they were led to believe, and when the time came to make a formal offer Eales and his consortium opened with a very low figure – rumoured to be as low as £5M up front with staged payments based on how well the club performed in the future. The figure offered was flat; there would be no extra payments to pay off Carson's loan or for any commission agreements with Pannu or anybody else. Pannu turned it down flat – it was also unacceptable to Carson who wanted to recoup the majority of the loan he had sunk into the club.

Pannu was playing a careful game but he had a vested interest in the sale of the club. As part of his negotiations with interested parties he was

286. Neil Moxley "Don't treat me like an idiot! Paladini blasts Birmingham Chief Pannu after takeover snub", Daily Mail, 15 November, 2012

demanding a payment to him as a golden handshake to leave the club[286]; on top of this he had negotiated a 7% cut from BIH as a commission for arranging the sale of the club – in effect, taking a slice of the pie from both sides. Eales's offer hadn't been divvied up at all; it was more a case of "this is the offer, split it between yourselves however you wish". This didn't satisfy Pannu, as he wanted any golden handshake payment to him on top of his commission for selling the club. The net result was a stalemate as neither party would budge from their position.

Former Birmingham City Vice-Chairman Sammy Yu Wai-ying was another interested party. He appeared on the scene around the same time as Eales and was negotiating directly with Carson because of his much publicised antipathy towards Pannu. Sammy had pulled together a consortium from mainland China who were looking for a club in Europe which could be used to improve the standard of the sport back home and he believed for a while that he could do a deal; particularly as he thought he had agreed terms with Carson to pay off what Carson was personally owed by the club in a time-scale suitable to them both.

It was never an easy negotiating process for Yu. After the deal collapsed, he told the press that he would "...guess there will not be any chance for anyone to buy the club as after six months trying I found a lot that is uncertain in BIHL and could not come into a proper way to get the matter to finalise."[287] Yu believed the club was out of reach because Carson had continually moved the goalposts of the price he demanded for the club and the repayment of his loan; what was apparently fine one day was no good the next. Yu never even had the chance to examine the books and he reluctantly pulled out in May 2013. He moved on to consider Sheffield Wednesday as a potential club for his PRC investors but that negotiation also fell flat as questions were asked whether Sammy really had the necessary backing in the first place.

By the summer of 2013, open insurrection amongst the fans had almost replaced the apathy that had predominated the previous season after the

287. Colin Tattum, *"Sammy Yu opens his heart on shock exit from Birmingham City", Birmingham Mail,* 26 September, 2012

twelfth placed finish in the Championship. With the sale of Curtis Davies for £2.25M[288] to Hull City and Nathan Redmond for £2.5M[289] to Norwich City, Birmingham City had sold every player with any significant value; players were brought in from much lower divisions like Matt Green[290] from Conference Champions Mansfield Town and, with much lower expectations, the fans were gearing themselves up for a difficult campaign. News of a takeover seemed as far away as ever and the BIH board were keeping any negotiations under wraps, in all probability because there were none.

The only time Pannu broke ranks was to slap down stories of a potential sale of the club that emerged from Tom Ross, who announced on 25 June 2013 on Twitter and Facebook that he understood a deal had been agreed and an announcement was imminent. Free Radio had gone as far as to book a studio in Spain where Tom was on holiday for him to report the news as it broke. Whether he had got the wrong end of the stick or had been led up the garden path only Tom knows, but BIH made no announcement to the HKSE and in August Pannu made a statement on the club website to confirm that no deal had been reached with anyone[291].

As Tom Ross took stick from all sides about his premature and inaccurate announcement, Gianni Paladini was quietly fuming. As far back as April 2013 he believed he had struck a deal with Peter Pannu only for the former police officer to change his mind. It was real hokey-cokey stuff from Pannu, with the deal being on again, off again which further infuriated Paladini, who unusually kept his own counsel rather than using the press – although a £1M penalty clause in a non-disclosure agreement might have had something to do with it.

Pannu was open in his dislike of the Italian, describing him around the offices at St Andrew's as a "toilet cleaning bastard[292]". The reason behind Pannu's open hostility remains unknown but it was crystal clear that he didn't want

288. "Curtis Davies: Hull City sign Birmingham Defender", BBC, 25 June, 2013
289. James Dickenson "Norwich and Swansea agree £2.5m fee for Birmingham youngster Nathan Redmond", Daily Express, 25 June, 2013
290. "Matt Green signs for Blues", Birmingham Mail, 3 July, 2013
291. Colin Tattum, "Blues: 'No sale of club is agreed or imminent'", Birmingham Mail, 7 August, 2013
292. Name withheld, Personal Interview, November 2013

to sell the club to Paladini. He may have tried to keep him hanging on to drum up interest from elsewhere but Paladini had other ideas – he knew there wasn't any other serious interest out there and he stuck with it.

By August 2013 rumours surrounding the club's future were at fever pitch. Social media and messageboards were abuzz with gossip as fans theorized, extrapolated and embellished on what little was known in the public domain in an attempt to try and get a grasp of the situation. Hope had been replaced by desperation because, from the outside, the club appeared to be teetering on the brink of financial collapse.

BIH was finally forced to confirm it was in negotiations to sell the club in an announcement to the HKSE on 19 August 2013[293]. With liquidity problems worsening and borrowings increasing, the holding company admitted it was in preliminary negotiations for the sale of the club and that due diligence had been conducted by third parties. It was the first public confirmation by BIH of anything tangible on the club's future.

Of course, this set off a veritable frenzy of speculation with the fans who seized on it as evidence that something was actually happening, that the sale of the club was just around the corner. Things had looked desperate on the pitch at the end of the season in April 2013 and now louder than ever the fans demanded a sale as they couldn't envisage any other outcome than relegation from the Championship and financial oblivion should Carson remain in control.

It just wasn't happening quickly enough. Pannu continued to drag his feet, making plans to visit the UK in September 2013, then changing them at the last minute leaving Paladini fuming. Carson wasn't happy with the protracted negotiations for the sale of the club either and took matters into his own hands. Knowing Sammy Yu had procured a Chinese consortium to make an offer for Sheffield Wednesday the BIH Chairman attempted to make contact and persuade them to buy Birmingham City instead – but all to no avail. When that initiative failed, Carson gave Yu a two month written agency agreement at the end of September for him to negotiate the sale of the club to other bidders as soon as possible.

293. *Birmingham International Holdings Announcement, 19 August, 2013*

The problem was that Carson's terms were ludicrous. Undeterred by his own fall from grace and the club's relegation, Carson wanted HK$400M for the club – around £32M – on top of the repayments of loans owed both to himself and BIH which the purchaser would have to also pay. He also wanted to sell the club in instalments to give himself the chance to buy it back should he defeat his money laundering charges; this also allowed him to retain control of the board room until the bitter end. Insiders privately wondered who in their right mind would ever go for such a deal.

The financial situation at the club was desperate now, with every penny a prisoner and rumours of dire warnings from the finance department that funds would finally run out at the end of December 2013[294]. Something had to give and after visiting the club at the start of October, Pannu confirmed to Paladini that he would take the Italian's offer to the boss and try and convince him to accept it. The endgame had arrived – or so Paladini thought. Even though he lodged an official bid of £17M with the club's solicitors and claimed he had placed £7M in an escrow account as proof of funds nothing happened. His only solution appeared to be to take the ball into Carson's court – to cut out the middle man and negotiate with the top dog himself.

Questions were asked about whether the top dog was still calling the shots; a rumour was doing the rounds that Carson had hocked his shareholding in BIH to Kingston Securities as collateral for a loan and that Kingston's owner Pollyana Chu had the final say on any sale.

As October 2013 ticked by without news, Paladini's patience started to wear thin. He believed that he had been messed around by Peter Pannu for months on end and was starting to weary of the negotiations, as were his backers. Days went by without an announcement and rumours abounded in Birmingham that Carson had declined the bid outright; continuing themes prevalent throughout his tenure at the club of prevarication and minimal public contact.

---

294. Neil Moxley, "EXCLUSIVE: Yeung has just six weeks to rescue cash-strapped Birmingham from plunging into administration", Daily Mail, 25 October, 2013

Into the void of hard information flooded rumour and counter-rumour, insinuation and innuendo as various parties presented themselves as "in the know" on social media. Some of this was fuelled by Paladini and his veritable posse of associates and hangers-on, all trying to push his agenda in order to land themselves a plush job and wage packet. But for all the talk in Birmingham, BIH remained resolutely quiet in Hong Kong. Carson was too busy concentrating on his trial to talk much about a sale – although, once his cross-examination was completed, he did tell reporters outside the District Court in a rare outburst that they'd "better ask him [Paladini] first if he has enough money"[295]; on the other hand Paladini was insistent that money had been lodged in an escrow account as proof of funds – whether it had or not or if it was enough cash has not been publicly demonstrated but it was clear that Carson wasn't convinced. Pannu had apparently gone to ground and there was no one else around who would comment on the situation.

It was all too much for Paladini. His frustration turned to anger and the Italian went on air with Tom Ross on 21 October 2013 with the intention of blowing wide open the whole sorry tale. In an exclusive interview he told listeners how much he wanted to buy the club, how he felt he was being mucked around by Pannu and how he had an agreement signed by Pannu in which Pannu agreed to his purchase of the club. He disclosed that he'd even been to Hong Kong to seek a direct meeting with executives of BIH without being able to track them down.

Social media exploded once more; fans clamoured to speak to Paladini on air and implored him to complete the deal. Vitriolic comments were made once more against Carson and Pannu for failing to complete the deal and questions were raised as to why nothing had been announced to the HKSE if indeed an official bid had been made. All this took place in Birmingham but in Hong Kong there was stony silence; as far as the people there were concerned, nothing had been agreed and the press remained absolutely disinterested in the purported deal – similarly, the HKSE weren't interested in BIH's failure to comment for now.

---

295. Thomas Chan, "Carson Yeung belittles talk of HK$248m takeover of Birmingham City FC", South China Morning Post, 13 November, 2013

Behind the scenes, an offer was made to Gianni Paladini to facilitate a direct meeting between Carson and one of his closest confidantes, Andrew Lam Ping-cheung, and in doing so be sure to flush out Pannu's influence over the whole process once and for all. Would Paladini acquiesce by making the long flight for a fireside chat, mano e mano with Carson? For someone who had gone on air and bragged that he was willing to catch the next flight to Hong Kong to sort it out, Paladini's interest quickly waned when the details were put to him of how such a meeting could come about.

This is where we, the authors came in. Ivery had been approached by people connected to Paladini to see if he knew anyone out in Hong Kong who could facilitate a meeting as he was out there at the time; Giles happened to know the right people who could set it up.

Paladini had assumed it would all be set up for him, gratis – that he would be able to fly to Hong Kong, walk into a meeting with Carson and his team and conclude a deal despite his earlier failed visit. He clearly had little understanding of how business is conducted in Hong Kong. If you want your seat at the negotiating table you need to show commitment, respect people's time and connections and – if necessary – cover the costs of those who are giving you the opportunity, even in deals done between friends. It might seem alien to some westerners, but in Hong Kong it's not unusual that time and effort in facilitating introductions are rewarded. The terms of the offer were simple – for a small fee (compared to the potential value of the deal) of £20,000 (a little more than the cost of two first class tickets from London) to cover the cost of our time, rearranged flights, hotel and entertainment expenses and of course some reward for our efforts we would arrange, as Paladini's exclusive agent, a meeting between Carson, Paladini and their respective advisors. Before any meeting took place Paladini would be advised what Carson would be looking for and, just as crucially, how it would be best to approach the negotiations because his reputation with Carson was at an all time low. In the event of a successful introduction that led to a deal, a negotiable commission was also proposed.

After a week or two of behind the scenes negotiations the whole proposal fell apart; it became clear that Paladini wasn't prepared to go for it; he wasn't prepared to spend £20,000 on pursuing a deal he had earlier insisted had already been done. We had assumed that these discussions were confidential and were surprised to see Neil Moxley's article in the Daily Mail dated 18 November 2013[296], which erroneously reported that Carson himself had demanded £20,000 from Paladini just to meet him. Mr Paladini denied any involvement in the article but we can assure you that none of that false information came from our side. It only served to embarrass Paladini further as the club put out an official statement from Carson denying the article's insinuation that he had demanded money to meet them and he threatened legal action against the newspaper[297].

In the meantime, BIH arranged more short term loans[298] to cover its immediate liquidity problems, set up deals[299] to bring in new share capital and to novate the outstanding loan from Carson from the club to BIH that had previously held up any sale. In principle the HKSE accepted the proposals, but BIH struggled to formulate the terms and again it was delay upon delay in calling the required EGM to approve the transaction. At the 10 January 2014 AGM, Peter Pannu confirmed there were potential bidders for Birmingham City – but that BIH were aiming to retain overall control of the club if other investors came in. The big issue was, of course, from where this alleged interest emanated and whether it had any strength.

It was also reported in the British media that Paladini had now turned his attention to South London club Millwall, leading a consortium seeking to buy the Lions. It would appear that the owner there swiftly had the measure of the Italian, with sources close to him saying he had spoken to Paladini but "it hadn't been worth the conversation.[300]"

296. Neil Moxley, "EXCLUSIVE: Yeung demands £20,000 from potential Birmingham City buyer Paladini just to meet him", Daily Mail, 18 November, 2013
297. "Statement on behalf of Carson Yeung", bcfc.com, 21 November, 2013
298. Birmingham International Holdings Announcement, 19 November, 2013
299. Birmingham International Holdings Announcement, 12 November, 2013
300. Alex Aldridge, "Millwall CEO quashes rumours of takeover after Paladini link", News at Den, 20 January, 2014

14

KICKING THE TYRE
DOWN THE ROAD

The scene was set for a big month – February 2014 would be the month of destiny for Blues fans. In the space of twenty-eight days, Carson would know if his company would be able to continue its restructuring, relist on the HKSE, and whether he would keep his liberty when the court reconvened on 28 February 2014 for the verdict, the day after his fifty-fourth birthday. If everything went to plan, he could look forward to March 2014 a free man, and return to his football club that he had been forbidden from visiting for two and a half years.

The EGM was the first thing up. After numerous delays through December and the early part of January 2014, the BIH board finally managed to put the refinancing deal together and requisition the general meeting. The deal itself wouldn't do many shareholders any favours – it would dilute their stake in the battered company, with the issue of convertible notes and new preference shares likely to push the total number of shares to 20BN from just over 4BN. A heavily diluted stake worth a little was preferable to no stake at all. The deal didn't do much in terms of raising cash other than provide working capital for BIH to pull itself up by the bootstraps and to free the football club from one of the major shackles holding back its sale: namely, the novation of Carson's loan from the club to BIH, taking the £15M liability off the club's books.

The EGM was held to approve seven resolutions[301]. The first resolution would see the placement of 1.26BN new shares in the company at a price of HK$0.05 each. These would be available immediately after the EGM and would bring in a much-needed injection of capital, raising a total of HK$63M (approx £4.84M) before the commission payable to the underwriters. As the placing was fully underwritten it would guarantee immediate cashflow for the company and would allow it to service its most pressing debts.

The second and third resolutions would see the issue of two convertible bonds to a company called U-Continent in their respective values of HK$50M and HK$125M. Neither bond carried any interest payable on the notes but they could be converted into 1.6BN and 4.16BN shares respectively at a price of

301. *Birmingham International Holdings Announcement, 16 January, 2014*

HK$0.03 per share. The idea apparently was to bring in a longer term investor rather than saddle the company with a huge interest bill that it couldn't pay. U-Continent is owned by Yang Yuezhou, a mainland businessman who had previously agreed to invest money in BIH by way of convertible notes, only for that deal to fail as the suspension of the listing continued far longer than anyone could have anticipated. This time was different because by the date of the EGM (although the shares were still suspended) BIH had obtained agreement from the HKSE that should the deals be ratified the HKSE would allow the resumption of trading in the shares[302].

The fourth, fifth and sixth resolutions would see the £15M debt Birmingham City Football Club owed to Carson assumed by BIH, which he could then convert to equity through a Debt Conversion bond with up to 6.45BN shares available at the agreed price of HK$0.03 per share. This was seen as crucial in making the football club more attractive to prospective purchasers who had previously baulked at paying off the loan in full and who had demanded extensive warranties from BIH because of the lack of any paperwork showing the origin of funds which made up the loans[303].

The BIH board recommended the deals as essential for the future of the company - without a resumption in trading of its shares attracting any further investment would be impossible and without the novation of Carson's debt the club would never be seen as a viable risk. Some of the shareholders didn't see it that way, though, as they saw that their stakes in the company would be heavily diluted. They also considered it unfair that they weren't allowed to buy into the company in the same way Yang Yuezhou was, for what they saw as a knockdown price. Both Liu Xingcheng and Vico Hui were opposed to the resolutions, which presented a problem for Carson: Liu and Hui controlled over 600M shares and Carson would not be allowed to vote his own shares on the third, fourth and fifth resolutions because of his own beneficial interest in the novation of his loan, as this made him a connected party. Something would have to be done to negate any risk of the deal falling over at the last hurdle.

302. *Birmingham International Holdings Announcement, 30 December, 2013*
303. *Birmingham International Holdings Announcement, 16 October, 2013*

On 29 January 2014, Liu Xingcheng received a letter from lawyers representing Kingston Securities demanding that he deposit HK$45M with them by noon, on 5 February – two hours before the EGM was due to start. Kingston's lawyers informed Liu that they were calling in the deficit on his margin account and should he not make payment, his shares in BIH would be taken against his debt. This presented a problem for Liu as he was stuck in Qingdao in northern China under house arrest, and wasn't allowed to travel. His detention allegedly resulted from a complaint by Carson that Liu had withdrawn money from a company there that Carson claimed was his. With the Chinese New Year celebrations about to start on 31 January, Liu had three days to sort out his account with Kingston in Hong Kong from his detention in northern China which would allow him to vote against the resolutions. It was never going to happen. After the EGM, it emerged Vico Hui had also received a similar letter and had not been able to vote his shares either.

One of the other conditions HKSE imposed for the resumption in trading of BIH shares was that Carson had to step down from his position as Chairman of the BIH board and relinquish his directorship. He had previously made a promise to step back before the resumption of trading[304] and now with the EGM drawing closer he finally had to bite the bullet. On 4 February 2014, Carson announced his resignation from the boards of BIH[305] and Birmingham City[306]. In his place, unknown mainlander Cheung Shing took the reins as Chairman of BIH, with Carson's brother-in-law Victor Ma Shui-cheong named as Vice-Chairman. Carson's ceremonial title President of Birmingham City was also renounced but two new directors were appointed to the board at St Andrew's – recent appointee to the BIH board Panagiotis "Panos" Pavlakis along with Ma[307]. Athens-born Pavlakis had a background in raising capital in the financial markets but, of course, there was also a familial connection in that he was the partner of Sayoko Yeung, a daughter of a step-brother of Carson's.

304. *Birmingham International Holdings Announcement, 19 August, 2013*
305. *Birmingham International Holdings Announcement, 4 February, 2014*
306. *"Carson Yeung steps down", bcfc.com, 4 February, 2014*
307. *"New Directors appointed", bcfc.com, 3 February, 2014*

Carson's resignation from the BCFC board allowed him to leave the football club boardroom on his own terms, rather than waiting to be forced out by the Football League should he be convicted at the end of the month. Social media was ablaze in Birmingham with the news that Carson had taken a step back, with many fans openly predicting it was the end of his era; the more sensible ones pointed to the fact that Carson still retained a sizeable stake in BIH and cast doubts as to whether Carson would relinquish control so easily.

With all the directorial manoeuvrings completed, the EGM went ahead smoothly and every single resolution was passed unanimously[308], although this was considerably helped by Liu and Vico being vetoed from voting. Peter Pannu was bullish when interviewed outside the meeting room at the Kowloon Shangri-La Hotel, informing reporters that: "I think today is a milestone in terms of what the group has achieved"[309]. He went on to play down problems at Birmingham City by asking "What troubles?"[310] before going on to point out that most football clubs in England were in the red.

Carson was in a defiant mood too, telling reporters "Why would I reduce my stake? I would increase it!"[311] Carson was in no mood for the press, storming to his car through the phalanx of reporters before berating his driver for not being in the right place at the right time, an accusation most Blues fans could level at Carson.

Despite his outburst at the EGM, Carson was satisfied with how things had turned out. The shares would resume trading on 7 February and, with that key event in place, there was only one thing to do. An extravagant dinner was held on 6 February at the Four Seasons Hotel to celebrate the resumption in trading of BIH shares. The dress code was black tie and the new Chairman of BIH, Cheung Shing, delivered the keynote speech in Mandarin. The attendees were predominately mainlanders, the vast majority of whom ignored the dress code by wearing jeans, leather jackets and trainers and

308. *Birmingham International Holdings Announcement, 5 February, 2014*
309. *Gregg Evans "The future is 'bright' for Birmingham City says Peter Pannu", Birmingham Mail, 5 February, 2014*
310. *"Pannu predicts 'bright' Blues future", BBC, 5 February 2014*
311. *Imogene Wong, "Defiant Carson Yeung vows to increase company stake", The Standard, 6 February, 2014*

who contributed to the evening turning into a shambolic display of drunken revelry. Carson's barrister Graham Harris wore a striking purple bow tie. Red envelopes – "lai see" packets – each containing a crisp new HK$500 note were handed out to each guest with additional lucky draw prizes which saw half of the room win another red packet which each contained HK$2000. All in all, at least HK$450,000 – some £35,000 – must have been spent on the evening: a considerable sum in view of the enforced cutbacks in the playing staff at Birmingham.

The shares resumed trading at 9:00am Hong Kong time on 7 February and, as expected, immediately fell. Over 1.2BN shares were traded – nearly half of those in the opening half hour – and the price tumbled from HK$0.154 to HK$0.101 as many shareholders scrambled to dump the BIH shares they had been stuck with for over two and a half years. Kingston was a notable trader in those early heavy dealings. Within a week many of those shareholders would come to regret that decision, as the share price almost tripled seeing them sit at HK$0.29 on 14 February. It was evident that someone out there had made a killing.

One such speculator was Luo Chao Kui. Stock exchange filings reveal that he bought 438M shares on 7 February[312] at an average price of HK$0.102 each, costing him HK$44.676M (about £3.46M). He then sold 81.9M of those shares at an average price of HK$0.373[313] ten days later, realising him HK$30.547M (about £2.38M), a net profit of HK$22.195M (about £1.7M) on those shares and still leaving him with a 6.92% stake in the company. No wonder people were being urged to invest in BIH at the Four Seasons dinner.

Insiders in Hong Kong may have been happy but back in Birmingham it was a different story. Tensions had been rising in the stands and the fans' apathetic moaning finally turned to vociferous protest at a game with Derby County on 1 February. For the first time since Carson's arrest, fans carried professionally made banners into the ground, proclaiming that the club had been "Made in Birmingham, Destroyed in Hong Kong" with profiles of both

312. HKSE filings
313. HKSE filings

Carson and Pannu and with the message to Carson to "Delay No More"[314].

"Delay No More" is a bilingual double entendre with its English implication clear that Carson should not hang around in selling the club; however, in Cantonese, which has an abundance of creative slang and swear words it means something entirely different. "Diu lay lo mo", which is pronounced in roughly the same way is a colloquial expression of abuse meaning "fuck your (old) mother" and is used in Hong Kong as a familiar insult in the same manner as "fuck you" or "piss off". It's not something you'd say in front of your mother but is a common phrase, particularly among blue-collar workers. The campaign[315], which was based by its leaders on Daniel Ivery's article on his Birmingham City fan site[316], was designed to exploit its double meaning, to show the strength of feeling on the terraces of St Andrew's and to attract Cantonese press attention. It worked on all fronts.

The fans rallied behind the flags, chanting anti-board songs demonstrating to the world their anger and disdain. At the next home game against Huddersfield, another banner appeared, this time exclaiming "BIHL Go Now"[317]. Ming Pao, a Cantonese language newspaper carried photos of the protest along with an interview with Ivery[318]. For the first time ever, the Cantonese language press were taking note of what was happening in Birmingham; soon other interview requests started to flood in.

Meanwhile Carson decided that, as his verdict was due the day after his birthday, it would be prudent for him to celebrate his fifty-fourth birthday somewhat earlier than normal on 17 February. As was his custom, the only way to mark the occasion was with another huge gala dinner, this time at the Aberdeen Marina Club on the south side of Hong Kong Island. On this occasion, Pannu gave a speech to the assembled throng and the unofficial MC for the night was Pollyanna Chu of Kingston Securities. There were

314. Steve Wollaston, "Video: Birmingham City fans protest against the board", Birmingham Mail, 1 February, 2014
315. Delaynomore.co.uk
316. "Postcards from HK: Delay No More", Often Partisan, 28 October, 2013
317. Bihlgonow.co.uk
318. News.sina.com.hk 22, February, 2014

rumours back in Birmingham that both had fallen out with Carson but it appeared that those stories couldn't be farther from the truth.

In the week before his birthday bash, BIH announced to the HKSE[319] that it had signed a binding memorandum of understanding to sell a 12% stake in the football club to "Beijing Liangzhu International Media Co Ltd" for a sum of HK$45M (about £3.5M). The MOU would see the deal completed within ten days and would allow the purchasing company, who were apparently in the advertising business, to put two directors on the Birmingham City board. It was all a bit surreal; after all this time dealing with numerous rumours of takeovers and press speculation, when a deal to sell shares in the club was actually announced it was met with a whimper. Furthermore the proposed purchaser barely seemed to exist judging by its feeble online presence. Who were these mainlanders and what interest did they have in the club?

Pannu surprisingly admitted to the Financial Times that he hadn't been "privy" to the deal[320], distancing himself and confirming that it had been negotiated by Carson and Victor Ma; strange given his position as Chief Executive Officer and Managing Director (not to mention "Acting Chairman" of the club) that apparently he had no idea of what had gone on. Ma had been involved in setting up the loans and convertible bonds with U-Continent and it now appeared that he had cemented his role as Carson's new "go-to" man; the familial connection proving to be thicker than the supposed two decades of friendship with Pannu.

Finding any information on Beijing Liangzhu turned out to be tricky. The only information held online about the company was a regulatory filing with Beijing's version of Companies House which did little more than confirm that the company was founded in 2005 and had RMB1.5M (about £145,000) paid up capital. It also gave the names of two investors – Guan Weixia and Su Zhongshan – and an executive director, Shang Hui. Nothing more was revealed about the company – not even a phone number. A credit check on the firm was a bit more revealing, confirming that the company had not filed

---

319. *Birmingham International Holdings Announcement, 12 February, 2014*
320. *Demetri Sevastopulo "Birmingham City FC Owner agreed stake sale to mystery buyer", Financial Times, 3 March 2014*

accounts since 2010 and was ranked 167 out of 180 media companies in Beijing. How and why would a mainland Chinese company with such a low profile and such a poor credit rating be able to afford nearly £3.5M to buy a stake in an English football club? One theory which remains unconfirmed was that Guan Weixia is in fact the mother of Joanna Wang Man li, Carson's common-law wife and mother of his two youngest children.

As with any deal connected to BIH, this one turned out to be problematic; however, this one was not only problematic but was also acutely embarrassing. On 25 February, BIH were forced to announce to the HKSE they had given Beijing Liangzhu an extension beyond the deadline to pay for its proposed acquisition of the 12% stake in BCFC[321]. On 7 March, the deal fell apart completely when Beijing Liangzhu were unable to pay the deposit and BIH cancelled the deal[322] – threatening legal action but apparently never actually doing anything more. Naturally, this news was met with howls of derision and scepticism in Birmingham and flew in the face of Pannu's promise of a "bright" future for Birmingham City.

The BIH board hadn't rested on its laurels in only having the suspension of trading shares lifted on the HKSE and failing to procure a small investment in the football club. If the holding company wanted to divest itself of the football club in its entirety, then BIH would need to diversify into another business to maintain its listing on the main board of the HKSE. With this in mind, BIH announced on 20 February that it had signed a non-binding MOU to buy a stake in an Indonesian oil and gas services firm named PetroPro PT[323]. The deal would see BIH take a 65% interest in the company for a price of HK$52M. The company was said to provide technical services and distribute software to the oil and gas industry in Indonesia.

It was a petrochemical deal for BIH, which had long been rumoured in Hong Kong and made some sense given the oil and gas executives from the mainland who had recently joined the board over the previous nine months. BIH were careful to insert many conditions into the agreement to make

321. *Birmingham International Holdings Announcement, 25 February, 2014*
322. *Birmingham International Holdings Announcement, 7 March, 2014*
323. *Birmingham International Holdings Announcement, 20 February, 2014*

sure that all approvals and guarantees were in place before handing over any cash; perhaps they were mindful of the troubles Nat Rothschild had experienced in the coal industry in Indonesia in 2013. There has been no further announcement on the progress of this deal and the question of how BIH would ever pay for its shares remains unanswered. Sceptics might say that these deals were really designed to create some froth in the share price and allow speculators to make a killing.

As the verdict edged ever closer, Carson's anxiety increased. He was worried by the speculation that he was going to be convicted and he wanted reassurance from his team that this wouldn't be the case. Even though his legal advisors tried to remain upbeat and bullish, Carson decided he had better make some contingency plans should the worse come to the worst. Andrew Lam was informally consulted in putting together the legal team which might be required for the appeal process. Harris is not a renowned appellate counsel and would need help, so the superstar English silk Clare Montgomery QC – who had represented Lam in his own appeals, winning famously in the Court of Final Appeal – was touted as leading counsel. Egan's role in the appeal team was never in doubt.

Carson may have been bullish after the EGM about buying more BIH shares but his actions appear contradictory. From 17 February to 18 March, according to Stock Market filings Carson sold shares in BIH that he held through his Great Luck Management investment vehicle on an almost daily basis. These shares were included in the restraint order the Department of Justice had obtained against Carson's assets. One theory was that the HK$52M deficit shown on the Great Luck Management account in the restraint order had been called in and that the shares the company held in BIH had been sold presumably by Kingston to cover that loss. Kingston were able to do this as they would have first call on any debt owed by Carson before the restraint order had been obtained.

When the day of judgement finally dawned, the Hong Kong press attended the District Court in their hordes. Carson arrived at court and was met by a scrum of photographers scrambling for his picture and the public gallery was filled by international reporters who had travelled to Hong Kong to witness the judge's verdict on the former hairdresser. There was a good smattering of journalists from the global media such as the BBC, the New York Times and Al Jazeera English.

Those hoping for a quick decision would be disappointed. The judge informed the courtroom that he would be reading his reasons for judgement in full in English – all 112 pages of it – which would then be translated to Cantonese for Carson's benefit. After arriving in court looking stoic and resolute, Carson turned slowly paler as he listened to the interpreter, rocking gently back and forth in his seat.

In the gallery, various directors of BIH including Panagiotis Pavlakis, Victor Ma Shui-cheong and Cheung Shing were present to show their support – even Peter Pannu appeared for a seventeen minute cameo. Birmingham City director and Carson's eldest son Ryan sat with them, watching and listening intently as judgement was passed on his father. It was too much for Cheung Shing though, with the mainlander spending the afternoon session asleep, his head resting against the back wall.

Judge Douglas Yau Tak-hong was careful as he read out his reasons in English. As he reached critical points in his reading he paused, allowing the interpreter to catch up and making sure he enunciated every word clearly so the defendant could have no doubts as to their meaning.

In Birmingham the mood was impatient. Fans had been waiting for this day of reckoning but it soon became obvious that 28 February was not to be that day. At 3:30pm local time, Judge Yau decided he was too tired to continue reading his judgement for that day and adjourned the hearing until the following Monday, much to howls of derision and frustration 6000 miles away. The result was far from clear and the judge's continuation of Carson's bail for the weekend gave at least one of his legal team a straw to clutch.

It can't have been easy for Carson. Having steeled himself for the worst, he now had the whole weekend to stew on his fate. On his return to court on

Monday, 3 March he angrily pushed his way through the mob of paparazzi waiting for him, shoving aside one cameraman who had got too close as he made for the relative sanctuary of the courtroom doors.

The judge picked up his judgement where he had left off on the Friday with no hesitation. The prosecution team had been reduced in number due to scheduling conflicts but the judge had allowed them to be represented by the most junior barrister on the team, Ella Liang, with Reading scheduled to arrive in court as soon as his other appointment was out of the way. It appeared to be slow going again but the pace noticeably quickened as the judge came to his findings on the evidence.

After deciding that the defence witnesses were telling the truth, the judge then tempered that pronouncement by noting that they did not have direct first hand knowledge of what Carson had been doing. Noticeably, later in his judgement he did find in one or two cases that the defence witnesses other than Carson had been dishonest in giving their evidence. The writing was on the wall when Judge Yau became scathing of Carson, concluding that he was "not a witness of truth" and was "someone who is prepared to, and did try to, lie whenever he saw the need to."

Judge Yau then proceeded to rip Carson's testimony to shreds, finding that he had exaggerated his income as a hair stylist, that he had concealed key details of share transactions, that he had lied in his explanations of how transactions had been processed and, crucially, where his money had come from. Over and over again, the judge repeated the same theme – that the lack of paperwork, his use of third parties to make payments and the contradictory answers he had given all painted a picture of money laundering.

Carson remained impassive as the judge convicted him on all five charges. No emotion betrayed his demeanour and he looked straight ahead, looking stoic and resolute. Maybe he knew it was coming but, even so, it showed a real strength in him to take his punishment like a man. The judge remanded him in custody pending the sentencing hearing on 7 March and, after waving goodbye to his BIH cohorts Panagiotis Pavlakis and Cheung Shing, Carson was taken down.

As all this went on, Harris and Reading congratulated each other on their work in the courtroom in a slightly unseemly display of backslapping. As lawyers you have to work against friends in some cases and you may well think your opponent a worthy one; but it's a matter of decorum and tact not to congratulate your opponent within sight of your client as he walks the long road to prison – save the old boys mutual admiration society for the bar in the evening.

The reaction in Birmingham was twofold. There was a large outpouring of a very schadenfreude-like joy as some fans delighted in Carson finally being convicted of crimes they were sure he had committed all along. There was also widespread relief – the trial was over and now Birmingham City could move forwards – or could it?

With the judge implying that he agreed with Pulvirenti's evidence that the club had been partly purchased with the proceeds of an indictable offence, as well as numerous other findings that the HK$721M which flowed through the five accounts were the proceeds of indictable offences, inevitable questions arose as to whether any further arrests will be made in connection with the case; furthermore, would the football club suffer because of the distinct possibility that it was at least in part bought with tainted cash? Finally, with BIH having confirmed to the HKSE the lack of documentation to back up the third party remittances that made up Carson's loan to the football club, would this also lead to a new investigation?

Pannu made statements on both the club website and at the behest of the HKSE in which he maintained that it was "business as usual"[324][325]; this was hardly convincing and a bit embarrassing following the money laundering headlines. The Football League confirmed they too were satisfied with things as they stood. Fans weren't so sure, though, and there was a growing movement that representations should be made to the Football League to force them to act – could they make Carson and by extension BIH sell up?

324. Birmingham International Holdings announcement, 3 March 2014
325. Www.bcfc.com "Statement: Carson Yeung", 3 March 2014

Gianni Paladini hoped so[326]. The day after Carson's conviction he was back in the Birmingham press pleading with BIH to sell him the club. Peter Pannu[327] had also admitted that the sale of the club had to happen sooner or later but was firm in his intent not to sell to the Solihull-based Italian.

On Friday 7 March, Carson was sentenced to six years imprisonment. That day he was transferred from Lai Chi Kok Remand Centre and taken to the maximum security Stanley Prison on the south of Hong Kong Island to start his sentence. His punishment was met with great joy back in Birmingham and fans expressed their delight at what they saw as justice delayed but not denied when it was finally meted out.

326. Paul Suart "Gianni Paladini: Sell me Birmingham City", Birmingham Mail, 4 March, 2014
327. Colin Tattum, "Under-fire Peter Pannu says Carson Yeung knows that he has to sell Birmingham City", Birmingham Mail, 8 February, 2014

15

THE STREISAND EFFECT

One of the more bizarre events to happen in the aftermath of Carson's verdict concerned Daniel Ivery. Having returned to Birmingham from Hong Kong where he had been reporting on the trial, he was summoned to St Andrew's for a "friendly chat" with lawyers representing Birmingham City to discuss his Often Partisan (OP) website.

Ivery had already received three legal letters demanding that he remove comments on the site in the previous twelve months; the first two threatened court action but after responding to the lawyers that any such legal action would be vigorously defended, things had gone quiet. Ivery hoped that having made clear to his readers that they needed to be more careful in what they wrote, and having clamped down heavily on the more vitriolic commenters along with his attempts to build better lines of communication with the board of the club, the relationship would improve.

When the call came, it was couched in friendly language but it was made plain that there wouldn't be any dodging the meeting; it was implied that the meeting was an alternative to some real legal pressure being cranked up against the website. Of course, when it comes to lawyers in this context, there is no such thing as a friendly chat; however, the truth be told, he figured it would be worth trying to have a dialogue face to face rather than have further legal correspondence about the website. The lawyers may have been acting for Birmingham City but there was no doubt in his mind that the lawyers were really there on the instruction of one person: Peter Pannu. Ivery had known for some time he wasn't on Pannu's Christmas card list after Pannu had berated him in an interview with local radio presenter Tom Ross, in which he had criticised OP on no less than four occasions. It was Ivery's hope that maybe he could pass a message to Pannu that his opinions weren't personal attacks – and that his only objective was truthful reporting for fellow fans.

It did not turn out that way. Ivery realised that it was to be a more serious encounter while he was waiting patiently in the club reception, as the lawyer was consulting with the club's Chief Coordinating Officer Jo Allsopp – ostensibly Pannu's number two. If this was happening before he was invited into the meeting, then it was likely that the meeting wasn't going to be a pleasant one – why would someone need to talk "tactics" before a friendly chat? Ivery's gut instinct was to walk straight back out of St Andrew's and not bother with the meeting at all but afflicted by natural curiosity as to what they would say and realising that he would only be inviting the inevitable legal threats if he didn't attend, he proceeded with the meeting.

Dean Dunham, the lawyer representing the club, was a stereotypical successful City lawyer. Bright red tie contrasting with a conservative suit jacket, Cheshire cat smile and a demeanour that warned of the caution this man should be treated with. There was no doubt that hiding behind his friendly-looking exterior was a clever legal mind and that everything he would say would be said for a particular reason. He smiled as he informed Ivery that the meeting was "without prejudice", that the contents of it couldn't be used by either side against the other and that it was just an informal setting to try and rectify what had become a fractious situation. Knowing that the meeting wasn't on the record eased Ivery's concerns somewhat but the impression was clear that this guy was going to use his knowledge of the law, his persuasiveness and his position of power to browbeat Ivery – who is relatively ignorant in terms of legal knowledge – into submission.

The first topic of conversation was the comments on the blog. Ivery had received legal letters before and he knew that this topic would come up, and so he headed it off at the pass by assuring Dunham before he went any further that he would disable the comments on the site for the time being. As much as the comments on the blog provided interaction with the readers, they were also a pain; no matter how much Ivery encouraged people to be careful in what they wrote, as he couldn't be there to moderate them all the time, a few commenters would continue to make statements that were either childish abuse or legally troublesome. In closing down the comments he hoped the situation would be resolved. It was not to be though.

The lawyer smiled – obviously thinking this was all going his way and moved on to his second topic – an article written on the Often Partisan site in October 2013, which had discussed the "Delay No More" slogan and its offensive homophone in the Cantonese dialect. Dunham accused Ivery that his statements had been tantamount to inciting people to commit a crime, and that he was lucky he wasn't facing criminal charges himself. He warned Ivery that he was responsible for anything people did after reading the website if a large enough group of people followed his lead – as if he were the Pied Piper of Hamelin merrily leading a pack of Bluenoses. Anyone who knows Birmingham City fans will know that as a fanbase they are anarchic, disparate and unpredictable; if you ask them to do one thing they will do another out of their pure, wilful contrariness and trying to lead them is about as successful as herding cats – a trait Ivery has specifically noted on other occasions in his posts on the website.

Having listened to what had been said Ivery asked what resolution they expected; and was informed that they were prepared to let it slide but they impressed upon him the need to be more "mindful" of what he said in the future on the website. This notion they were prepared to "let it go" was puzzling - if it had really caused problems for the club, surely they would have pushed it legally? The fact they weren't suggested that it wasn't anywhere near as cut and dried as they made out and Ivery realised that this meeting had been called purely to try and put the frighteners on him, to control what was seen as a loose cannon by muzzling him from feeding information that they'd rather keep quiet to the fans.

Ivery asked them if they had taken any action against the fans who had sung songs about Carson every single home game since his arrest, using far more defamatory and abusive messages – referring to the then-Birmingham City President by an Anglo-Saxon term for the female anatomy. Dunham said that they hadn't, as they had no documentary evidence to use against those fans; Ivery promptly rebutted this by pointing out that the club took CCTV footage of the fans during every game for crowd control purposes. Ivery went on to remind them that those kinds of chants were illegal, they were also against the rules of the club and the Football League and it seemed odd and hypocritical that no action (however hard it would be to enforce) had been taken against those fans. He also added that a significant period of time had elapsed since the "Delay No More" piece had been published and, since then, he had written another article subsequent to being contacted by a graphic designer to discuss an idea for a protest banner and – in all that time – there had been no contact from the club or its lawyers about it; this was particularly strange as the lawyers had been in contact with him about other comments on the site in that time frame. Ivery also told Dunham that he believed the club had made no attempt at mitigating any loss or damage which was promptly shot down - "mitigation isn't necessary" but there seemed to be a bit of doubt in Dunham's mind as to whether Ivery was the complete legal ignoramus that he appeared to be on first impression.

Dunham proceeded to what Ivery believed was the core issue that he wanted him to address; that Pannu didn't like the "personalisation" of the campaign against him. Ivery laughed and replied that he should advise his client that going on the radio and having a go at the Often Partisan website wasn't exactly objective either. The tension was becoming quite palpable in the room but the balance of power had slowly shifted; the lawyer had gone into the meeting believing he held all the cards but this scruffy blogger presented him with a bit more than he had estimated, even without representation or any legal training.

They then talked about this book. Jo Allsopp told Ivery that she hadn't even considered the book as being problematic before the meeting; however, the lawyer wanted to know if he would provide a copy pre-publication for them to vet. Dunham said that while he understood the book was about Carson – and he didn't represent Carson – he had a duty to ensure it wasn't defamatory about the club, adding that, for example, if a sponsor pulled out of a deal with the club then Ivery could be held legally responsible for that loss of business.

As the book has two authors, even if Ivery had been minded to agree he knew he couldn't speak for Will Giles, so Ivery told them they would have to speak to him. He informed them that Giles was a solicitor of 24 years standing in

Hong Kong and, as well as his writing, that Giles was also involved to ensure the book stayed on the right side of the law and to give it a professional legal perspective. Ivery hoped this would ease their mind – that if their intentions had been straightforward it would have been enough – but evidently this wasn't the case. Ivery got the impression as he handed over Giles's business card that the involvement of a solicitor in the writing of the book was the last thing they wanted to hear.

Dunham said it was normal publishing practice to allow a subject of a book to view it beforehand, to which Ivery replied that if that was the case, he was sure that Giles would agree when they approached him. Dunham told Ivery he represented many celebrities in similar projects, to which Ivery repeated that if it was standard, he couldn't see Giles having a problem and that he should speak to him. Dunham then threatened that they would go to court and injunct publication if they felt it necessary, but they didn't want to go down that path. Ivery knew this was bluster - they could try to prevent publication, win damages, close down the OP website but the negative PR generated would be so bad in doing so and the backlash so great that the club could not justify those risks.

Ivery became angry. He'd been led into this meeting under false pretences; what was supposed to be a "friendly" chat was in fact a blatant attempt at intimidation. Like most right-minded people, Ivery hates bullies and he had spotted Dunham trying to baffle him with legalese a mile off. He looked the lawyer in the eye and told him in no uncertain terms that he'd been dealing with far scarier people than him; that he was used to treading a careful line with people who didn't use court action to get across their displeasure and that he wouldn't be pushed into doing something he didn't want to. Ivery reaffirmed to him that he should speak to Giles – which Dunham confirmed he would and the meeting finished – but not before Allsopp said she wanted to buy a copy of the book when it came out.

The rest is a matter of public record – Ivery released a statement the following day to explain what had happened and the proverbial muck hit the fan. Local media asked for Ivery's comments and raised the issue of the club trying to gag a fan; social media was hot with fans disgusted with what they saw as a clumsy attempt by the club to silence someone who had been publishing a steady stream of detailed information on the governance of the club and BIH. The club refused to comment, and unsurprisingly no attempt was made to contact Giles. They failed in their attempt to scare Ivery off – but, what is more, they had ignited a well-known internet phenomenon known as the "Streisand Effect".

Put simply, the Streisand effect produces the anomaly where an attempt to hide, remove, or censor a piece of information has the unintended consequence of publicizing the information more widely, usually facilitated by the internet. The moniker developed after 2003 when Barbra Streisand attempted to suppress photos of her Malibu residence that had been taken as part of a project examining coastal erosion along the entire California coast. Before her lawsuit, the photos had been downloaded six times from the project website, two of those were by her own lawyers. In the month following the lawsuit, 420,000 people visited that site alone and the picture of her house is now on the Wikipedia page that describes the phenomenon.

By trying to frighten Ivery into compliance and self-censorship, they forced his hand into telling people why he was having to disable comments on the website, albeit only for a short period. This in turn led a backlash of comments against those people at the club who were perceived to be responsible – especially Peter Pannu – and generated more interest in this book because surely it must be more interesting than first thought if the club's lawyers had tried to influence its publication. It is notable that rather than respond to questions put to him by email in an open, engaging manner, Pannu had decided that he would try and control the information we can publish.

What is even more incredible is that it has since emerged that Peter Pannu has commented on the website anonymously. Rather than engage the fans by answering interview requests, Pannu posted comments on the website using the pseudonym "Lover Blue Nose" or "Lover B" purely to try and raise his standing and to promote himself. When his high wages were criticised in a post in December 2013, Pannu posted:

"It seems none of the fans can see thro the justifications for his [Pannu's] high pay, if it can ever be termed as high. He [Pannu] is obviously the highest qualified executive in UK football and now has ensured that we won a cup and after Carson s arrest, had further made sure that we did not go bust. With the arrest of Carson and withdrawal of the credit by the bankers, we would have been in bankruptcy but due to him who are still here and efforts are made to dispose of the club which is still available for sale thanks to him. [Pannu]"

In February 2014, when discussions were on the website about the EGM Pannu again went on the offensive, telling people

"share prices had shot up again 50%..where are the doom blowers and critics... Carson has made a lot of money with the his loan sent to HK and according to the circular converts at 0.03 and today the share is at 0.15.... so he has made a massive 80M pounds profits on paper already..... is this not a master stroke by Pannu ... all admits now the club is in a better shape for sale...thanks again to Pannu..."

yet curiously wouldn't respond to email requests about what was happening about the sale of the club. His last comment in March 2014 shows just how highly he thought of himself.

"For me Pannu is the super star. He kept us alive and going and showed tremendous loyalty to Carson. These days no one is loyal to no one...."

Pannu may see himself as a superstar but his standing both in Hong Kong and in Birmingham is considerably less than that.

THE STREISAND EFFECT

16

THE CHIPS WERE STACKED AGAINST CARSON IN THE DISTRICT COURT BY WILL GILES

There is a rather unfair joke in legal circles that the last time "The Edwardian" Graham Harris SC kept a man out of prison was when he was prosecuting him. It's unfair because although Harris' record of achieving acquittals in the District Court is on the face of it extremely poor – he is certainly not alone in his high conviction rate, which unfortunately for Carson increased with his guilty verdict. In the preface to the criminal law 'bible' Archbold in 2010, Clive Grossman SC, former vice chairman of the Hong Kong Bar Association and Deputy Director of Public Prosecutions, expressed his concerns about the high conviction rates in Hong Kong which he claimed as "probably approaching that of North Korea". He went on to say "any person who is arrested on a serious or relatively serious charge is almost certain to be convicted, and since the convictions are in the District and High Courts, imprisonment is almost always the norm. Given the paucity of successful appeals (save for the Department of Justice's Review of Sentences) an arrested person is, statistically, almost certain to face imprisonment."[328] The Chief Justice described this remark as an "ill-considered and intemperate outburst" and "is totally unjustified and wholly misconceived"[329].

Who is right? If we confine the argument to the District Court, as that was the venue where Carson would be forced to face the money laundering charges, then in 2012 (the most recent year in which statistics are available) in contested cases where the defendants pleaded not guilty, 135 defendants were acquitted after trial, against 204 convicted after trial – a conviction rate of 60.2%. Once guilty pleas are included, the conviction rate soared to 91.4% – a remarkably consistent rate of over 90% has been achieved since 2006. But is this an unusually high rate compared to other jurisdictions? Is the explanation that the Department of Justice only lays charges when they have a sure-fire winner?

The Legislative Council ("LegCo") in Hong Kong considered the statistics from other comparable jurisdictions; England and Wales, Canada and Australia[330] in 2010 using statistics for 2006 to 2009.

328. Archbold Hong Kong: Criminal Law, Pleading, Evidence and Practice 2010 (Hong Kong: Sweet & Maxwell/Thomson Reuters, 2009), preface
329. Albert Wong, "Courts' 90pc conviction rate stirs up row", South China Morning Post, 15 September 2009
330. Legislative Council Secretariat, Research and Library Services Division, Information Note: Conviction rates in selected places, 2010, File Ref.: IN19/09-10, Fourth Legislative Council (Year 2009-2010)

Overall conviction rates, guilty pleas and convictions after trial in selected places and Hong Kong (in %)

	Hong Kong (1) (2) District Court	England and Wales Crown Court	Canada (3)	Australia District Court & Supreme Court (4)
2006-2007				
Overall conviction rates	91.8	77.3		79.1
Guilty pleas	65.5	68.1	Not comparable	69.9
Convictions after trial	26.3	9.2		8.8
2007-2008				
Overall conviction rates	90.5	79.3		78.9
Guilty pleas	69.5	71.4	Not comparable	69.7
Convictions after trial	21.0	7.9		8.2
2008-2009				
Overall conviction rates	92.6	80.9	69.4	78.6
Guilty pleas	72.4	73.2	61.8	68.7
Convictions after trial	20.2	7.7	7.6	8.2

Notes: (1) Statistics are in calendar year, which are figures in the years 2006 to 2008 respectively.

(2) Statistics are provided by the Department of Justice. According to the Department of Justice, these figures are calculated on a basis consistent with those of the selected places. Such calculation method is different from the one used in LC Paper No. CB(2)2613/08-09(01) that the Department submitted to the Panel on Administration of Justice and Legal Services in October 2009.

(3) The method of presenting statistics in 2008-2009 differs from the previous two years, making the figures not comparable.

(4) The total figures include a small number of "charges proven not further defined".

The figures are startling. For convictions after trial in which the defendants pleaded not guilty, Hong Kong's rate of conviction was around 2.5 times higher than each of England and Wales, Canada and Australia.

Various explanations were examined by LegCo, such as the lack of criminal legal aid provision for defendants and that the Department of Justice only prosecutes when they have overwhelming evidence which produces a high success rate, neither of which proved conclusive. One of the key sentences in the LegCo Secretarial report is this:

"Hong Kong's high conviction rate has also raised concern in the legal profession about the lack of jury trials in the District Court. Although the impartiality of judges sitting alone in the District Court has not been questioned, some lawyers in Hong Kong have asked for the extension of the jury system to the District Court."[331]

The impartiality of the judges sitting alone in the District Court should be examined – which should be a function of the Hong Kong Bar Association and Law Society of Hong Kong, independent professional bodies which represent both branches of the legal profession and hold themselves out as the bastions and protectors of civil liberties and the rule of law which made representations to LegCo. It should also be the function of LegCo itself, as LegCo is a quasi-democratic body which is supposed to act as a check and balance in overseeing Hong Kong's system of the administration of justice. It is not that the District Court Judges are biased; it is simply that the statistics are so alarming that all factors should be considered in explaining why the conviction rates in Hong Kong are so out of kilter with the rest of the common law world. In its report dated 23 June 2010, the Law Society concluded that "the conviction rates in Hong Kong do not appear to be particularly high compared with those overseas jurisdictions."[332] With respect, the figures don't lie and nor do experienced counsel like Clive Grossman SC who regularly emerge from the District Court complaining about yet another guilty verdict against what they maintain was the weight of the evidence.

331. Albert Wong, "Lawyers hope to reopen debate on jury system", South China Morning Post, 5 October 2009
332. Hong Kong Law Society, Submissions on "Conviction Rates", 23 June 2010, LC Paper No.
    CB(2)197/09-10(01), paragraph 19(a)

One aspect we believe should be considered is the background and experience of the District Court Judges who handle criminal trials, which we suggest inevitably influences their decisions. Of the judges who preside over criminal trials in the District Court, around 25% have only ever acted as prosecution counsel before being promoted to their judicial posts. They inevitably consider cases through what could be called "the prosecutor's prism" in arriving at their verdicts.

One such candidate on being interviewed for this prestigious position was reportedly asked this very question, "having acted only as a prosecutor would it have any bearing on [her] judgements?" To which, of course, she replied "No". She obviously knew how to answer a leading question!

The criticism of the composition of an unbalanced judiciary weighted disproportionately in favour of former prosecutors is not new. In his wonderful book Tales from No. 9 Ice House Street[333], the first Chinese Crown Counsel Patrick Yu Shuk-siu described the remarkable case of Father Sheridan, a Jesuit priest at Wah Yan College in 1951. Father Sheridan was the editor of the school magazine Echo and in one of its issues he criticised the Hong Kong judicial system in its appointment of judges not from the private bar as in the UK but from the Colonial Legal Service. Patrick Yu reported Father Sheridan's opinion in this way:

"Without having practised in the private sector, they could hardly be expected to appreciate or sympathize with the difficulties of defence counsel in criminal trials. If at all, they would have appeared hitherto in court only as counsel representing the Crown and would more likely than not be biased subconsciously in favour of the prosecution."[334]

We hope that a similar view expressed today would be viewed as fair comment but the then acting Attorney-General George Strickland decided to charge the Irish priest with contempt of Court as his criticism of judicial appointments, "was likely to prejudice and undermine the due

333. Patrick Yu Shuk-siu, Tales from No. 9 Ice House Street, Hong Kong University Press, 2002
334. Ibid. p.11

administration of justice in Hong Kong by bringing it into disrepute."[335]

The trial was held before Chief Justice Sir Gerald Lewis Howe, himself an Irishman and well known to the Jesuits, who convicted Father Sheridan of the contempt and fined him HK$200 (a not inconsiderable sum given that Elsie Tu GBM, CBE, a former LegCo member, says she could live on that sum for a whole month around that period[336]) to be paid within a fortnight, in default of which he would go to prison for one week. At an emergency meeting held at Wah Yan College, it was decided unanimously not to pay the fine as a protest against the charging and conviction of their brother priest. The fine was eventually paid on the last day not by the Jesuits but by a stranger with money believed to have been sourced from the Chief Justice himself!

The perception of partiality to the prosecution is what needs to be addressed. The point was better made in the Australian High Court by Heydon J in **AK v The State of Western Australia**[337] in which he said this:

"The perception is not so much that the judge may assume that the police always get the right man, but that once the prosecution has tendered enough evidence to make out a case to answer, the possible answers to that case which may be derived from the prosecution evidence and any evidence which the defence calls are not attended to sufficiently closely, because the judge has rejected those explanations in so many earlier cases. The perception is likely to be that when it comes to criminal defences, judges feel that they have heard it all before...and there is no new thing under the sun...Where trial is by jury, these perceptions do not matter: for factual findings are for the jury alone..."[338]

---

335. *Ibid.*
336. "A century of distinction", *Post Magazine, 2 June 2013*
337. *(2008) 232 CLR 438*
338. *Ibid. paragraph 101 (Heydon J)*

Patrick Yu was appointed to the first ever Judicial Services Committee in the mid-1970s to represent the Bar. The function of the Committee was to recommend and approve the appointment of judges. It was not until 1977 that Archie Zimmern became the first Hong Kong Supreme Court Judge to be appointed from the local Bar and not from the Colonial Legal Service. Now such appointments are made by the Judicial Officers Recommendation Committee – "an independent statutory body" – whose proceedings are secret and is, of course, dominated by judges. One wonders how far we have progressed since the 1970s in the appointment of judges. In 2012 the House of Lords Constitution Committee in the UK said this, "'Appointments panels must include lay persons who can bring a different perspective to the assessment of candidates' abilities,' the report says, in order to prevent a 'self-replicating' caste within the legal system".[339]

How did District Court Judge Douglas Yau end up with the exclusive power to convict Carson (without a jury) and imprison him for 6 years? The District Court was established in Hong Kong in 1953 and in its criminal jurisdiction it tried cases before a Judge alone with a maximum sentencing power of 5 years imprisonment. The need for the District Court was described in the District Court Bill which was first read on 31 December 1952:

From The 'Objects and Reasons' for the Bill

"...2. The volume of litigation, civil and criminal, passing through the courts of this Colony is such that it cannot be adequately and rapidly dealt with by the present establishment of judges and magistrates. At first sight, the solution to this problem might appear to lie in a further increase in the number of judges and magistrates...It is also anomalous that there should be no court with jurisdiction and powers of punishment greater than those now conferred upon magistrates but less than those conferred upon the Supreme Court. Here again, in other colonial territories the problem has been solved either by conferring greater powers and jurisdiction on magistrates or by the creation of District Courts. It is considered that the best solution is to create a District Court of Hong Kong." [340]

339. Owen Bowcott, "Judiciary needs to be more diverse, peers say", The Guardian, 28 March 2012,
340. Hansard (31 December 1952, p. 301) (First Reading of the District Court Bill)

Its criminal jurisdiction was established by an amendment to the Magistrates Ordinance which provided for the transfer to the District Court, on the exclusive application of the Attorney General (the Defendant had no say in the matter), of charges and complaints in relation to indictable offences, except serious offences like murder set out in a separate schedule which were automatically transferred to the Supreme Court for trial by jury. On the absence of the right to a jury trial, the District Court Bill said this:

"Moreover, provision is made for appeals in criminal cases to go to the Full Court, and the trial judge is required (clause 30) to place on record a short statement of the reasons for his verdict. It is considered that these provisions are an adequate safeguard against miscarriages of justice. To provide for trial by jury in the District Court would place a grave additional burden on an already over-worked jury list, and to provide for a right to elect to be tried by jury would be to introduce something which is not at present available to an accused person, and might very well defeat one of the main objects of the Bill."[341]

And Mr. Arthur Ridehalgh, Q.C., the Attorney General, in an astonishing diatribe further justified the absence of the right to a jury trial (which had originally been introduced in 1845 in Hong Kong as a jury of '6 men' with the first recorded Chinese name appearing as a juror in 1858) in the second reading of the bill in 1953:

"**THE ATTORNEY GENERAL:**— ... the absence of provision in this legislation for trial by jury, I would like to say that the view is taken that such a provision is unnecessary. I would like to point out that trial by jury is not an end in itself but is a means to an end and a means which was particularly devised in England. I would like also to say that juries are not infallible even where they are composed of twelve persons and unanimity is essential to their verdict. I would interpolate that here a jury is composed of seven persons and a majority verdict of five to two is allowable in any but capital cases. As I have said, juries are not infallible and those who have had

---

341. *Hansard (31 December 1952, p. 303) (First Reading of the District Court Bill)*

experience in the practice of the law have seen them err on both sides of the line. There are cases in England where the Court of Criminal Appeal has upset a verdict of guilty by a jury on the ground of unreasonableness. On the other side of the line, the practitioner who has been in practice for any length of time must have come across cases where a verdict of not guilty has been either a stupid or perverse one.

Now, I would say this in relation to trial by jury, that it is much more difficult to upset a verdict on fact than it is to upset a finding by a judge on a question of fact, and the reason for that is this, that you cannot go behind a verdict of a jury and start inquiring into the reasons why they arrived at their verdict. Now, in this legislation provision is made whereby a judge on coming to a decision that a person is guilty of an offence shall give a short statement of his reasons for his finding and that finding will therefore be subject to scrutiny if an appeal is taken to the Full Court.

It is suggested, Sir, that that provides an adequate safeguard against miscarriages of Justice which, of course, is the due end of the processes of law."[342]

The District Court was established with trial by Judges sitting alone as a purely pragmatic colonial measure to alleviate an "already over-worked jury list" supported by the most senior government prosecutor's undermining critique of the principle of trial by jury "which was particularly devised in England" and "not infallible"; this was balanced by the supposed safeguards of a right of appeal and the trial judge's responsibility to make a short statement of the reasons for his verdict. One could be forgiven for thinking that "one country, one system" had come ninety-four years early and "the party" had done away with what should have been an inalienable human right, at the stroke of the executive pen.

---

342. *Hansard (14 January 1953, pp. 4-5) (Second Reading of the District Court Bill)*

The birth of the modern jury is often traced to the abolition of the Star Chamber, a "Court" in name but which in reality wielded and abused its unshackled power to support the crumbling regime of Charles I, by the passing of the Habeas Corpus Act on 5 July 1641 whose long title simply reads:

"An Act for the Regulating of the Privy Council and for taking away the Court commonly called the Star Chamber."

The Act provided that anyone imprisoned by order of the King, Privy Council or any councillor could apply for a writ of habeas corpus but just as importantly:

Whereas by the Great Charter many times confirmed in parliament, it is enacted, that no freeman shall be taken or imprisoned or disseised of his freehold or liberties, or be outlawed or exiled or otherwise destroyed, and that the King would not pass upon him, or condemn him; but by lawful judgment by his peers...

Lord Devlin described trial by jury as "the lamp that shows that freedom lives"[343], and listed five advantages of trial by jury over trial by judge alone: [344]

(1) Juries are superior to judges in assessing defence points: "the hope of the defence very often lies in impalpabilities – the willingness to make allowances for muddle-headedness, illogicalities, and unreasonableness – impalpabilities that are less appealing to the legal mind than to the lay"[345], and, "[I]t is an essential part of the system that the law should recognize that there are cases in which such factors should be dominating";[346]

(2) Juries are superior to judges in assessing credibility;[347]

343. *The Hon Sir Patrick Devlin, Trial by Jury (The Hamlyn Lectures, Eighth Series, Stevens & Sons Limited, 1956) p. 164*
344. *ibid. p. 120*
345. *ibid, p.122*
346. *ibid, p.123*
347. *ibid, p.149*

(3) Juries are better able to see the justice of a case, as opposed to the judge who is sworn to strictly follow the law;[348]

(4) Trial by jury helps to ensure the independence and quality of judges;[349]

(5) Trial by jury gives protection against laws which ordinary men may regard as harsh and oppressive.[350]

This ancient tenet described by 'Liberty' director of policy Isabella Sankey as ... "The right to jury trial isn't just a hallowed principle but a practice that ensures that one class of people don't sit in judgment over another and the public have confidence in an open and representative justice system" has been deprived to all defendants in the District Court since 1953, including of course Carson.

The apparent institutional bias in favour of the prosecution in the District Court is compounded by its right under section 88 of the Magistrates Ordinance to elect to transfer the charges of indictable offences (save the category of offences such as murder set out in a separate schedule) to the District Court rather than the High Court – the Magistrate has absolutely no discretion in the matter. It is the prosecution's sole right to elect whether to try a case like Carson's in the District Court before a judge alone or before the High Court with a jury. Given the statistics, it is not surprising that the District Court is a popular choice. The prosecution's only real concern in reality in its 'choice' of venue would be whether the power of sentencing in the District Court is sufficient for its and the Government's penal and political purposes.

The maximum sentence a judge can impose in the District Court was increased from five to seven years by the District Court (Amendment)

348. ibid, p.154
349. ibid p.158-159
350. ibid, p.160
351. "First trial without jury approved", BBC News, 18 June 2009

Ordinance in 1973 but, more importantly, its jurisdiction was increased to entitle it to hear an even greater array of cases.

The Explanatory Memorandum of that Bill reads:

"The great increase in the amount of serious crime during the past few years has imposed severe burdens on the Supreme Court and the District Court.

It is therefore proposed that some of the more serious cases now tried in the Supreme Court should be tried in the District Court. In order to enable the District Court to deal adequately with such cases this Bill increases the maximum sentence which may be imposed by a District Judge from 5 to 7 years."[352]

The colonial pragmatism and creeping increase in the expansion of trials without juries continued unabated. Carson added to a long line of challenges to the deprivation of his right to a jury trial but he came up against the same High Court Judge, the Honourable Mr. Justice Alan Wright, as Lily Chiang who in 2009 had sought a judicial review of the prosecution's election to try her in the District Court. In her case, the judge said:

"The decision as to whether an indictable offence be tried in the Court of First Instance [the High Court] by a judge and jury or in the District Court by a judge alone is the prerogative of the Secretary for Justice." His decision was upheld in the Court of Final Appeal.

In Carson's case, the same judge said,

"28. I am satisfied that the purpose of these proceedings [Carson's judicial review] is to attempt to disrupt the forthcoming trial and is an abuse of the process of this court. There are clear indicators that this is even so, even leaving aside the chronology submitted by the putative respondent.

...34. Then there is the nature of the application itself which, as obvious

352. Hansard (23 May 1973, p. 814) (Second Reading of the District Court (Amendment) Bill 1973)

from the background I have outlined, is frivolous."[353]

Carson was stuck in the District Court without the right to a trial by his peers, a right often taken for granted in the rest of the common law world. With the institutional element of justice seemingly against him would the judge's interpretation of the charges he faced give him any hope of being that one person in ten or eleven to emerge from the District Court with an acquittal?

Carson was charged with five charges of dealing with property having reasonable grounds to believe it represented the proceeds of an indictable offence. The prosecution did not at any time seek to prove or even allege a 'predicate' offence – an underlying crime – which led to the cash in Carson's accounts which he then 'dealt' with. The judge himself throughout his judgment says it was not his function to speculate what that offence or offences might be. He was simply concerned whether the 'reasonable man' would come to the conclusion that the money represented the proceeds of an indictable offence, which was never defined. It begs the question whether the judge could properly direct himself in his fact finding "jury" role before reaching his verdict without knowing how the money was at least alleged to represent the proceeds of an indictable offence or offences.

To these 2 questions:

(1) Is the prosecution required to prove the property is derived from a predicate offence?

(2) Is the prosecution required to prove the defendant actually believed the property was the proceeds of an offence?

District Court Judge Douglas Yau followed established case-law from higher courts in answering "No".

---

353. *Yeung Ka Shing Carson v. Secretary for Justice, HCAL 59 of 2013 (DHCJ Wright) paras. 28 and 34*

Was the legislation ever intended to be so wide as to enable the conviction of someone where no underlying offence was proved and even if the person (even correctly) believed the proceeds were not the proceeds of an indictable offence?

There is no doubt that in answering question (2) the judge followed established case law in adopting "the reasonable man" objective test in considering Carson's intention and whether he had "reasonable grounds to believe". This "Mens Rea" or mental element requirement under "the second limb" of section 25(1) Organised and Serious Crimes Ordinance (Cap. 455) ("**OSCO**") is minimal as confirmed by Lord Woolf when considering the equivalent legislation covering the proceeds of drug trafficking:

"Furthermore the only "mens rea" which the prosecution is required to establish, if mens rea is an appropriate description of the necessary mental element, is that the defendant should know or have reasonable grounds to believe that the relevant person is connected with drug trafficking. **This mental element can exist, even if the defendant does not have the required belief**, if there are reasonable grounds for holding the belief. The offence is therefore a Draconian one. [**emphasis added**]"[354]

The notion that you cannot 'know' that property was the proceeds of an offence unless it actually was such property, which should also apply to "having reasonable grounds to believe" it was the proceeds of an indictable offence has been rejected by the Court of Final Appeal in **Oei Hengky Wiryo vs HKSAR**[355].

An observation by Lunn JA in the Court of Appeal decision in **HKSAR vs Pang Hung Fai**[356] demonstrates a possible divergence of opinion in the appeal courts:

Lunn JA:

"196. …it would be a defence that the defendant **honestly and reasonably did not suspect the property to represent the proceeds of an indictable**

354. AG of Hong Kong v Lee Kwong Kut & Others [1993] AC 951 (Lord Woolf) p.964 G-H
355. Oei Hengky Wiryo v HKSAR FACC 4/2006 (Mr Justice McHugh NPJ) paras. 106-109.
356. HKSAR v Pang Hung Fai CACC 34/2012 (Hon Lunn JA) para. 196.

offence. Of course, such a person would be morally blameless. I agree with his observation (paragraph 214) that **it would be "unattractive" to conclude that the legislature intended such a person to be caught by the offence. [emphasis added]**"

The unsatisfactory state of the money laundering law under OSCO is best shown in **Pang Hung Fai** in which the defendant faced one charge of dealing with property known or believed to represent the proceeds of an indictable offence. Pang was a successful business man with two factories in the mainland and his friend Kwok who he had known for many years was the chairman of a listed company. Kwok asked Pang to receive some money from two mainland friends and Pang did not ask about the nature of the transaction. Pang said he had no reason to ask Kwok who was a successful businessman, because he had known him and trusted him for thirty years. It never occurred to Pang that the money might have originated from the proceeds of an illegal transaction. Two sums amounting to HK$14M were received after this instruction (which was prepared by Pang's bookkeeper for accounting records purposes) from Kwok:

"I will remit a sum of HK$14,049,380 to your company on the 1st day of August 2008. Please receive (it) for (me). (I) will inform you of the information of the bank account later to have (the money) transferred back to me."[357]

At Kwok's request about four weeks later, Pang remitted the HK$14,049,380 less bank charges to Kwok's company in Cambodia. It later transpired Kwok and his two mainland friends had conspired to defraud his own public company from the sale proceeds of shares issued after they exercised options which the company never received – the HK$14,049,380 was the proceeds of an indictable offence. Kwok absconded and Pang was left to face the music.

The same judge as in Carson's case, District Court Judge Douglas Yau convicted Pang on the grounds that it was a substantial sum of money, the

---

357. *Ibid. para.13*

money was coming from overseas, Pang didn't know the two mainlanders who remitted the funds, no reason had been given by Kwok as to why he needed Pang to receive and hold the money and the money was then remitted to Cambodia without anything else being done with it; all facts together would lead "a common sense, right-thinking member of the community" to have reasonable grounds to believe that the money dealt with by Pang represented proceeds of an indictable offence. Pang was sentenced to 2.5 years in prison. The judge's decision was upheld in the Court of Appeal.

The "Mens Rea" or mental element, the criminal intent required for this offence under the second limb – the "having reasonable grounds to believe" ingredient – is a complex question which is still evolving and further answers may come from the Court of Final Appeal in the **Pang Hung Fai** case to be heard in autumn 2014.

So on the present state of the "Mens Rea" requirement of the law, Carson's own subjective intention – whether he himself believed the property in his accounts to be the proceeds of an indictable offence or offences was not relevant.

Of even greater interest in the search for a true definition of this offence was the judge's answer "No" to the first question – his acceptance again following established case-law that in proving the "Actus Reus" – the criminal act – the prosecution need not show the property came from a predicate indictable offence or even that they were required to allege an underlying indictable offence.

Our research appears to indicate that this approach is against the original legislative intent of the law:

1) The Long Title of the OSCO is concerned with property that is **actually** the proceeds of crime:

"An Ordinance to create new powers of investigation into organized crimes and certain other offences and into the proceeds of crime of certain offenders; provide for the confiscation of proceeds of crime;

make provision in respect of the sentencing of certain offenders; **create offences relating to the proceeds of crime or property representing the proceeds of crime**; and for ancillary and connected matters. [**emphasis added**]"[358]

2) There is no discussion in the legislative materials relating to the original bill or the amendment to the bill about property which was not actually the proceeds of an offence. The purpose of the money laundering offence was to target the actual (not suspected) proceeds of crime which was made clear in what was originally entitled the Organized Crime Bill 1991: "Explanatory Notes on the Organized Crime Bill 1991 Money Laundering Offence (Clause 7) 25. This offence is created to deter people, including professional investment advisers, from getting involved in laundering money or other **property representing the proceeds of crime** for a member of an OCG [Organized Crime Group]. 26. The basic elements of the offence are –

(b) that the relevant money or property **was the proceeds** (directly or indirectly, wholly or partly) of crime; [**emphasis added**]"[359]

In 1992, after the Organized Crime Bill – the first White Bill was proposed and in particular with regard to the money laundering offences proposed, it was suggested that the provision "should be more widely available against the proceeds of crime, and not limited to the proceeds of organized crime and drug trafficking".[360]

The Bill was accordingly renamed "The Organized and Serious Crimes Bill" ("**OSCO Bill**") and its scope was changed:
"Scope of the [OSCO Bill]

5. The offence provisions in the White Bill which involved proving that a person was a member of an organized crime group (OCG) when he

---

358. *Organized and Serious Crimes Ordinance (Cap. 455), Long Title*
359. *Security Branch, Legislative Council Brief on the Organized Crime Bill 1991, 5 August 1991, File Ref.: SCR 3/2831/87, Annex B, paras. 25-26*
360. *Security Branch, Legislative Council Brief on the Organised and Serious Crimes Bill 1992, 7 July 1992, File Ref.: SBCR 3/2831/87, para. 4(c)*

committed a specified offence were strongly criticised during the public consultation exercise on the grounds that they were complex and were unfair to the accused. We drop such offence provisions and move away altogether from the OCG concept.

6. [The proposed]…definition of organized crime, coupled with the offences in Schedule 1, will capture the vast majority of the serious offences committed by triad societies."[361]

In the OSCO Bill, the money laundering offence was finally enacted in October 1994 after amendment as section 25. The description of the new offence in the LegCo brief was as follows:

"36. Clause 25 provides that a person commits a money laundering offence if, knowing or having reasonable grounds to believe that another person has carried on a criminal activity or has benefited from crime, he enters into an arrangement that assists that person to retain his proceeds of crime."[362]

The offence proposed and ultimately enacted was:

"25. Assisting a person to retain proceeds of indictable offence
(1) Subject to subsection (3), a person who enters into or is otherwise concerned in an arrangement whereby -

(a) the retention or control by or on behalf of another ("the relevant person") of the relevant person's proceeds of an indictable offence is facilitated (whether by concealment, removal from the jurisdiction, transfer to nominees or otherwise); or

(b) the relevant person's proceeds of an indictable offence -

(i) are used to secure funds that are placed at the relevant person's disposal;
   or

---

361. *Ibid., paras. 5 and 6*
362. *ibid, para. 36*

(ii) are used for the relevant person's benefit to acquire property by way of investment, knowing or having reasonable grounds to believe that the relevant person is a person who has committed or has benefited from an indictable offence, commits an offence.

(2) In this section, references to any person's proceeds of an indictable offence include a reference to any property which, in whole or in part, directly or indirectly, represented in his hands his proceeds of an indictable offence."

The proposed section also set up a specific defence if the defendant did not know or suspect that the arrangement related to any person's proceeds of crime. The proposed offence clearly encompassed the actual proceeds of crime – the proceeds of an indictable offence – and also set up the subjective defence that the defendant could not be convicted if he himself did not know the money related to proceeds of crime.

3) In addition the promoters of the OSCO assured LegCo the bill did not target innocent third parties: "Money Laundering Offence

Clause 25 proposes a general money laundering offence which is an extension from the current provision in Cap. 405 relating to drug money.

The ad hoc group recognised the merit of a wider provision against money laundering. Yet, the present proposal to enlarge the provision to such an extent as to cover all proceeds of crime will net even trivial cases. **It may create unnecessary burden on innocent third parties who routinely handle money on behalf of their clients, for instance, bankers, lawyers, estate agents, and so on. The Administration has assured us that these legitimate trades are not their target.** It has been agreed to limit the provision to proceeds of indictable offences; and proceeds of foreign offences which would amount to an indictable offence in Hong Kong. This latter application will help combat the internationalization of crime and prohibit criminals from making Hong Kong a haven of money laundering. **[emphasis added]**"[363]

4) The funds targeted by the OSCO were the finances of criminal syndicates, not legitimate funds as debated in LegCo:

"Turning now to the money laundering provisions, the third major proposal in the Bill, these create a general money laundering offence to cover the proceeds of all crime, modelled also upon the provisions in the Drug Trafficking (Recovery of Proceeds) Ordinance. Again, I am pleased that the ad hoc group supports **the objective of this provision, which will help destroy the financial strength of criminal syndicates.** Some ad hoc group Members, however, have pointed out that the money laundering offence was unusually wide. **We have therefore agreed to limit the money laundering offence to the proceeds of indictable offences. [emphasis added]**"[364]

5) OSCO was enacted in October 1994 but section 25 was swiftly amended. The current section 25 of the OSCO was amended in July 1995 under pressure from the Administration in what we say was undue haste supposedly to bring it in line with the changes being made to the similar offence under the Drug Trafficking (Recovery of Proceeds) Ordinance (Cap. 405) ("**DTRPO**")

The offence of "dealing with property known or believed to represent proceeds of an indictable offence" – section 25 of the OSCO – as it is now and as Carson was charged with, was enacted in 1995 under the Organised and Serious Crimes (Amendment) Ordinance ("**OSCO Amendment Ordinance**") and brought into force just nine months after the original section (as set out above in 2)) took effect, replacing it entirely. It was said in the LegCo discussions:

"**MR JAMES TO**:- Initially the Bills Committee had some reservation on the Bill mainly because the Organized and Serious Crimes Ordinance

363. *Hansard (12 October 1994, p. 124) (Resumption of debate on Second Reading of the Organized and Serious Crimes Bill 1992)*
364. *Ibid., p. 140*

had only been implemented for a few months. However, the Administration pointed out that since the amendments proposed to the Ordinance were modelled on the Drug Trafficking (Recovery of Proceeds) (Amendment) Bill to maintain the correspondence between the two Ordinances and to enhance the law enforcement authority's ability to tackle triads and organized crime, it firmly believed the two Bills should be examined together.[365]

…**SECRETARY FOR SECURITY [(Mr. Peter Lai Hing-Ling, J.P.)]:-** The confiscation and money laundering provisions of the Organized and Serious Crimes Ordinance were modelled on the provisions of the Drug Trafficking (Recovery of Proceeds) Ordinance. To maintain compatibility and to achieve effective enforcement, the present Bill proposes amendments to the Organized and Serious Crimes Ordinance similar to those proposed for the Drug Trafficking (Recovery of Proceeds) Ordinance."[366]

When the above is read together with the discussion in the LegCo on the Drug Trafficking (Recovery of Proceeds) (Amendment) Bill 1995 ("**DTRP Amendment Bill**") and the LegCo brief prepared on the amendments to the two Ordinances concerned, two matters immediately become clear.

Firstly, the offence in section 25 of the DTRPO was replaced to reflect the 1988 United Nations Convention Against Illicit Traffic in Narcotic Drugs and Psychotropic Substances. Secondly, section 25 of the OSCO was amended simply to mirror those changes in the DTRPO.

As was said in the LegCo Brief on the DTRP Amendment Bill and Organised and Serious Crimes (Amendment) Bill 1995 ("**OSCO Amendment Bill**"):

"…5. In addition, certain amendments to the Ordinance are also required to enable Hong Kong to comply more fully with the latest international standards and recommendations.

---

365. Hansard (28 July 1995, p. 6491) (Resumption of debate on Second Reading of the Organised and Serious Crimes (Amendment) Bill 1995)
366. Ibid., p.6492

6. The United Nations Convention Against Illicit Trafficking in Narcotic Drugs and Psychotropic Substances 1988, is directed at improving international co-operation in the suppression of trafficking and money laundering. The following amendments are proposed to bring the Drug Trafficking (Recovery of Proceeds) Ordinance in line with **Articles 3 and 5 of the Convention**:

(a) to establish a criminal offence of **dealing in property**, knowing that it is the proceeds of drug trafficking;

(b) to provide for the recovery of income or other benefits derived from property which represents the proceeds of drug trafficking. [**emphasis added**]"[367]

As further explained in the explanatory memorandum to the DTRP Amendment Bill:

"16. Clause 20 repeals section 25 and substitutes new sections 25 and 25A. New section 25 **creates the offence of dealing with property** knowing or believing it to represent the proceeds of drug trafficking. [**emphasis added**]"[368]

Similarly, in the explanatory memorandum to the OSCO Amendment Bill:

"13. Clause 19 repeals section 25 and substitutes new sections 25 and 25A. New section 25(1) **makes it an offence for a person to deal with any property** knowing or having reasonable grounds to believe that it in whole or in part directly or indirectly represents any person's proceeds of an indictable offence. [**emphasis added**]"[369]

---

367. Security Branch, Government Secretariat, Legislative Council Brief on the Drug Trafficking (Recovery of Proceeds) (Amendment) Bill 1995 and the Organized and Serious Crimes (Amendment) Bill 1995, 10 April 1995, File Ref.: NCR 3/1/8 (G) VII, paras. 5 and 6
368. Ibid., Annex A, para. 16
369. ibid Annex B, para.13

If the present section 25 in the DTRPO was enacted with the specific ingredient of the offence being proceeds of drug trafficking then it appears to us that the legislature had a similar intention for the indictable offence to be identified in this new offence of 'dealing' with its proceeds.

Of course that is not how things have turned out. The Courts have adopted the "reasonable man" test when looking at the "Mens Rea" requirement of the offence and have so far refused to interpret section 25 of the OSCO as requiring proof that property actually represents the proceeds of crime[370][371][372].

Apart from the "Mens Rea" and the definition of "proceeds of an indictable offence" the Judgment in Carson's case also raises another issue fundamental to the fair administration of justice. As a result of the "objective man" test – the judging of the defendant's intention by the judge himself – defendants like Carson come under pressure to give evidence and provide an explanation of how the alleged laundered funds came to be in their possession and why they dealt with them. This is the case even though there is no requirement or "onus" on them to do so, unlike section 10 of the Prevention of Bribery Ordinance (Cap. 201), which specifically obliges the charged party to satisfactorily explain to the court how he maintains such a standard of living if he is to escape conviction.

This 'onus' in Carson's case could be labelled the 'evidential' onus or, as Graham Harris SC put it in the trial, 'the tactical onus'. As can be seen from the judgement, the judge put great store in labelling Carson a liar and found in his findings that Carson had reason to believe that the funds in his accounts were the proceeds of an indictable offence. Yet did the prosecution really prove that his explanations were false and even if they were, is the creation of the "reverse onus" and then the rejection of his explanation in convicting him, a correct implementation of this law? This is particularly pertinent

370. *Oei Hengky Wiryo v HKSAR FACC 4/2006*
371. *Au Hau Ching v HKSAR FAMC 61/2009*
372. *Wong Ping Shui Adam v HKSAR FAMC 1/2001*

when one considers key elements of the criminal justice system – that the accused is "innocent until proven guilty" and the need for the prosecution to prove its case "beyond a reasonable doubt." Surely it's not for the defendant to prove his innocence "beyond a reasonable doubt"? This is a further question which will no doubt exercise the appeal courts in Carson's case.

In addition we understand that the principle of legal certainty, established under Article 49 of the Basic Law and Article 11(1) of the Hong Kong Bill of Rights will be considered by the Court of Final Appeal in the **Pang Hung Fai** case. Is the offence too imprecise to enable a citizen to foresee whether his course of conduct is unlawful, as the facts may enable more than one reasonable belief? All of these issues and no doubt more will be raised before the appeal courts.

There is no doubt in our minds that the legislature only intended the section to catch the proceeds of actual indictable offences not notional, unnamed, unalleged offences. The definition is so wide that we believe that normal business conduct which has been practised hundreds if not thousands of times a day for decades in Hong Kong – for example, "mirror banking" where business people deposit mainland currency Yuan with a "money-changer" over the border and their bank account is then credited with Hong Kong Dollars in Hong Kong – would be caught. On the face of it, this is an illegal practice in the mainland that is designed to avoid the foreign exchange controls; the recipient would be unable to identify the source of funds deposited in Hong Kong but such dealings have contributed to Hong Kong's commercial success and its key role in China's growth as its "banker". Whether the appeal courts will allow consideration of the legislative intent is another matter but Carson's legal team will for sure be giving it their best shot in urging them to do so.

The Hong Kong Administration has been quick to seize on Carson's and other convictions in demonstrating its commitment to international standards in enforcing its anti-money laundering laws.

"The [Financial Action] Task Force recognised Hong Kong's efforts and agreed unanimously among members in October 2012 to remove Hong Kong from its "follow-up process" in its regular mutual evaluation.

Successful conviction of recent cases shows our determination and efficacy among law enforcement agencies and financial regulators in combating money laundering."[373]

In our view, their political means do not justify the legal ends of a law which catches "criminals" who have no criminal intent and who are simply conducting business as they always have.

Why do we raise these complex legal issues here? To demonstrate that although Carson is currently languishing in prison his legal battle has not even reached half time and those Blues fans who thought it was all over will need to think again. He is after all still the effective owner of the club and he, his barristers Harris, Egan and Tsoi and his friend Lam all know how to play a long game.

373. *Jackie Liu (Principal Assistant Secretary for Financial Services and the Treasury (Financial Services)), Letter to the Editor: "Hong Kong's efforts against money laundering", South China Morning Post, 19 March 2014*

17

WHAT NEEDS TO CHANGE

All said and done Birmingham City fans have been lucky, although we doubt many Blues fans would agree. The club hasn't been forced to play in Northampton like Coventry City and has survived in the Championship for at least four seasons, unlike Portsmouth who dropped down the leagues like a stone, languishing in League Two in May 2014, just six years after winning the FA Cup.

In no small part due to the persistence of the staff at the club who did what they could to maximise commercial and fan revenue from minimal resources, along with the good fortune to shed most of its high earners, the club has been able to find relative financial self-sufficiency. It is ironic that if Carson had been able to secure the signings he wanted in 2011 – particularly if they were on similar incremental contracts without relegation clauses to the one Nikola Zigic signed – then the situation would have been a lot worse and not dissimilar to Portsmouth's, who are still paying off players who no longer play for them like Birmingham City's own Hayden Mullins. It's possible that those additional wages could have forced the club into administration on relegation – much as happened at Portsmouth.

Both the Premier League and the Football League have rules that require clubs to maintain their finances within fairly tight limits – the "Financial Fair Play" rules – or they will face fines and more severe penalties for bad financial management. Queens Park Rangers are likely to be heavily fined between £25M and £35M for making a loss of £65.4M in 2012/3[374]. Failing to publish accounts can be punished by a transfer embargo, such as the one suffered by Birmingham City between 1 March 2012 and 4 July 2012. Should an owner be found guilty of financial wrong-doing, clubs can be penalised even if the owner has long departed – as Watford found to its cost after Laurence Bassini was fined and banned from football on charges of misconduct and dishonesty over financial dealings on behalf of the football club. Bassini was found guilty of not informing the league of the forward funding of £2.6M of TV income and transfer fees; Birmingham City have forward funded parachute payments themselves in the past two years but

---

374. Glenn Moore, "QPR Financial Results: Rangers face huge fine in top flight of debtors", *The Independent*, 6 March, 2014

have obtained league permission first.

Apart from the rare examples of enforcement, the laissez-faire attitude of the Football League in its failure to investigate issues proactively has led to dire consequences for several clubs. In Coventry City's case, the Football League merely imposed a "performance bond" of £1M on the new owners of the club, Otium Entertainment, and extracted a promise to return to the city of Coventry within five years after Otium uprooted the club and moved it to a groundshare with Northampton after a financial disagreement regarding rent and matchday revenues with the owners of their home ground, the Ricoh Stadium. There are mitigating circumstances in that Otium had good reason to believe that the club could not be sustainable at the Ricoh but equally the Football League's reluctance to act allowed that situation to fester and develop into the standoff it became. Had the Football League refused Otium permission to groundshare with Northampton, then the respective owners of the football club and the stadium would have been more likely to have reached some sort of compromise that would have kept the football club in the city of Coventry.

The statement the Football League issued after Carson's conviction[375] supports this perception that they are a soft touch. After noting that BIH had "revised arrangements" including Carson's resignation from all directorships and the introduction of new working capital, they confirmed they "did not require financial assurances beyond this point". With the failure of BIH to sell 12% of the club to Beijing Liangzhu, did they press the question whether any working capital was in fact provided by BIH or did the Football League merely accept the assurance from the club that it would complete its fixtures in the 2013/4 season? In short, they were quick to wash their hands of the affair – it mattered not that the convicted money launderer continued to own apparently the controlling stake in Birmingham City, or that the club was potentially implicated in receiving funds that were the proceeds of an indictable offence – they were happy with what they saw as a short term solution. Needless to say, Birmingham City fans were not impressed by this statement, as Steve McCarthy, Chairman of the Blues Trust emphasised:

375. *Football League Statement on Birmingham City, 3 March, 2014*

"We are very disappointed that the Football League is not actively planning to investigate the ownership and running of the club in the light of Carson Yeung's conviction. We are desperate for these people to go now and hand the club to somebody who will have its best interests at heart, ideally with the involvement of supporters in owning a stake."[376]

In 2011, Portsmouth fans complained that the Football League were slow to act as their club was used as a pawn in the financial dispute between Balram Chainrai and Arcadi Gaydamak over money allegedly owed to the Nepalese born Hong Kong-based Chainrai. It was only after the hard investigative work of some very dedicated Portsmouth fans like the blogger Micah Hall that the true picture came to light. At a Supporters Summit panel held by Supporters Direct at St. George's Park in July 2013 Hall confirmed that the Football League had been reticent to act on the information he had gathered, and that they had given little support to the Pompey fans as the club unwound around them despite clear evidence of convicted forger Daniel Azougy acting as a shadow director of the club.[377]

It took Hall an inordinate amount of diligent research to identify one of the owners of his football club – the mysterious Ali al-Faraj – at the time when Portsmouth were in the Premier League, which is a shocking indictment on the business of football. There is no doubt that financially sensitive information requires confidentiality but the issue of beneficial ownership of the clubs – who actually owns the clubs – has in some cases been ignored by the authorities. In both the Premier League and the Football League the identities of those who have a beneficial interest in 10% or more of a football club must be made public in a document available online but even this is a fudge; for example, almost anyone could see at one point that Liu Xingcheng and Zhou Xin owned over 10% of Blues; however, without any further disclosures, those names are anonymous and meaningless and serve to make the rule redundant.

376. David Conn, "Birmingham City fans concerned at Carson Yeung's continued influence", *The Guardian*, 4 March, 2014

377. Micah Hall "Hall Right Now: Revealed – The true story behind Ali Al Faraj", *fansnetwork.co.uk*, 7 October, 2012

Interestingly, Hall was another fan who attracted the lawyers when he was sued in connection with his investigative work into his football club, although in his case it was prospective purchaser Pascal Najadi who filed a writ against him – and in Hall's case the "Streisand effect" also took hold with fans of other clubs taking up the cudgels and reproducing his piece to a wider audience.

In Carson's case he was in the habit of using nominees to hold his shares, as demonstrated in the Kanstar and Neptune deals which were the subject of evidence at his trial. This is not illegal in Hong Kong except when it breaches disclosure requirements of the Securities and Futures Ordinance ("SFO"). It is a breach of the SFO to hide your ownership behind a nominee where your interest in shares in listed companies is a 5% or above stake. Carson has been convicted on 2 occasions of breaches of this nature – in 2004 he was convicted on fourteen counts in relation to Cedar Base and in 2010 he was convicted in connection with his BIH shareholding. One benefit of hiding ownership of shares would be to keep the shareholding below the 30% threshold, which would trigger a general offer. In the same way Carson has been able to hide his true shareholdings from the HKSE, it is easy to envisage owners hiding their true interests behind nominees away from the oversight of the seemingly toothless Premier League and Football League.

Both the Football League and the Premier League define an owner of a club as someone with a beneficial interest of 30% or more of the club or is acting in concert with other shareholders which would take them above that threshold. Carson has never declared ownership of more than a 28% stake of BIH and so has never been considered by the football authorities as a beneficial owner of Birmingham City, despite acting in a manner that would suggest he has complete control of the club and being recognised as such by the shareholders, fans and press alike.

The "fit and proper" test is a sop to the conscience of the authorities – it has been so ineffectual only three people ever failed the test in its existence with one of those (Massimo Cellino) beating it on appeal. Carson took the test in September 2009 on becoming a director of Birmingham City FC and passed it – even though he was then under investigation in Hong Kong for money laundering. Those investigations weren't public – but if the test had required him to disclose any current or pending investigations then there would have been cause to examine his credentials more closely. He also slipped through an apparent loop-hole in the test in that his conviction for his failure to disclose his beneficial interest in BIH dating back to 2010, although a criminal offence in Hong Kong is no longer equivalent in the UK and would not have been taken into account. As it was, he was a shoe-in – exactly the type of international owner the Premier League and Football League desired to spread their "brand" to the lucrative Asian market.

The solution appears to be obvious – to lower the threshold for someone to be considered a beneficial owner under The Owners and Directors Test to force more people into taking it. As an example, the HKSE have the limit of 5% for disclosure of ownership in a listed company when buying and selling its shares; if it has to be reported to the HKSE that a person has taken a 5% stake in a company, why does this not have to be declared to the Premier League and Football League? If it puts off people who have something to hide and wouldn't want to take the test or make such disclosures it might hurt clubs in the short-term commercially but it would benefit the game in the long-term as it would increase the transparency and accountability of owners of the clubs and possibly avoid English clubs becoming bastions for rogues like Carson.

Of course, that would require the Football League to toughen up and be ready for any legal challenge, as it isn't beyond the realms of improbability that someone would challenge such a change in the rules in the courts as a restraint of trade. Some people may despise the franchise system of American sports, where teams can be sold and transported by new owners, but lessons can be learned from their strict governance on transparency of ownership. As an example, barring the Green Bay Packers who are owned by their fans under a grandfather clause, NFL rules limit the number of owners of any team to 32 and at least one of those owners must hold a 30% stake, although that stake can be split between a family[378]. If the Football League won't drop

378. Daniel Kaplan, "NFL pares ownership rule", Sports Business Daily, 26 October, 2009

the reporting threshold, then forcing at least one person to hold 30% and be in control and fully accountable may improve the financial dealings of the clubs. If a club happens to be on a stock exchange triggering the threshold for a general offer a waiver can always be sought.

The last time the TV rights for the Premier League were sold in 2012 BT and BSkyB paid more than £3BN, making it the richest league in the world. Even at the Championship level, the money in the game dwarfs many European leagues making that competition the seventh richest in Europe. With so much money awash in the game it has become a honeypot for investors looking for a quick buck and with the additional element of the business in international transfers which involve numerous unregulated intermediaries you can easily understand why it would be attractive to a money launderer. [379]

They will not publicly admit it, but it's well known within media circles that the Football League and the Premier League do not make resources available or have any desire to vet prospective owners before they buy football clubs under their jurisdictions. This is understandable given their historical functions as administrators rather than regulators. Financing a club's running costs from overseas can easily be made into a complex labyrinthine web of business that hides the real financiers. It would require an enormous team of professionals to check funds originated from the owners, so the Premier League and Football League rely on a club's own auditors to spot anything untoward. Neither the Football League nor the Premier League conduct any spot checks of their own. Where the club is a subsidiary of a foreign company it is difficult to see how their cursory analysis of a club's historical accounts or future budgets is any guarantee the club will be sustainable. Of course auditors can always be changed as well, as happened at BIH and Birmingham City.

Fans would do well to appreciate these facts as well. Birmingham City came to rely on two sources of income – television money from Sky from its time in the Premier League and infusions of cash from its owner. In the season Birmingham City finished ninth, fully three-quarters of its revenue came

379. James Munro, *"Money Laundering Risk to Football", BBC, 1 July, 2009,*

from television rights. Relegation was always going to cost the club dearly and as much as Carson's arrest and the freezing of his assets affected his ability to fund the club, relegation hit the club much harder. Parachute payments are designed to soften the blow of relegation from the Premier League to the Championship but there is still a steep drop in a club's income. Unless a new owner is truly a billionaire willing to risk throwing his money away, it is very much a case of it's the better the devil you know.

In line with the Football League or Premier League requirements of furnishing financial budgets showing sustainability of a club's business, they could also implement the real benefit of demanding a bond to insure the club in the event of an owner's financial difficulties. A bond system should be in place to protect those vulnerable people who end up losing in a club's liquidation like the ordinary rank and file staff and small business suppliers who are not protected like the players because players get paid before anyone else does under the football creditor rule. Under the football creditor rule, "football debts" have to be paid in full first before any other debtors, including HMRC– something that we mentioned the HMRC are extremely unhappy about. If a new owner really is so rich, he would have such a good credit rating that such a bond from a bank or insurance policy should be relatively affordable, not to mention showing the owner's commitment to his staff and the club's suppliers.

If the Football League and Premier League can maintain the "football creditor" rule and fight off challenges to it in the court system[380], as they have done so far, then logic dictates that they could also impose stricter ownership rules; it begs the question whether it is really a case of the Football League and Premier League wishing not to derail the foreign gravy train in football?

Their failure to have any kind of failsafe mechanism in their system requires the authorities to share some of the blame for Birmingham City's predicament, at least in the eyes of many Blues fans. The Football League, the Premier League and the FA are the guardians of the game, who are charged

380. Bill Wilson "Football repels taxman's bid to change creditors ruling", BBC, 25 May, 2012

not just with drafting and maintaining the financial rules of the sport but also with enforcing them too. When the authorities are as reticent as they have been in enforcing the rules, then the fans will eventually lose faith in them and eventually in the game itself. The fact that the Football League will not even talk to the press about how they police the game, preferring to hide behind soundbites and confidentiality disclaimers makes it hard to feel any sympathy for them when they are lambasted for the vulnerability of many of the clubs under their jurisdiction to appalling financial mismanagement.

It's easy though to blame the glut of foreign owners in the professional game as the root cause of many of the issues we have seen. It has been said that foreign owners don't understand the culture and history of clubs in England and why fans might react to their actions in the way they do – for example Cardiff City's Malaysian owner Vincent Tan changing their shirts from blue to red to reflect the perceived luck attached to the colour red in the owner's home country as the fans continue to wear blue in protest, or Hull-based Egyptian Aseem Allam pursuing the unsuccessful name change from Hull City to Hull Tigers in the face of a huge backlash from the fans – but English owners are also guilty of antagonising fans by making changes which they perceive as against the interests of their club. One doesn't have to delve very far back into Birmingham City's history to see the antipathy that built up around Messrs Gold and Sullivan when the fans believed that they had been treated as customers ready to be exploited rather than valued assets when ticket prices were raised extortionately on promotion to the Premier League.

This difference is all too often forgotten by owners of football clubs: they are not just businesses which make profits (or in most cases in the Championship, losses) by selling a service to a customer – they are institutions with deep-rooted historical connections in local communities, where whole families have followed their team and passed their fanaticism down through the generations. As more money has come into the game and the costs of operating clubs has risen exponentially as a result of –principally – the increase in players' wages, clubs have found themselves chasing corporate clients, television viewers at home and abroad and foreign partners to the detriment of the match day experience of fans who buy the season tickets, who come well down the pecking order. The onus should be on the Football League and Premier League to make sure that the paying fans – who provide direct revenue from ticket sales, indirect revenue from purchasing the TV packages, retail revenue from shirt sales and all of the atmosphere which is a large part of the product they sell to the domestic and international TV audiences – are not marginalised by the commercialisation of the football landscape. Gate receipts may be dwarfed by commercial revenue in the club accounts, but try selling a Premier League package to Asia with empty terraces, no shirts, no singing, no chanting and no noise.

For all his faults, Carson's tenure at Birmingham City wasn't as bad as it could have been. He did invest in the team and in the club's infrastructure right up to the point of his arrest, with the club intending to purchase its training ground from the University of Birmingham. For all the passing good Carson did Blues, fans saw their team deteriorate in a steady decline as a consequence of his dodgy deals. The worst thing for the fans was that when the chips were down there was absolutely nothing they or anyone else could do to persuade Carson to fold. The fit and proper person test is supposedly designed to prevent a criminal convicted of financial crimes from buying a club but it seems that the Football League were powerless to force a company in the control of an alleged and subsequently convicted money launderer into selling up – even as the club collapsed with him.

It would be unfair to say that Carson was a totally malign influence. Birmingham City enjoyed its best ever period of success under his stewardship – winning its first major trophy in a Wembley showpiece final, finishing a creditable ninth in the Premier League and acquitting themselves well in European competition; all of which gave Blues fans some of their best times. It's hard to reconcile those recent memories with the sight of seeing the team heavily beaten in the Championship, especially at home by average teams just because the manager cannot afford to bring in anyone with any proven quality and has to rely on loaning untried youngsters, signing raw talent on free transfers and playing the best youngsters that the academy can produce before they are ready.

For Carson, his Birmingham City years represented the best and worst of his life. He was as happy as any fan when Blues won the League Cup. As Blues fans now hurl abuse at him as their team languishes a division lower and struggling to make ends meet, Carson has lost his house, his money and his liberty. For a man who started off sweeping up hair in a hotel hairdressing concession, it's been an extraordinary tale but it's unlikely his own immaculately-coiffed locks have survived the prison barber.

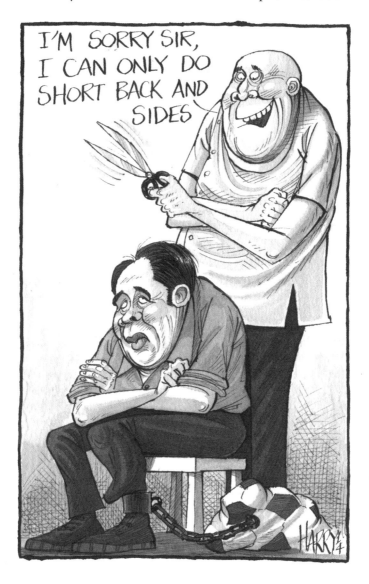

David Sullivan, David Gold and Carson - © Birmingham Mail

Carson Yeung at Wast Hills © Birmingham Mail

Sammy Yu, Mike Wiseman, Carson, Vico Hui, Peter Pannu © Birmingham Mail

Casino Lisboa, Macau © Daniel Ivery

Alex McLeish, Peter Pannu, Carson Yeung © Birmingham Mail

Angry Carson © Daniel Ivery

Carson Entering the District Court - © Daniel Ivery

Graham "the Edwardian" Harris
© Daniel Ivery

Zhou Xin © Daniel Ivery

Vico Hui © Daniel Ivery

John Reading on the District Court steps
© Daniel Ivery

Liu Xingcheng © Daniel Ivery

Kevin Egan © Will Giles

LEGAL CORRESPONDENCE WITH BCFC'S SOLICITORS
AS OUTLINED IN "THE STREISAND EFFECT"

Dan Ivery

By email only: Daniel.ivery@gmail.com

26 March 2014

NOTICE UNDER DATA PROTECTION ACT 1998 ("the Act")

Dear Mr Ivery,

RE: www.oftenpartisan.co.uk ("the Site")
Birmingham City Football Club ("BCFC")

As you are aware from previous correspondence this firm acts for BCFC and its management.

In previous correspondence we have brought various defamatory and misleading statements, posted on the Site, to your attention. Further and as you are aware, our client has had an on-going concern with the nature of statements/comments posted on the Site and motivation behind such statements.

You are clearly a 'controller' under the Act as you are processing personal data on the Site. In this respect you have a duty to comply with the data protection principles set out within the Act (*section 4(4)*).

Notwithstanding the above, we note that neither yourself personally nor Often Partisan (as an entity) have actually obtained a registration under the Act. In the circumstances you are in breach of the Act and pursuant to *section 17* our client is entitled to obtain an injunction to effectively close down the Site until such time as the appropriate registration has been dealt with.

Our client does not wish for the Site to close down. However, on the basis that you are processing personal data on the Site it must insist that you deal with the registration under the Act, which is a simple process, so that it has the remedy of complaining to the Information Commissioner should you breach the data processing principles.

DEBELLO *law*

33rd Floor, Euston Towers,
286 Euston Road, London, NW1 3DP
t 0203 137 7126 *f* 0207 681 1603
w www.debellolaw.co.uk

Debello Law is a trading name of Debello Law Limited. Company No. 7236891.
Authorised and regulated by the Solicitors Regulation Authority.

Please can you confirm that you will commence the process of registration within the next 7 days, failing which our client reserves its right to apply for injunctive relief. If you require any guidance on how to register under the Act we will be happy to provide this to you.

We look forward to hearing from you as a matter or urgency. In the meantime, our clients reserve all their rights.

Yours faithfully

DEBELLO LAW

Dan Ivery

By email only: Daniel.ivery@gmail.com

26 March 2014

Dear Mr Ivery

RE: www.oftenpartisan.co.uk ("the Site")

We write further to the meeting that took place between yourself, Joanne Allsopp (BCFC) and Dean Dunham of this firm on 12th March 2014 ("the Meeting").

At the start of the Meeting it was explained to you that our intention was for the meeting to be held on an 'informal' basis. It was stressed to you that the purpose of the meeting was simply to have an honest and open discussion and to explain some of the concerns that BCFC has with certain comments being made on the Site, both by yourself and users of the Site in the comments section. You said that you were happy with this from the outset. It was also agreed that the meeting should be held on a 'without prejudice' basis.

During the Meeting BCFC's various concerns were explained to you. These principally surrounded on-going defamatory statements that were being made by users of the Site when commenting on articles written by you. You clearly agreed with this and in fact stated there and then that you would disable the 'comment' function on the Site, as you did not have time to monitor the comments and filter those that were defamatory. You went on to say that you had been considering doing this for some time.

On 13th March 2014 you released a statement on the Site explaining why you had disabled the comment function. This effectively stated that i) you had been called in to a legal meeting with BCFC's lawyers ii) that you had been asked by BCFC's lawyers not to mention the Meeting on the Site and iii) you had been "intimidated into silence" ("the Statement").

Both this firm and BCFC are disappointed with certain parts of the Statement, which frankly are misleading and as a consequence untrue. At no time were you asked not to mention the Meeting on the Site. In this respect you appear to be confusing both sides agreement to the Meeting being held on a Without Prejudice basis with a request for silence and as a consequence you have misled the

DEBELLO *law*

33rd Floor, Euston Towers,
286 Euston Road, London, NW1 3DP
t 0203 137 7126 *f* 0207 681 1603
w www.debellolaw.co.uk

Debello Law is a trading name of Debello Law Limited. Company No. 7236891.
Authorised and regulated by the Solicitors Regulation Authority.

public. On the basis that you did not have legal representation at the meeting it was suggested to you that the meeting be held on a without prejudice basis so that *you* would have the protection of BCFC not being able to use anything that you said during the meeting against you in subsequent court proceedings (if such proceedings ever transpired). This was your option as BCFC were happy for the Meeting to be 'open' as opposed to being without prejudice. You elected for it to be without prejudice. Further, at no time were the words "do not mention the meeting on the Site" or any similar words communicated to you in the Meeting. The only reference made, that was remotely close to this, was that when you took the decision to disable the comment function you were asked not to tell users of the Site that BCFC had asked or indeed demanded that you do this. On the basis that this was clearly your decision and BCFC had at no time asked you to take this step, you agreed.

Following publication of the Statement the Birmingham Mail reported on the Meeting, using words "gagged" "ordered" and "told you" to describe how you had been treated. This publication was clearly the product of your misleading and untrue Statement and demonstrates the influence that you have over third parties and indeed the trust that they place on what you say. In this respect we would ask that you publish a further statement to correct the misleading and untrue statements that you have made and that you agree the wording of such statement with us before publication.

We have asked to see a copy of the book that you have co-written about Carson Yeung ("the Book") before it is published and released to the public. The purpose of our request was to ensure that the Book does not contain any defamatory or otherwise misleading statements about BCFC or that would have a negative impact on BCFC. You have declined our request. In this respect we hereby put you on notice that should it transpire, after publication, that the Book does contact such statements legal proceedings will be instigated against both yourself and your co-writer.

We look forward to hearing from you as a matter or urgency. In the meantime, our clients reserve all their rights.

Yours faithfully

Debello Law
DEBELLO LAW

Our Ref: RM/EW/43564.1

Your Ref:

Debello Law
33rd Floor
Euston Towers
286 Euston Road
London
NW1 3DP

Summit House
12 Red Lion Square
London WC1R 4QD
DX 37954 Kingsway

www.mishcon.com

9 April 2014

BY E-MAIL: (enquiries@debellolaw.co.uk) AND POST

Dear Sirs

www.oftenpartisan.co.uk (the "Blog")

We understand that you act for Birmingham City Football Club ("BCFC"). Please confirm whether you also act for Peter Pannu, the Acting Chairman of BCFC.

We have very recently been instructed by Mr Daniel Ivery, and have been passed copies of your two letters dated 26 March 2014. Please direct all future correspondence on this matter to this Firm.

Your letters refer to "*various concerns*" about the Blog and "*ongoing defamatory statements*" published by users of the Website. However, you fail to set out any specific words which you complain are defamatory of your client, whether in our client's own posts or in readers' comments. If you are asserting – as your letter suggests – that the Blog is defamatory of your client, you must set out: (i) the words complained of; (ii) any factual inaccuracies or unsupportable comment within the words complained of; and (iii) the meaning you attribute to the words complained of. Please also set out what evidence you propose to rely on to demonstrate the publication of any such statements either have caused or are likely to cause your clients serious harm, the threshold below which any publications are not actionable following the coming into force of section 1 of the Defamation Act 2013.

Our client does not agree with your assessment of the Statement published on 13 March 2014. It constitutes his honest assessment of the meeting you called him to – without notice - on 12 March 2014. It is surprising that you complain about any confusion surrounding whether or not Mr Ivery was at liberty to mention the fact and detail of the meeting, given that you expressed the discussions to be "without prejudice", a legal term, without giving him – a legally unrepresented and inexperienced individual – any opportunity to understand what that this meant. The Statement makes clear, in its second paragraph, that it was Mr Ivery's decision to disable the comments function, made in light of the issues you had raised.

Our client has no control over the *Birmingham Mail*, and is neither obliged nor inclined to publish any further statement in response to its independent reporting.

20868479.2
Switchboard: +44 20 7440 7000
Main Fax: +44 20 7404 5982

London: Mishcon de Reya Solicitors
New York: Mishcon de Reya New York LLP

Authorised and regulated by the
Solicitors Regulation Authority, SRA
Number 68218.

A list of partners is available for
inspection at the above address.

We are considering your second letter, and the extent to which our client processes personal data, as defined by the DPA. If it is necessary for our client to register, he will do so shortly. Any application for injunctive relief would be unnecessary, disproportionate and oppressive. Kindly ensure that – in the event that you make an application to the Information Commissioner – a copy of this letter is included within your application, as it is relevant to issues of damage and legal costs.

We trust that this letter deals with your concerns, and that you will let us know if it does not.

Yours faithfully

Mishcon de Reya

EPILOGUE

Carson Yeung wasn't the only Blues fan to have reason to dread the Ides of March 2014 as he started his six year prison sentence. On 15 March 2014 the Blues lost 4-1 away at Sheffield Wednesday and in the seven games that month they won only once – away at Millwall – and picked up only four points from a possible twenty-one. The team began an inexorable slide down the table towards the relegation zone. After a rare win at the start of April away at Doncaster Birmingham City lost their next five consecutive games to find themselves on the last day of the season in the bottom three, reliant on results elsewhere if they were to avoid the drop to the third tier of English professional football.

Behind the scenes the situation was far from rosy. BIH and BCFC director Panos Pavlakis had returned to Birmingham ostensibly to agree a sale of the club and as he courted various parties in an attempt to arouse interest and bids, infighting started between him and Acting Chairman Peter Pannu, as they competed to arrange the sale of the club. With commission and "face" on the line, both directors were anxious to emerge as a triumphant saviour; the one to deliver Birmingham City from the hands of its now reluctant and impecunious overlords into the hands of a new (and hopefully spendthrift) owner. The performances on the pitch weren't helping as Panos and Pannu haggled; bidders were aware that relegation would cause another hefty drop in the valuation of the club and as the season neared its conclusion the atmosphere around St Andrew's was fraught with tension as staff, players and fans feared the worst.

The fans did their bit to try and help; responding to an offer of cheaper tickets, they turned up to the last three home games in their droves hoping to cheer their beleaguered team to victory. Blues had suffered a wretched run of form which had seen them fail to win a league game at home since October 2013, eventually equalling an unwanted all-time League record for the most consecutive home games without a win at eighteen. It was to be the worst home season ever for the club in its lack of wins, the number of defeats suffered and the meagre points accrued – all three standing at record levels. The manager Lee Clark's stock dipped further and further as he grew more and more desperate in his attempts to fix the problem; recalling players who had been out of favour for months and playing them in untried positions in increasingly bizarre attempts to fashion a victory.

The final game of the season was against Bolton away at the Reebok Stadium on 3 May; Birmingham City knew that a draw would be good enough if Doncaster Rovers lost their final game away to the Championship winners Leicester, but if Rovers came away with anything then Birmingham City would need a win and hope that Blackpool or Millwall would lose. Blues hadn't won away at the Reebok since 2003 and were coming into the game on the back of five straight defeats. For many fans, it was already over.

Clark stuck to a fairly regular 4-2-3-1 formation, recalling previously suspended skipper Paul Robinson to the side in central defence, with Jonathan Spector moving to right back and Callum Reilly to left-back. Fans were left disappointed that the on-loan Manchester United striker Federico Macheda, who had scored ten goals in his previous seventeen appearances for Blues, was left on the bench as Nikola Zigic was preferred up front on his own.

A tense first half finished goalless and with news that results elsewhere were not going in Blues' favour the outlook appeared bleak. Clark was forced into substituting the injured Emyr Huws at half time for Mitch Hancox, with Callum Reilly moving into a more favoured central midfield position and right-back Paul Caddis playing in "the hole" behind Zigic. The situation went from bad to worse as Blues fell behind to a Lee Chung-yong goal on fifty-seven minutes. As news filtered through that Leicester had taken the lead against Doncaster through a penalty and Blues required just a single goal for a draw to stay up, it quickly increased to two goals needed as Lukasz Jutkiewicz scored a second for Bolton in the seventy-sixth minute. It looked like Blues were dead and buried.

By this point Federico Macheda and Jordon Ibe had been introduced for the ineffectual Chris Burke and Callum Reilly as Blues had to go for broke. The fans on the terraces in the South Stand of the Reebok knew time was running out and sung their hearts out as Blues kicked off again, 0-2 down.

They were almost immediately rewarded when a perfectly-hit Hancox cross was nodded home by the giant Zigic. Could the team redeem themselves at the death? The players pressed Bolton continuously; the fans sang "We're Birmingham City, we fight to the end" in relentless encouragement as Blues piled forwards searching for the equaliser. As ninety minutes approached the fourth official held up his board to indicate a minimum of six additional minutes; six minutes for Blues to save themselves from a relegation that would cause heartache and increase doubts about the very future of the club.

Three minutes into injury time, Jordon Ibe had a shot charged down on the left side of the penalty area, Macheda found his follow up shot blocked but the ball rebounded up to Nikola Zigic who believed he had headed it home... only to find two Bolton players on the line. The ball looped back up from Tim Ream's head and all alone in the box was the diminutive Paul Caddis who usually played right-back, who timed his leap to perfection and nodded the ball back across the line from a distance of four yards to an explosion of noise from behind the goal. Somehow, Blues had done it – they had rescued themselves from the brink of oblivion and condemned Doncaster Rovers to the fate that many believed would befall them.

Around Birmingham there were shouts of joy and exuberance as fans watching on pirated internet streams saw Caddis nod home; at the Reebok in Bolton the delirious reactions of the 3800 travelling fans as the final whistle went told the story. This was not a celebration; this was sheer relief that Blues would be spared the drop to the third tier for only the third time in their history and for the first time in twenty years.

381. Youtube.com, "Colin Tattum reaction to Blues victory", 3 May 2014

In the press gallery reporter Colin Tattum recorded an emotional video for the Birmingham Mail, on the verge of tears as he proclaimed that this should never happen to the club again – that things must change so Birmingham City wouldn't find themselves in the same situation next season[381].

Director Panos Pavlakis was on the pitch to celebrate with the players, hugging scorer Paul Caddis and no doubt secretly thanking him for making his job selling the club a bit easier.

At the player awards dinner the next day, the feeling was one of relief – it was, as one club insider described it, as if the club had been given the all-clear by the doctors following surgery and that – although things weren't perfect – recovery was now possible.

For Pavlakis and Pannu the hard work could start again – with the season over the sale of the club had to be concluded, as there was now no more revenue to come in from gate receipts and BIH had no funding of its own – yet alone any money for BCFC. Its finances were desperate.

SOURCE LIST

1. HKSAR v Yeung Ka Sing, Carson. DCCC860 of 2011 (DJ Douglas Yau) para 215. Legal Reference System, The Judiciary of the Hong Kong SAR. 28 February 2014. http://legalref.judiciary.gov.hk/lrs/common/search/search_result_detail_frame.jsp?DIS=91968&QS=%2B&TP=RV

2. Oliver Chou. "The last bell". South China Morning Post. 29 July 2012. http://www.scmp.com/article/1007958/last-bell

3. HKSAR v Yeung Ka Sing, Carson. DCCC860 of 2011 (DJ Douglas Yau) para 212. Legal Reference System, The Judiciary of the Hong Kong SAR. 28 February 2014. http://legalref.judiciary.gov.hk/lrs/common/search/search_result_detail_frame.jsp?DIS=91968&QS=%2B&TP=RV

4. ibid para 212

5. Next Media, 6 March, 2014 http://hk.next.nextmedia.com/article/1252/17203021

6. HKSAR v Yeung Ka Sing, Carson. DCCC860 of 2011 (DJ Douglas Yau) para 214. Legal Reference System, The Judiciary of the Hong Kong SAR. 28 February 2014. http://legalref.judiciary.gov.hk/lrs/common/search/search_result_detail_frame.jsp?DIS=91968&QS=%2B&TP=RV

7. ibid para 221

8. -

9. HKSAR v Yeung Ka Sing, Carson. DCCC860 of 2011 (DJ Douglas Yau) para 226. Legal Reference System, The Judiciary of the Hong Kong SAR. 28 February 2014. http://legalref.judiciary.gov.hk/lrs/common/search/search_result_detail_frame.jsp?DIS=91968&QS=%2B&TP=RV

10. ibid para 243

11. ibid para 232

12. ibid para 157

13. ibid para 567

14. ibid para 258

15. ibid para 259

16. ibid para 264

17. ibid para 266

18. ibid para 272

19. ibid para 296

20. ibid paras 311-313

21. ibid para 321

22. ibid para 313

23. ibid para 313

24. ibid para 575

25. Companies Winding Up Proceedings 33 of 2003, (Kwan J). Legal Reference System, The Judiciary of the Hong Kong SAR. 23 September 2004. http://legalref.judiciary.gov.hk/lrs/common/ju/ju_frame.jsp?DIS=43270&currpage=T

26. HKSAR v Yeung Ka-Sing, Carson. DCCC860 of 2011 (DJ Douglas Yau) para 115. Legal Reference System, The Judiciary of the Hong Kong SAR. 28 February 2014. http://legalref.judiciary.gov.hk/lrs/common/search/search_result_detail_frame.jsp?DIS=91968&QS=%2B&TP=RV

27. ibid para 124

28. ibid para 127

29. ibid para 617

30. 'SFC Prosecutes Yeung Ka Sing Carson for Breaching the Securities (Disclosure of Interests) Ordinance'. Hong Kong Securities and Futures Commission Enforcement News, 27 September 2004. http://webb-site.com/codocs/SFC040927.pdf

31. Next Media. 6 March, 2014. http://hk.next.nextmedia.com/article/1252/17203021

32. Retrieved April 18 2011. http://images.yule.tom.com/vw/275543-1.html

33. Wing Hang Bank v Success Orient Investment Ltd and others. HCMP2457 of 2011 (R Lung KW). Legal Reference System, The Judiciary of the Hong Kong SAR. 31 January 2013. http://legalref.judiciary.gov.hk/lrs/common/search/search_result_detail_frame.jsp?DIS=85594&QS=%2B&TP=JU

34. Success Orient Investment Ltd Annual Return 2010, 2011 retrieved December 2013

35. James Nursey. "Blueprint for Glory". Daily Mirror. 16 July 2007. http://www.mirror.co.uk/sport/football/blueprint-for-glory-712958

36. HKSAR v Yeung Ka-Sing, Carson. DCCC860 of 2011 (DJ Douglas Yau) para 410. Legal Reference System, The Judiciary of the Hong Kong SAR. 28 February 2014. http://legalref.judiciary.gov.hk/lrs/common/search/search_result_detail_frame.jsp?DIS=91968&QS=%2B&TP=RV

37. ibid para 411

38. ibid para 345

39. Aaron Tam. "Birmingham City owner Carson Yeung guilty of money laundering". AFP. 4 March 2014. https://uk.news.yahoo.com/birmingham-city-boss-yeung-faces-money-laundering-verdict-022245532.html#7XKKOWp

40. HKSAR v Yeung Ka-Sing, Carson. DCCC860 of 2011 (DJ Douglas Yau) para 346. Legal Reference System, The Judiciary of the Hong Kong SAR. 28 February 2014. http://legalref.judiciary.gov.hk/lrs/common/search/search_result_detail_frame.jsp?DIS=91968&QS=%2B&TP=RV

41. Ibid para 347

42. ibid para 577

43. ibid para 428

44. ibid paras 431-432

45. East Week. Volume 393. 11 March 2011.

46. John Garnaut. "Macau's seedy casino war turns to gold". Sydney Morning Herald. 22 September 2009. http://www.smh.com.au/business/macaus-seedy-casino-war-turns-to-gold-20090921-fyn5.html

47. Jonathan Kaiman. "Macau betting on a new kind of Chinese tourism". The Guardian. 5 January 2014 http://www.theguardian.com/business/2014/jan/05/macau-gambling-tourism-money-laundering

48. Christine Duhaime. "Hong Kong – organised crime visits the film set of Transformers 4 for alleged extortion and other thoughts on triads and money laundering". Duhaime's Anti-Money Laundering Law in Canada. 24 October 2013. www.antimoneylaunderinglaw.com/2013/10/organized-crime-visits-the-film-set-of-transformers-4-for-alleged-extortion-and-other-thoughts-on-triads-and-money-laundering.html

49. Matt Isaacs and Reuters Staff. "Special Report: High Rollers, triads and a Las Vegas Giant". Reuters. 29 March 2010. http://www.reuters.com/article/2010/03/29/us-casinos-macau-sands-idUSTRE62S34020100329

50. Steven Stradbrooke. "Junket Operator Neptune Group linked to Bo Xilai Corruption Allegations". Calvinayre.com February 27 2013 http://calvinayre.com/2013/02/27/casino/junket-operator-neptune-group-bo-xilai-corruption-allegation/

51. Jason Dean and Jeffrey Ng. "Ex Gome Chairman Sentenced to 14 years in prison". Wall Street Journal. 18 May 2010. http://online.wsj.com/news/articles/SB10001424052748703315404575251271890222924?mg=reno64-wsj&url=http%3A%2F%2Fonline.wsj.com%2Farticle%2FSB10001424052748703315404575251271890222924.html

52. Shai Oster and Simon Lee. "Jailed Birmingham City Owner Shows China Shadow Bank Link". Bloomberg. 7 March 2014. http://www.bloomberg.com/news/2014-03-06/china-crime-ties-seen-in-money-laundering-investor-s-fall.html

53. HKSAR v Yeung Ka-Sing, Carson. DCCC860 of 2011 (DJ Douglas Yau) para 440. Legal Reference System, The Judiciary of the Hong Kong SAR. 28 February 2014. http://legalref.judiciary.gov.hk/lrs/common/search/search_result_detail_frame.jsp?DIS=91968&QS=%2B&TP=RV

54. Webb-site.com http://webb-site.com/dbpub/orgdata.asp?p=3855

55. HKSE filings http://sdinotice.hkex.com.hk/di/NSAllFormList.aspx?sa2=an&sid=30400102&corpn=China+Nan+Feng+Group+Ltd.&sd=26/01/2005&ed=31/03/2005&sa1=cl&scsd=01%2f01%2f2005&sced=31%2f12%2f2005&sc=979&src=MAIN&lang=EN&

56. HKSE filings http://sdinotice.hkex.com.hk/di/NSForm1.aspx?fn=22018&sa2=an&sid=29480107&corpn=Golden+Resorts+Group+Ltd.&sd=31%2f05%2f2005&ed=29%2f01%2f2008&sa1=cl&scsd=04%2f03%2f2005&sced=04%2f03%2f2008&cn=1&src=MAIN&lang=EN&sa2p=1&

57. HKSAR v Yeung Ka-Sing, Carson. DCCC860 of 2011 (DJ Douglas Yau) para 450. Legal Reference System, The Judiciary of the Hong Kong SAR. 28 February 2014. http://legalref.judiciary.gov.hk/lrs/common/search/search_result_detail_frame.jsp?DIS=91968&QS=%2B&TP=RV

58. ibid para 451

59. ibid para 585

60. China United International Holdings Announcment. 15 March 2005. http://202.66.146.82/listco/hk/willie/announcement/a050315.pdf

61. HKSAR v Yeung Ka-Sing, Carson DCCC860 of 2011 (DJ Douglas Yau) para 491. Legal Reference System, The Judiciary of the Hong Kong SAR. 28 February 2014. http://legalref.judiciary.gov.hk/lrs/common/search/search_result_detail_frame.jsp?DIS=91968&QS=%2B&TP=RV

62. ibid para 492

63. ibid para 628

64. ibid paras 596 and 599

65. Matt Isaacs and Reuters Staff. "Special Report: High Rollers, triads and a Las Vegas Giant". Reuters. 29 March 2010. http://www.reuters.com/article/2010/03/29/us-casinos-macau-sands-idUSTRE62S34020100329

66. Evan Osnos. "The God of Gamblers". New Yorker. 9 April 2012. http://www.newyorker.com/reporting/2012/04/09/120409fa_fact_osnos

67. BBC Sport. 11 May 2006. http://news.bbc.co.uk/sport1/hi/football/teams/b/birmingham_city/4762319.stm

68. L Wilkins. "Your Shout: Kenny Cunningham was right all along". Birmingham Mail,.28 July 2006. http://www.thefreelibrary.com/Letter%3A+Your+Shout+-+KENNY+Cunningham+was+right+all+along.-a0148761061

69. Graham Hill, "Blues in serious financial mess; exclusive: Sullivan bombshell", Sunday Mercury, 7 May 2006 http://www.thefreelibrary.com/

70. Grandtop Announcement. 29 June 2007. http://www.irasia.com/listco/hk/birminghamint/announcement/a16388-e290607.pdf

71. Thomas Chan. "Carson Yeung planned mainland soccer empire, he tells money laundering trial". South China Morning Post. 22 October 2013. http://www.scmp.com/news/hong-kong/article/1336751/carson-yeung-planned-mainland-soccer-empire-he-tells-money-laundering

72. HKSE filings http://sdinotice.hkex.com.hk/di/NSForm1.aspx?fn=18656&sa2=an&sid=10204100&corpn=Grandtop+International+Holdings+Ltd.&sd=06%2f02%2f2007&ed=29%2f11%2f2007&sa1=cl&scsd=01%2f01%2f2007&sced=31%2f12%2f2007&sc=02309&src=MAIN&lang=EN&

73. Thomas Chan. "Carson Yeung lost HK$15.4m in stocks: prosecution". South China Morning Post. 6 November 2013. http://www.scmp.com/news/hong-kong/article/1348543/carson-yeung-lost-hk154m-stocks-prosecution

74. Grandtop Announcement, 3 July 2007 http://www.irasia.com/listco/hk/birminghamint/announcement/a16433-e_02309_20070703.pdf

75. Grandtop Announcement, 7 August 2007 http://www.irasia.com/listco/hk/birminghamint/announcement/a17806-ew_02309ann.pdf

76. Grandtop Announcement, 5 November, 2007 http://202.66.146.82/listco/hk/birminghamint/announcement/a071105.pdf

77. Grandtop Announcement. 20 July 2007 http://www.irwebcast.com/cgi-local/report/redirect.cgi?url=http://www.irasia.com/listco/hk/birminghamint/announcement/a17130-eltn20070720362.pdf

78. Neil Gough and Ben Kwok. "The man behind the Birmingham bid." South China Morning Post. 29 June 2007. http://www.scmp.com/article/598563/man-behind-birmingham-bid

79. HKSAR v Yeung Ka-Sing, Carson. DCCC860 of 2011 (DJ Douglas Yau) para 625. Legal Reference System, The Judiciary of the Hong Kong SAR. 28 February 2014. http://legalref.judiciary.gov.hk/lrs/common/search/search_result_detail_frame.jsp?DIS=91968&QS=%2B&TP=RV

80. The report of the Market Misconduct Tribunal into dealings in the shares of ABC Communications (Holdings) Limited on and between 31 March 2008 and 2 May 2008 http://www.mmt.gov.hk/eng/reports/ABC_Communications_Holdings_Limited_Report_PartI.pdf

81. David Conn. "Watford's former owner banned from football for three years". The Guardian. 18 March 2013. http://www.theguardian.com/football/2013/mar/18/watford-former-owner-banned-three-years

82. The Football League "Owners & Directors Test & Publication of Ownership". Retrieved 3 February 2014. http://www.football-league.co.uk/staticFiles/0/8c/0,,10794~166912,00.pdf

83. Colin Tattum. "Karren Brady spells it out for Carson Yeung". Birmingham Mail. 21 February 2008. http://www.birminghammail.co.uk/sport/football/football-news/karren-brady-spells-it-out-for-carson-58842

84. "Cellino argues convictions 'spent' as he attempts to take over Leeds". The Herald. 4 February 2014. http://www.heraldscotland.com/sport/football/cellino-argues-convictions-spent-as-he-attempts-to-take-over-leeds.1391510057

85. "Sullivan Raises Yeung Concerns". Metro. 27 October 2007. http://metro.co.uk/2007/10/27/sullivan-raises-yeung-concerns-426105/

86. Matt Lawton. "Wigans £3M tempts Birmingham to release Bruce". Daily Mail. 15 November 2007. http://www.dailymail.co.uk/sport/football/article-494135/Wigans-3m-tempts-Birmingham-release-Bruce.html

87. Peter Ferguson and Neil Moxley. "Steve Bruce's switch to Wigan from Birmingham turns farcical", Daily Mail. 21 November 2007. http://www.dailymail.co.uk/sport/football/article-495442/Steve-Bruces-switch-Wigan-Birmingham-turns-farcical.html

88. Mark Ryan. "David Sullivan declares a truce with Carson Yeung after stormy return to St Andrew's". Daily Mail. 8 November 2010. http://www.dailymail.co.uk/sport/football/article-1327367/David-Sullivan-declares-truce-Carson-Yeung-stormy-return-St-Andrews.html

89. Grandtop Announcement, 2 August 2007 http://www.irasia.com/listco/hk/birminghamint/announcement/a17671-ew_02309ann.pdf

90. Grandtop Announcement, 19 September 2007 http://www.irwebcast.com/cgi-local/report/redirect.cgi?url=http://202.66.146.82/listco/hk/birminghamint/announcement/a080919.pdf

91 name withheld, Personal Interview, August 2013

92 SMI Publishing Group Announcement, 24 April 2008 http://www.hkexnews.hk/listedco/listconews/GEM/2008/0424/GLN20080424054.pdf

93. Natalie Wong. "The Final Whistle?". The Standard. 8 July 2011. http://www.thestandard.com.hk/news_detail.asp?pp_cat=36&art_id=112865&sid=32967447&con_type=3&d_str=20110708&sear_year=2011

94. Albert Wong. "Sex, scars and soured affairs". The Standard 1 April 2006. http://www.thestandard.com.hk/archive_news_detail.asp?art_id=15633&archive_d_str=20060401

95. Grandtop Announcment, 12 August 2009 http://www.irwebcast.com/cgi-local/report/redirect.cgi?url=http://202.66.146.82/listco/hk/birminghamint/announcement/a090812.pdf

96. James Nursey. "Blue Murder: Takeovers all change at the top for Birmingham City and Portsmouth". The Mirror. 7 October 2009. http://www.thefreelibrary.com/BLUE+MURDER%3B+TAKEOVERS+ALL+CHANGE+AT+THE+TOP+FOR+BIRMINGHAM+CITY+AND...-a0209124618BLUE+MURDER%3B+TAKEOVERS+ALL+CHANGE+AT+THE+TOP+FOR+BIRMINGHAM+CITY+AND...-a0209124618

97. name withheld, Personal interview, October 2013

98. Chris Noon. "Aston Villa Approves Billionaire's takeover". Forbes. August 14 2006. http://www.forbes.com/2006/08/14/lerner-villa-soccer-cx_cn_0814autofacescan01.html

99. Grandtop Announcement, 21 August, 2009 http://www.irwebcast.com/cgi-local/report/redirect.cgi?url=http://202.66.146.82/listco/hk/birminghamint/announcement/a090821a.pdf

100. Malcolm Moore. "Carson Yeung's team hoping to unlock lucrative Chinese market for Birmingham City". Daily Telegraph. 26 August. 2009.

101. Grandtop Announcment, 21 August 2009 http://202.66.146.82/listco/hk/birminghamint/announcement/a090821a.pdf

102. HKSE filings http://sdinotice.hkex.com.hk/di/NSForm2.aspx?fn=124496&sa2=an&sid=10204100&corpn=Grandtop+International+Holdings+Ltd.&sd=03%2f03%2f2009&ed=21%2f10%2f2009&sa1=cl&scsd=26%2f02%2f2009&sced=26%2f02%2f2010&sc=2309&src=MAIN&lang=EN&

103. Colin Tattum. "Birmingham City: Carson Yeung tipped to start throwing money at Blues". Birmigham Mail. 19 September 2009. http://www.birminghammail.co.uk/sport/football/football-news/birmingham-city-carson-yeung-tipped-103635

104. Colin Tattum. "Cheerio, Cheerio, Cheerio". Birmingham Mail. 17 September 2009. http://blogs.birminghammail.co.uk/birminghamcity/2009/09/cheerio-cheerio-cheerio.html

105. Sportsmail Reporter. "Birmingham chairman David Gold wants St Andrew's stay but no deal with Carson Yeung finalised". Daily Mail. 30 September 2009. http://www.dailymail.co.uk/sport/football/article-1217237/Birmingham-chairman-David-Gold-wants-St-Andrews-stay-deal-Carson-Yeung-finalised.html

106. Colin Tattum. "Birmingham City: Why Michael Dunford was chosen as CEO". Birmingham Mail. 13 October 2009. http://www.birminghammail.co.uk/sport/football/football-news/birmingham-city-why-michael-dunford-was-chosen-105630

107. Grandtop Announcement, 23 September 2009 http://www.irwebcast.com/cgi-local/report/redirect.cgi?url=http://202.66.146.82/listco/hk/birminghamint/announcement/a090923.pdf

108. Grandtop Announcement, 25 September 2009 http://www.irwebcast.com/cgi-local/report/redirect.cgi?url=http://202.66.146.82/listco/hk/birminghamint/announcement/a090925.pdf

109. "Carson Yeung's lawyer asks for case to be thrown out". ITV. 29 April 2013. http://www.itv.com/news/central/update/2013-04-29/carson-yeung-lawyer-asks-for-case-to-be-thrown-out/

110. "Twelve O'Clock High: Court upholds 'tail-gunner' clause and awards success fee to former financial advisor". Norton Rose Fulbright. June 2010. http://www.nortonrosefulbright.com/knowledge/publications/28897/twelve-oclock-high-court-upholds-tail-gunner-clause-and-awards-success-fee-to-former-financial-adviser

111. Sportsmail Reporter. "Carson Yeung regains control at Birmingham after settling £2.2million debt with Seymour Pierce". Daily Mail. 27 April 2010. http://www.dailymail.co.uk/sport/football/article-1269195/Carson-Yeung-regains-control-Birmingham-settling-2-2million-debt-Seymour-Pierce.html

112. Grandtop Announcment, 6 October, 2009 http://www.irwebcast.com/cgi-local/report/redirect.cgi?url=http://202.66.146.82/listco/hk/birminghamint/announcement/a091006a.pdf

113. "Carson Yeung to splash out £40million on Birmingham City", Metro, 15 October 2009 http://metro.co.uk/2009/10/15/carson-yeung-to-splash-out-40million-on-birmingham-city-491046/

114. "Birmingham City is for the people". Birmingham Mail. October 13 2009. http://www.birminghammail.co.uk/sport/football/football-news/birmingham-city-is-for-the-people---vico-105683

115. Colin Tattum. "Colin Doyle downs Birmingham City chairman Vico Hui in pint contest". Birmingham Mail. 16 January 2010. http://www.birminghammail.co.uk/sport/football/football-news/birmingham-city-is-for-the-people---vico-105683

116. East Week. Volume 393. 9 March 2011.

117. Naomi Rovnick and Daniel Ren. "Kai Yuan strikes it rich but lands in steel war". South China Morning Post. 2 April 2010. http://www.scmp.com/article/710315/kai-yuan-strikes-it-rich-lands-steel-war

118. Stuart James. "David Gold and David Sullivan to sue new Birmingham City Owners". The Guardian. 8 April 2010. http://www.theguardian.com/football/2010/apr/08/birmingham-david-gold-david-sullivan-rift

119. David Conn. "Birmingham City face questions as emails show Pannu's demands for cash". The Guardian. 27 March 2013. http://www.theguardian.com/football/2013/mar/27/birmingham-city-peter-pannu

120. ibid

121. ibid

122. Mark Hughes. "Court victory raises hope of reinstatement". South China Morning Post. 23 February 1994. http://www.scmp.com/article/64028/court-victory-raises-hope-reinstatement

123. ibid

124. Charlotte Parsons. "Witness Blow Frees Pannu". South China Morning Post. 8 February 1996. http://www.scmp.com/article/149058/witness-blow-frees-pannu

125 Barclay Crawford and Greg Torode. "Cleared officer takes post at UK soccer club". South China Morning Post. 8 October 2009. http://www.scmp.com/article/694762/cleared-officer-takes-post-uk-soccer-club

126. Vaudine England. "Hong Kong's lavish nightclubs lose their appeal". The Guardian. 12 December 2012.

127. Colin Tattum, "Full interview: Birmingham City chief Peter Pannu tells of triad battles", Birmingham Mail, 9 October, 2009 www.birminghammail.co.uk/news/local-news/full-interview-birmingham-city-chief-105409

128. Charlotte Parsons. "Trials of force's golden boy". South China Morning Post. 8 February 1996. http://www.scmp.com/article/149057/trials-forces-golden-boy

129. Colin Tattum. "Blues chief: My triad battles; INTERVIEW EXCLUSIVE: Dealings in a danger zone". Birmingham Mail. 9 October 2009. http://www.thefreelibrary.com/Blues+chief%3A+My+Triad+battles%3B+INTERVIEW+EXCLUSIVE%3A+Dealings+in+a...-a0209391296Blues+chief%3A+My+Triad+battles%3B+INTERVIEW+EXCLUSIVE%3A+D-ealings+in+a...-a0209391296

130. HKSAR v Yeung Ka-Sing, Carson. DCCC860 of 2011 (DJ Douglas Yau) para 440. Legal Reference System, The Judiciary of the Hong Kong SAR. 28 February 2014. http://legalref.judiciary.gov.hk/lrs/common/search/search_result_detail_frame.jsp?DIS=91968&QS=%2B&TP=RV

131. HKSE filings http://sdinotice.hkex.com.hk/di/NSAllFormList.aspx?sa2=an&sid=30400102&corpn=China+Nan+Feng+Group+Ltd.&sd=28/04/2004&ed=31/03/2005&sa1=cl&scsd=01%2f01%2f2004&sced=31%2f12%2f2005&sc=00979&src=MAIN&lang=EN&

132. HKSAR v Yeung Ka-Sing, Carson. DCCC860 of 2011 (DJ Douglas Yau) para 450. Legal Reference System, The Judiciary of the Hong Kong SAR. 28 February 2014. http://legalref.judiciary.gov.hk/lrs/common/search/search_result_detail_frame.jsp?DIS=91968&QS=%2B&TP=RV

133. ibid, para 364

134. ibid, para 444

135. ibid, para 451

136. HKSE filings http://sdinotice.hkex.com.hk/di/NSForm1.aspx?fn=8442&sa2=an&sid=22090101&corpn=Massive+Resources+International+Corporation+Ltd.&sd=04%2f03%2f2004&ed=07%2f06%2f2005&sa1=cl&scsd=01%2f01%2f2004&sced=31%2f12%2f2005&sc=0070&src=MAIN&lang=EN&

137. Massive Resources Announcement, 21 January, 2005 http://www.hkexnews.hk/listedco/listconews/SEHK/2005/0124/LTN20050124025.pdf

138. HKSE filings http://sdinotice.hkex.com.hk/di/NSForm1.aspx?fn=6921&sa2=an&sid=22090101&corpn=Massive+Resources+International+Corporation+Ltd.&sd=04%2f03%2f2004&ed=07%2f06%2f2005&sa1=cl&scsd=01%2f01%2f2004&sced=31%2f12%2f2005&sc=0070&src=MAIN&lang=EN&

139. HKSE filings http://sdinotice.hkex.com.hk/di/NSForm1.aspx?fn=7016&sa2=an&sid=22090101&corpn=Massive+Resources+International+Corporation+Ltd.&sd=04%2f03%2f2004&ed=07%2f06%2f2005&sa1=cl&scsd=01%2f01%2f2004&sced=31%2f12%2f2005&sc=0070&src=MAIN&lang=EN&

140. HKSAR v Yeung Ka-Sing, Carson. DCCC860 of 2011 (DJ Douglas Yau) para 442. Legal Reference System, The Judiciary of the Hong Kong SAR. 28 February 2014. http://legalref.judiciary.gov.hk/lrs/common/search/search_result_detail_frame.jsp?DIS=91968&QS=%2B&TP=RV

141. ibid, para 446

142. China Energy Announcement, 4 February 2009 http://www.hkexnews.hk/listedco/listconews/SEHK/2009/0204/LTN20090204955.pdf

143. China Energy Announcement, 30 July 2009 http://www.hkexnews.hk/listedco/listconews/SEHK/2009/0730/LTN20090730615.pdf

144. China Energy Announcement, 21 September 2009 http://www.hkexnews.hk/listedco/listconews/SEHK/2009/0921/LTN20090921506.pdf

145. China Energy Announcement, 8 October 2009 http://www.hkexnews.hk/listedco/listconews/SEHK/2009/1008/LTN20091008223.pdf

146. China Energy Announcement, 31 December 2009 http://www.hkexnews.hk/listedco/listconews/SEHK/2009/1231/LTN20091231240.pdf

147. China Energy Announcement, 28 January 2010 http://www.hkexnews.hk/listedco/listconews/SEHK/2010/0128/LTN20100128573.pdf

148. China Energy Announcement, 22 February 2010 http://www.hkexnews.hk/listedco/listconews/SEHK/2010/0222/LTN20100222154.pdf

149. China Energy Announcement, 30 April 2010 http://www.hkexnews.hk/listedco/listconews/SEHK/2010/0430/LTN20100430817.pdf

150. China Energy Announcement, 13 July 2010 http://www.hkexnews.hk/listedco/listconews/SEHK/2010/0713/LTN20100713442.pdf

151. China Energy Announcement, 28 September 2010 http://www.hkexnews.hk/listedco/listconews/SEHK/2010/0928/LTN20100928579.pdf

152. China Energy Announcement, 3 December 2010 http://www.hkexnews.hk/listedco/listconews/SEHK/2010/1203/LTN20101203273.pdf

153. China Energy Announcement, 16 September 2013 http://www.hkexnews.hk/listedco/listconews/SEHK/2013/0916/LTN20130916776.pdf

154. "IFJ Report lists China's Secret Bans on Media Reporting". International Federation of Journalists. 31 January 2010. http://www.ifj.org/en/articles/ifj-report-lists-chinas-secret-bans-on-media-reporting

155. James Anderlini. "Bo fallout theatens China's security chief". Financial Times. 12 April 2012. http://www.ft.com/intl/cms/s/f978ce9c-8ae6-11e1-b855-00144feab49a,Authorised=false.html?_i_location=http%3A%2F%2Fwww.ft.com%2Fcms%2Fs%2F0%2Ff978ce9c-8ae6-11e1-b855-00144feab49a.html%3Fsiteedition%3Dintl&siteedition=intl&_i_referer=http%3A%2F%2Fen.wikipedia.org%2Fwiki%2FZhou_Yongkang#axzz2v9VkxQ7u

156. Zhou Dan, Personal interview, 22 February 2014

157. webb-site.com http://webb-site.com/dbpub/positions.asp?p=33417

158. webb-site.com http://webb-site.com/dbpub/positions.asp?p=12295

159. webb-site.com http://webb-site.com/dbpub/positions.asp?p=36604

160. webb-site.com http://webb-site.com/dbpub/positions.asp?p=46181

161. webb-site.com http://webb-site.com/dbpub/positions.asp?p=44711

162. webb-site.com http://webb-site.com/dbpub/positions.asp?p=44709

163. Yeung Ka Sing Carson v Chen Lixue HCA221 of 2014

164. Birmingham International Holdings Announcement, 27 April 2012 http://www.irwebcast.com/cgi-local/report/redirect.cgi?url=http://202.66.146.82/listco/hk/birminghamint/announcement/a120427a.pdf

165. iMerchants Announcement, 5 May 2009 http://www.hkexnews.hk/listedco/listconews/GEM/2009/0505/GLN20090505147.pdf

166. Zhou Dan, Personal interview, 22 February 2014

167. iMerchants Announcement, 31 August 2009 http://www.hkexnews.hk/listedco/listconews/GEM/2009/0831/GLN20090831074.pdf

168. iMerchants Announcement, 17 September 2009 http://www.hkexnews.hk/listedco/listconews/GEM/2009/0917/GLN20090917019.pdf

169. iMerchants Announcement, 23 October 2009 http://www.hkexnews.hk/listedco/listconews/GEM/2009/1023/GLN20091023036.pdf

170. iMerchants Announcement, 18 November 2009 http://www.hkexnews.hk/listedco/listconews/GEM/2009/1118/GLN20091118024.pdf

171. China Water Announcement, 3 August 2012 http://www.hkexnews.hk/listedco/listconews/sehk/2012/0803/LTN20120803951.pdf

172. Colin Tattum. "Colin Tattum reflects on Birmingham City's remarkable 2009-10 Premier League Season". Birmingham Mail. 11 May 2010. http://www.birminghammail.co.uk/sport/football/football-news/colin-tattum-reflects-on-birmingham-citys-124618

173. Colin Tattum. "Birmingham City 1, West Ham 0, Colin Tattum's Big Match Verdict". Birmingham Mail. 14 December 2009. http://www.birminghammail.co.uk/sport/football/football-news/birmingham-city-1-west-ham-219314

174. "Birmingham forced to abandon Tuncay Sanli signing". The Telegraph. 27 August 2009. http://www.telegraph.co.uk/sport/football/teams/birmingham-city/6099972/Birmingham-forced-to-abandon-Tuncay-Sanli-signing.html

175. Colin Tattum. "Mood around Birmingham City has changed – Trevor Francis". Birmingham Mail. 3 November 2009. http://www.birminghammail.co.uk/sport/football/football-news/mood-has-changed-at-birmingham-city---107350

176. Sportsmail Reporter. "Birmingham face relegation if Carson Yeung reduces ticket prices claims ex-chairman David Gold". Daily Mail. 14 October 2009. http://www.dailymail.co.uk/sport/football/article-1220407/Birmingham-face-relegation-Carson-Yeung-reduces-ticket-prices-claims-ex-Blues-chairman-David-Gold.html

177. Colin Tattum. "Sammy Yu opens his heart on his shock exit from Birmingham City". Birmingham Mail. 26 September 2010. http://www.birminghammail.co.uk/sport/football/football-news/sammy-yu-opens-his-heart-on-his-shock-249492

178. "Carson Yeung to splash out £40million on Birmingham City", Metro, 15 October 2009 http://metro.co.uk/2009/10/15/carson-yeung-to-splash-out-40million-on-birmingham-city-491046/

179. "Birmingham sign Michel from Sporting Gijon". The Guardian. 11 January 2010. http://www.theguardian.com/football/2010/jan/11/birmingham-city-michel-alex-mcleish

180. Sandy Macaskill. "Birmingham seal £3 million move for Aston Villa defender Craig Gardner". Daily Telegraph. 26 January 2010. http://www.telegraph.co.uk/sport/football/teams/birmingham-city/7078517/Birmingham-seal-3-million-move-for-Aston-Villa-defender-Craig-Gardner.html

181. Colin Tattum. "Birmingham City remain in talks for Tottenham Hotspur star Roman Pavlyuchenko". Birmingham Mail. 28 January 2010. http://www.birminghammail.co.uk/sport/football/football-news/birmingham-city-remain-in-talks-for-tottenham-117607

182. "EPL Table 2009-10". EPLMatches.com. http://www.eplmatches.com/tables/english-premier-league/epl-table-2009-2010/

183. Sportsmail Reporter. "Ben Foster challenged to make a name for himself after clinching £6m move from Manchester United to Birmingham City". Daily Mail. 19 May 2010. http://www.dailymail.co.uk/sport/football/article-1279652/Ben-Foster-completes-6m-switch-Manchester-United-Birmingham-City.html

184. "Birmingham complete £6m deal for Serbia striker Nikola Zigic". The Guardian. 26 May 2010. http://www.theguardian.com/football/2010/may/26/birmingham-nikola-zigic-serbia-premier

185. "Birmingham recruit Hleb, Jiranek and Beausejour". BBC. 31 August 2010. http://news.bbc.co.uk/sport1/hi/football/teams/b/birmingham_city/8956520.stm

186. "Birmingham City urged not to sign Bobby Zamora". Birmingham Mail. 5 July 2010. http://www.birminghammail.co.uk/sport/football/football-news/birmingham-city-urged-not-to-sign-127651

187. Sportsmail Reporter. "Wigan lead race to sign Estudiantes £7m striker Mauro Boselli". Daily Mail. 31 May 2010. http://www.dailymail.co.uk/sport/football/article-1282837/Wigan-lead-race-sign-Estudiantes-7m-striker-Mauro-Boselli.html

188. "Birmingham close to £5m signing of Moussa Dembélé fom AZ Alkmaar". The Guardian. 5 August 2010. http://www.theguardian.com/football/2010/aug/05/birmingham-moussa-dembele-az-alkmaar

189. Colin Tattum. "Match Report Beijing Guoan 0 Birmingham City 1". Birmingham Mail. 22 July 2010. http://www.birminghammail.co.uk/sport/football/football-news/match-report-beijing-guoan-0-128663

190. "Carling Cup Final: Arsenal 1 Birmingham City 2 – Full Time Match Report". Birmingham Mail. 27 February 2011. http://www.birminghammail.co.uk/sport/football/football-news/carling-cup-final-arsenal-1-149321

191. Colin Tattum. "Birmingham City 3 Rochdale 2: Colin Tattum's big match verdict and player ratings". Birmingham Mail. 27 August 2010. http://www.birminghammail.co.uk/sport/football/football-news/birmingham-city-3-rochdale-2-130831

192. Colin Tattum. "Birmingham City 1 Brentford 1 (aet, Blues win 4-3 on penalties): Colin Tattum's big verdict". Birmingham Mail. 27 October 2010. http://www.birminghammail.co.uk/sport/football/football-news/birmingham-city-1-brentford-1-134324

193. Phil McNulty. "Birmingham City 2 – 1 Aston Villa". BBC. 1 December 2010. http://news.bbc.co.uk/sport1/hi/football/9233759.stm

194. Phil McNulty. "Birmingham City 3 – 1 West Ham". BBC. 26 January 2010.

195. Brendon McLoughlin. "Birmingham City owner Carson Yeung gives 18-year-old son a seat on the club's board of directors". The Telegraph. 18 July 2011. http://www.telegraph.co.uk/sport/football/teams/birmingham-city/8646209/Birmingham-City-owner-Carson-Yeung-gives-18-year-old-son-a-seat-on-clubs-board-of-directors.html

196. Birmingham International Holdings Announcement, 3 March, 2011 http://202.66.146.82/listco/hk/birminghamint/interim/2011/int1.pdf

197. Bill Wilson. "Football repels taxman's bid to change creditor's ruling". BBC. 25 May 2012. http://www.bbc.co.uk/news/business-18208076

198. Nabil Hassan. "Financial Fair Play: A third of owners considering selling club". BBC. August 13 2013. http://www.bbc.co.uk/sport/0/football/23669759

199. BCFC accounts, retrieved from Companies House

200. Birmingham International Holdings announcement, 24 October 2010 http://202.66.146.82/listco/hk/birminghamint/announcement/a101024.pdf

201. Birmingham International Holdings announcement, 22 February 2011 http://www.irwebcast.com/cgi-local/report/redirect.cgi?url=http://202.66.146.82/listco/hk/birminghamint/interim/2011/int.pdf

202. Nick Harris. "Birmingham tempting fate with their financial plans". Daily Mail. 8 January 2011. http://www.dailymail.co.uk/sport/football/article-1345400/Nick-Harris-Birmingham-tempting-fate-financial-plans.html

203. Birmingham International Holdings announcement, 14 April 2011 http://www.irwebcast.com/cgi-local/report/redirect.cgi?url=http://202.66.146.82/listco/hk/birminghamint/announcement/a110414.pdf

204. HKSE filings http://sdinotice.hkex.com.hk/di/NSForm1.aspx?fn=44759&sa2=an&sid=10204100&corpn=Birmingham+International+Holdings+Ltd.&sd=15%2f03%2f2011&ed=11%2f02%2f2014&sa1=cl&scsd=13%2f02%2f2011&sced=13%2f02%2f2014&sc=2309&src=MAIN&lang=EN&

205. Birmingham International Holdings announcement, 4 May 2011 http://www.irwebcast.com/cgi-local/report/redirect.cgi?url=http://202.66.146.82/listco/hk/birminghamint/announcement/a110504.pdf

206. "Birmingham City Blues". The Swiss Ramble. 14 January 2011. http://swissramble.blogspot.co.uk/2011/01/birmingham-city-blues.html

207. Colin Tattum. "Birmingham City Talking Point: Colin Tattum explains why Nikola Zigic deserves more credit". Birmingham Mail. 13 November 2013. http://www.birminghammail.co.uk/sport/football/football-news/birmingham-city-talking-point-colin-6298920

208. Nick Harris. "Birmingham tempting fate with their financial plans". Daily Mail. 8 January 2011. http://www.dailymail.co.uk/sport/football/article-1345400/Nick-Harris-Birmingham-tempting-fate-financial-plans.html

209. Peter Scrivener. "Birmingham 0 – 2 Fulham". BBC. 15 May 2011. http://www.bbc.co.uk/sport/0/football/13364707

210. "Birmingham City: Craig Gardner joins Sunderland and describes moving as a 'no-brainer'". Birmingham Mail. 1 July 2011. http://www.birminghammail.co.uk/sport/football/football-news/birmingham-city-craig-gardner-joins-157083

211. Sandy Macaskill. "Birmingham City owner Carson Yeung arrested on suspicion of money laundering". The Telegraph. 29 June 2011. http://www.telegraph.co.uk/sport/football/teams/birmingham-city/8607022/Birmingham-City-owner-Carson-Yeung-arrested-on-suspicion-of-money-laundering.html

212. OCSO http://www.assetrecovery.org/kc/resources/org.apache.wicket. Application/repo?nid=728d9f3e-b73f-11de-a008-b1bed31c538f

213. name withheld, Personal Interview, August 2013

214. Birmingham International Holdings announcement, 30 June 2011 http:// www.irwebcast.com/cgi-local/report/redirect.cgi?url=http://202.66.146.82/ listco/hk/birminghamint/announcement/a110630.pdf

215. "Birmingham City owner Carson Yeung refused permission to attend Championship match against Coventry City". The Telegraph. 11 August 2011. http://www.telegraph.co.uk/sport/football/teams/birmingham-city/8694963/ Birmingham-City-owner-Carson-Yeung-refused-permission-to-attend-Championship-match-against-Coventry-City.html

216. "Birmingham owner Carson Yeung refused right to fly back for Braga game". The Guardian. 14 September 2011. http://www.theguardian.com/ football/2011/sep/14/birmingham-carson-yeung-braga

217. HCMP 1254 of 2011 (V. Bokhary J.)

218. Natalie Wong. "The Final Whistle". The Standard. 8 July 2011. http://www.thestandard.com.hk/news_detail.asp?pp_cat=36&art_ id=112865&sid=32967447&con_type=3&d_str=20110708&sear_year=2011

219. Birmingham International Holdings announcement, 3 August 2011 http:// www.irwebcast.com/cgi-local/report/redirect.cgi?url=http://202.66.146.82/ listco/hk/birminghamint/announcement/a110803.pdf

220. Birmingham International Holdings announcement, 31 August 2011 http:// www.irwebcast.com/cgi-local/report/redirect.cgi?url=http://202.66.146.82/ listco/hk/birminghamint/announcement/a110831a.pdf

221. Brett Gibbons. "Birmingham City: Fans plan protest before Everton clash". Birmingham Mail. 29 July 2011. http://www.birminghammail.co.uk/news/ local-news/birmingham-city-fans-plan-protest-158542

222. Birmingham International Holdings announcement, 31 October 2011 http:// www.irwebcast.com/cgi-local/report/redirect.cgi?url=http://202.66.146.82/ listco/hk/birminghamint/announcement/a111031a.pdf

223. Birmingham International Holdings announcement, 17 March 2013 http:// www.irwebcast.com/cgi-local/report/redirect.cgi?url=http://202.66.146.82/ listco/hk/birminghamint/annual/2011/res.pdf

224. "Birmingham City placed under transfer embargo". BBC. 2 March 2012. http://www.bbc.co.uk/sport/0/football/17232625

225. Birmingham International Holdings announcement, 31 January 2012 http:// www.irwebcast.com/cgi-local/report/redirect.cgi?url=http://202.66.146.82/

listco/hk/birminghamint/announcement/a120131.pdf

226. Birmingham International Holdings announcement, 27 April 2012 http://www.irwebcast.com/cgi-local/report/redirect.cgi?url=http://202.66.146.82/listco/hk/birminghamint/announcement/a120427.pdf

227. Brett Gibbons. "Birmingham City FC tell fans: 'Wait for accounts before judging'". Birmingham Mail. 6 March 2012. http://www.birminghammail.co.uk/news/local-news/birmingham-city-fc-tell-fans-180401

228. "A statement from Peter Pannu". BCFC.com. 6 May 2013. http://www.bcfc.com/news/article/a-statement-from-peter-pannu-806262.aspx

229. Brett Gibbons. "Blues paid more out to Xtep than they received in kit supply deal". Birmingham Mail. 8 January 2013. http://www.birminghammail.co.uk/sport/football/football-news/birmingham-city-paid-more-to-xtep-430912

230. Birmingham International Holdings announcement, 18 January 2010 http://202.66.146.82/listco/hk/birminghamint/announcement/a100118.pdf

231. Brett Gibbons. "Blues paid more out to Xtep than they received in kit supply deal". Birmingham Mail. 8 January 2013. http://www.birminghammail.co.uk/sport/football/football-news/birmingham-city-paid-more-to-xtep-430912

232. "Xtep Gone". Often Partisan. 29 June 2012. http://www.oftenpartisan.co.uk/archives/5788/xtep-gone.html

233. Colin Tattum. "Birmingham City rip up kit contract with Xtep". Birmingham Mail. 29 June 2012. http://www.birminghammail.co.uk/sport/football/football-news/birmingham-city-rip-up-kit-187736

234. Jon Griffin. "Birmingham City hit by boardroom split". Birmingham Mail. 27 June 2012. http://www.birminghammail.co.uk/news/local-news/birmingham-city-hit-by-boardroom-split-187602

235. BCFC accounts year ending 2012

236. Jon Griffin. "Birmingham City hit by boardroom split". Birmingham Mail. 27 June 2012. http://www.birminghammail.co.uk/news/local-news/birmingham-city-hit-by-boardroom-split-187602

237. Jeanette Oldham, "Special Investigation: Birmingham City chief Peter Pannu's secret £1.5m pay deal", Birmingham Mail, 26 April, 2013 http://www.birminghammail.co.uk/news/local-news/special-investigation-birmingham-city-chief-3156172

238. document withheld

239. Jeanette Oldham. "Special Investigation: Birmingham City chief Peter

Pannu in 'threat' to club's auditor". Birmingham Mail. 27 April 2013. http://www.birminghammail.co.uk/incoming/birmingham-city-chief-peter-pannu-3182817

240. Austin Chiu. "Carson Yeung granted four months to prepare defence". South China Morning Post. 29 November 2012. http://www.scmp.com/news/hong-kong/article/1093274/carson-yeung-granted-four-months-prepare-his-defence

241. Wing Hang Bank v Success Orient Investment Ltd and others, HCMP2457 of 2011 (R Lung KW)

242. Birmingham International Holdings announcement, 19 September 2012 http://www.irwebcast.com/cgi-local/report/redirect.cgi?url=http://202.66.146.82/listco/hk/birminghamint/announcement/a120919a.pdf

243. Birmingham International Holdings announcement, 11 January 2013 http://www.irwebcast.com/cgi-local/report/redirect.cgi?url=http://202.66.146.82/listco/hk/birminghamint/announcement/a130111.pdf

244. Colin Tattum. "Birmingham City: It looks like we have no deal – Gianni Paladini". Birmingham Mail. 15 September 2011. http://www.birminghammail.co.uk/sport/football/football-news/birmingham-city-it-looks-like-we-have-no-4005

245. ibid

246. Jeanette Oldham. "Special Investigation: Birmingham City chief Peter Pannu's secret £1.5m pay deal". Birmingham Mail. 26 April 2013. http://www.birminghammail.co.uk/news/local-news/special-investigation-birmingham-city-chief-3156172

247. "A statement from Peter Pannu", BCFC.com. 6 May 2013. http://www.bcfc.com/news/article/a-statement-from-peter-pannu-806262.aspx

248. Daniel Ivery. "Birmingham City shareholder launching bid to force Carson Yeung and Peter Pannu out". Birmingham Mail. 2 May 2013. http://www.birminghammail.co.uk/news/local-news/birmingham-city-shareholder-launching-bid-3315138

249. "BIH AGM News – Liu Xingcheng Vote Denied". Often Partisan. 10 May 2013. http://www.oftenpartisan.co.uk/archives/8697/bih-agm-news-liu-xingcheng-vote-denied.html

250. Birmingham International Holdings announcement,10 May 2013 http://www.irwebcast.com/cgi-local/report/redirect.cgi?url=http://202.66.146.82/listco/hk/birminghamint/announcement/a130510.pdf

251. Birmingham International Holdings announcement, 13 May 2013 http://

www.irwebcast.com/cgi-local/report/redirect.cgi?url=http://202.66.146.82/listco/hk/birminghamint/announcement/a130513.pdf

252. "BIH Embroiled in New Court Battle". Often Partisan. 5 June 2013. http://www.oftenpartisan.co.uk/archives/8877/bih-embroiled-in-new-courtroom-battle.html

253. Birmingham International Holdings announcement, 19 August 2013 http://www.irwebcast.com/cgi-local/report/redirect.cgi?url=http://202.66.146.82/listco/hk/birminghamint/announcement/a130819.pdf

254. Birmingham International Holdings announcement, 19 November 2013 http://www.irwebcast.com/cgi-local/report/redirect.cgi?url=http://202.66.146.82/listco/hk/birminghamint/announcement/a131119.pdf

255. Birmingham International Holdings announcement, 1 August 2013 http://www.irwebcast.com/cgi-local/report/redirect.cgi?url=http://202.66.146.82/listco/hk/birminghamint/announcement/a130801a.pdf

256. Candy Chan. "Yeung Funeral Request Denied". The Standard, 31 July 2012. http://www.thestandard.com.hk/news_detail.asp?art_id=124867&con_type=1

257. "VIDEO: Carson Yeung Trial – Birmingham City owner denies money-laundering", Birmingham Mail, 29 April 2013 http://www.birminghammail.co.uk/news/local-news/birmingham-city-carson-yeung-trial-3306608

258. Daniel Ivery "Haggard and under scrutiny from the press", Birmingham Mail, 30 April 2013 http://www.birminghammail.co.uk/news/local-news/birmingham-city-carson-yeung-trial-3306608

259. HKSAR v Pang Hung Fai. CACC34 of 2012 (Hon Stock VP, Lunn JA and McWalters J). Legal Reference System, The Judiciary of the Hong Kong SAR. 31 May 2013. http://legalref.judiciary.gov.hk/lrs/common/search/search_result_detail_frame.jsp?DIS=87746&QS=%2B&TP=JU

260. "Birmingham City's Carson Yeung loses bid to stop trial". BBC. 3 May 2013. http://www.bbc.co.uk/news/business-22397327

261. Matt Isaacs and Reuters Staff. "Special Report: High Rollers, triads and a Las Vegas Giant". Reuters. 29 March 2010. http://www.reuters.com/article/2010/03/29/us-casinos-macau-sands-idUSTRE62S34020100329

262. Diana Lee. "Showstopper as 'Uncle Ba' gets 3 years", The Standard. 12 July 2011. http://www.thestandard.com.hk/archive_news_detail.asp?art_id=112978&archive_d_str=20110712

263. Thomas Chan. "Carson Yeung's margin account traded more than HK$500m". South China Morning Post. 16 May 2013. http://www.scmp.com/news/hong-kong/article/1238463/carson-yeungs-margin-account-traded-more-hk500m

264. Thomas Chan. "Soccer Boss Carson Yeung had money woes since 2002: prosecution". South China Morning Post. 29 October 2013. http://www.scmp.com/news/hong-kong/article/1342111/soccer-boss-carson-yeung-had-money-woes-2002-prosecution

265. Thomas Chan. "Former lawmaker Chim Pui-chung chastises judge". South China Morning Post. 27 June 2013. http://www.scmp.com/news/hong-kong/article/1269665/former-lawmaker-chim-pui-chung-chastises-judge

266. Thomas Chan. "Carson Yeung's access to his father's account disputed in court". South China Morning Post. 20 June 2013. http://www.scmp.com/news/hong-kong/article/1264489/carson-yeungs-access-fathers-account-disputed-court

267. Thomas Chan. "Carson Yeung shuttles between hospital and trial". South China Morning Post. 13 July 2013. http://www.scmp.com/news/hong-kong/article/1281321/carson-yeung-shuttles-between-hospital-and-trial

268. ICAC Press Release, 3 March, 2005 http://webb-site.com/codocs/ICAC050303.pdf

269. ICAC Press Release, 12 June, 2006 http://webb-site.com/codocs/ICAC060612.pdf

270. HKSAR v Kevin Barry Egan. CACC140 of 2007. Legal Reference System, The Judiciary of the Hong Kong SAR. 12 February 2009. http://legalref.judiciary.gov.hk/lrs/common/ju/ju_frame.jsp?DIS=64338&currpage=T

271. HKSAR v Kanjanpas Chong Kwong Derek and Others. CACC 248 of 2006. Legal Reference System, The Judiciary of the Hong Kong SAR. 21 May 2009. http://legalref.judiciary.gov.hk/lrs/common/ju/ju_frame.jsp?DIS=65877&currpage=T

272. HKSAR v Kevin Barry Egan FACC 3 of 2009, Mandy Chui v HKSAR FACC 4 of 2009, Andrew Lam v HKSAR FACC 5 of 2009. Legal Reference System, The Judiciary of the Hong Kong SAR. 28 June 2010. http://legalref.judiciary.gov.hk/lrs/common/ju/ju_frame.jsp?DIS=71692&currpage=T

273. Thomas Chan. "Carson Yeung will take the stand at his money laundering trial after u-turn". South China Morning Post. 27 September 2013. http://www.scmp.com/news/hong-kong/article/1318446/carson-yeung-will-take-stand-his-money-laundering-trial-after-u-turn

274. Thomas Chan. "Carson Yeung says styling and stocks made his fortune". South China Morning Post. 15 October 2013. http://www.scmp.com/news/hong-kong/article/1332438/carson-yeung-explains-fortune-money-laundering-trial

275. Thomas Chan. "The money I took was from my own investments: Carson Yeung". South China Morning Post. 31 October 2013. http://www.scmp.com/news/hong-kong/article/1344708/money-i-took-was-my-investments-carson-yeung

276. Julie Chu. "Carson Yeung demands money laundering trial halt over unfair evidence". South China Morning Post. 9 November 2013. http://www.scmp.com/news/hong-kong/article/1351199/carson-yeung-demands-money-laundering-trial-halt-over-unfair-evidence

277. Thomas Chan. "Carson Yeung belittles talk of HK$248m takeover of Birmingham City FC". South China Morning Post. 13 November 2013. http://www.scmp.com/news/hong-kong/article/1354707/carson-yeung-belittles-talk-hk248m-takeover-birmingham-city-fc

278. Thomas Chan. "Birmingham City chief Carson Yeung accused over "inconsistent evidence". South China Morning Post. 13 December 2013. http://www.scmp.com/news/hong-kong/article/1379245/birmingham-city-chief-carson-yeung-accused-over-inconsistent-evidence

279. "Gianni Paladini pledges to take Birmingham City back to the biggest stage". Birmingham Mail. 13 September 2013. http://www.birminghammail.co.uk/news/local-news/gianni-paladini-pledges-to-take-birmingham-3790

280. "QPR Report Friday: Gianni Paladini speaks". QPR Report. 18 November 2011, http://qprreport.blogspot.hk/2011/11/qpr-report-friday-gianni-paladini.html

281. Colin Tattum. "Birmingham City: It looks like we have no deal – Gianni Paladini". Birmingham Mail. 15 September 2012. http://www.birminghammail.co.uk/sport/football/football-news/birmingham-city-it-looks-like-we-have-no-4005

282. Colin Tattum. "Gianni Paladini throws down the gauntlet to Peter Pannu... again". Birmingham Mail. 26 November 2012. http://www.birminghammail.co.uk/sport/football/football-news/gianni-paladini-throws-down-the-gauntlet-335458

283. Colin Tattum"Birmingham City Gianni Paladini deal to be struck 'within 10 days'", Birmingham Mail, 12 November 2012 http://www.birminghammail.co.uk/sport/football/football-news/birmingham-city-takeover-gianni-paladini-308030

284. Colin Tattum. "Pannu is ready to do business". Birmingham Mail. 19 December 2012. http://www.birminghammail.co.uk/sport/football/football-news/birmingham-citys-acting-chairman-peter-378737

285. Birmingham International Holdings Announcement, 21 October 2013 http://202.66.146.82/listco/hk/birminghamint/announcement/a131021.pdf

286. Neil Moxley. "Don't treat me like an idiot! Paladini blasts Birmingham Chief Pannu after takeover snub". Daily Mail. 15 November 2012. http://www.dailymail.co.uk/sport/football/article-2233530/Gianni-Paladini-blasts-Birmingham-City-chief-Peter-Pannu-takeover-snub.html

287. Colin Tattum. "Sammy Yu opens his heart on shock exit from Birmingham City". Birmingham Mail. 26 September 2012. http://www.birminghammail.co.uk/sport/football/football-news/sammy-yu-opens-his-heart-on-his-shock-249492

288. "Curtis Davies: Hull City sign Birmingham Defender". BBC. 25 June 2013. http://www.bbc.com/sport/0/football/23030343

289. James Dickenson. "Norwich and Swansea agree £2.5m fee for Birmingham youngster Nathan Redmond". Daily Express. 25 June 2013. http://www.express.co.uk/sport/football/409998/Norwich-and-Swansea-agree-2-5m-fee-for-Birmingham-youngster-Nathan-Redmond

290. "Matt Green signs for Blues". Birmingham Mail. 3 July 2013. http://www.birminghammail.co.uk/sport/football/transfer-news/birmingham-city-matt-green-signs-4863487

291. Colin Tattum. "Blues: 'No sale of club is agreed or imminent'". Birmingham Mail. 7 August 2013. http://www.birminghammail.co.uk/sport/football/football-news/birmingham-city-no-sale-club-5676652

292. name withheld, Personal interview, November 2013

293. Birmingham International Holdings Announcement, 19 August 2013 http://202.66.146.82/listco/hk/birminghamint/announcement/a130819.pdf

294. Neil Moxley. "EXCLUSIVE: Yeung has just six weeks to rescue cash-strapped Birmingham from plunging into administration". Daily Mail. 25 October 2013. http://www.dailymail.co.uk/sport/football/article-2477098/Carson-Yeung-weeks-rescue-cash-strapped-Birmingham-City-administration--exclusive.html

295. Thomas Chan. "Carson Yeung belittles talk of HK$248m takeover of Birmingham City FC". South China Morning Post. 13 November 2013. http://www.scmp.com/news/hong-kong/article/1354707/carson-yeung-belittles-talk-hk248m-takeover-birmingham-city-fc

296. Neil Moxley. "EXCLUSIVE: Yeung demands £20,000 from potential Birmingham City buyer Paladini just to meet him". Daily Mail. 18 November 2013. http://www.dailymail.co.uk/sport/football/article-2509633/Carson-Yeung-told-Gianni-Paladini-pay-20-000-wants-talk-buying-Birmingham-City.html

297. "Statement on behalf of Carson Yeung". bcfc.com. 21 November 2013. http://www.bcfc.com/news/article/201311121-statement-on-behalf-of-carson-yeung-1186640.aspx

298. Birmingham International Holdings Announcement, 19 November 2013 http://www.irwebcast.com/cgi-local/report/redirect.cgi?url=http://202.66.146.82/listco/hk/birminghamint/announcement/a131119.pdf

299. Birmingham International Holdings Announcement, 12 November 2013 http://www.irwebcast.com/cgi-local/report/redirect.cgi?url=http://202.66.146.82/listco/hk/birminghamint/announcement/a131112.pdf

300. Alex Aldridge. "Millwall CEO quashes rumours of takeover after Paladini link". News at Den. 20 January 2014. http://www.newsatden.co.uk/30786-millwall-ceo-quashes-takeover-rumours-after-paladini-link.html

301. Birmingham International Holdings Announcement, 16 January 2014 http://202.66.146.82/listco/hk/birminghamint/announcement/a140116.pdf

302. Birmingham International Holdings Announcement, 30 December 2013 http://202.66.146.82/listco/hk/birminghamint/announcement/a131230.pdf

303. Birmingham International Holdings Announcement, 16 October 2013 http://202.66.146.82/listco/hk/birminghamint/announcement/a131021.pdf

304. Birmingham International Holdings Announcement, 19 August 2013 http://202.66.146.82/listco/hk/birminghamint/announcement/a130819.pdf

305. Birmingham International Holdings Announcement, 4 February 2014 http://202.66.146.82/listco/hk/birminghamint/announcement/a140204b.pdf

306. "Carson Yeung steps down". bcfc.com. 4 February 2014. http://www.bcfc.com/news/article/20140204-carson-yeung-steps-down-1340115.aspx

307. "New Directors appointed". bcfc.com. 3 February 2014. http://www.bcfc.com/news/article/20140203-new-directors-appointed-1338070.aspx

308. Birmingham International Holdings Announcement, 5 February 2014 http://202.66.146.82/listco/hk/birminghamint/announcement/a140205b.pdf

309. Gregg Evans. "The future is 'bright' for Birmingham City says Peter Pannu". Birmingham Mail. 5 February 2014. http://www.birminghammail.co.uk/sport/football/football-news/future-bright-birmingham-city-says-6675300

310. "Pannu predicts bright future", BBC, 5 February, 2014 http://www.bbc.co.uk/sport/0/football/26052372

311. Imogene Wong. "Defiant Carson Yeung vows to increase company stake". The Standard. 6 February 2014. http://www.thestandard.com.hk/news_detail.asp?we_cat=2&art_id=142218&sid=41500090&con_type=1&d_str=20140206&fc=8

312. HKSE filings http://sdinotice.hkex.com.hk/di/NSForm1.aspx?fn=61808&sa2=an&sid=10204100&corpn=Birmingham+International+Holdings+Ltd.&sd=05%2f02%2f2014&ed=18%2f02%2f2014&sa1=cl&scsd=25%2f02%2f2013&sced=25%2f02%2f2014&sc=2309&src=MAIN&lang=EN&

313. HKSE filings http://sdinotice.hkex.com.hk/di/NSForm1.aspx?fn=61972&sa2=an&sid=10204100&corpn=Birmingham+International+Holdings+Ltd.&sd=05%2f02%2f2014&ed=18%2f02%2f2014&sa1=cl&scsd=25%2f02%2f2013&sced=25%2f02%2f2014&sc=2309&src=MAIN&lang=EN&

314. Steve Wollaston. "Video: Birmingham City fans protest against the board". Birmingham Mail. 1 February 2014. http://www.birminghammail.co.uk/sport/football/football-news/video-birmingham-city-fans-protest-6658374

315. delaynomore.co.uk

316. "Postcards from HK: Delay No More". Often Partisan. 28 October 2013. http://www.oftenpartisan.co.uk/archives/10054/postcards-from-hk-delay-no-more.html

317. bihlgonow.co.uk

318. news.sina.com.hk. 22 February, 2014. http://news.sina.com.hk/news/20140223/-2-3196188/1.html

319. Birmingham International Holdings Announcement, 12 February, 2014 http://www.irwebcast.com/cgi-local/report/redirect.cgi?url=http://202.66.146.82/listco/hk/birminghamint/announcement/a140212a.pdf

320. Demetri Sevastopulo, "Birmingham City FC Owner agreed stake sale to mystery buyer", Financial Times, 3 March 2014 ft.com (behind paywall)

321. Birmingham International Holdings Announcement, 25 February 2014 http://www.hkexnews.hk/listedco/listconews/SEHK/2014/0225/LTN20140225426.pdf

322. Birmingham International Holdings Announcement, 7 March 2014 http://www.irwebcast.com/cgi-local/report/redirect.cgi?url=http://202.66.146.82/listco/hk/birminghamint/announcement/a140307.pdf

323. Birmingham International Holdings Announcement, 20 February 2014 http://www.irwebcast.com/cgi-local/report/redirect.cgi?url=http://202.66.146.82/listco/hk/birminghamint/announcement/a140220.pdf

324. Birmingham International Holdings Announcment, 3 March 2014 http://www.irwebcast.com/cgi-local/report/redirect.cgi?url=http://202.66.146.82/listco/hk/birminghamint/announcement/a140303a.pdf

325. "Statement: Carson Yeung", bcfc.com, 3 March 2014 http://www.bcfc.com/news/article/20140303-statement-carson-yeung-1393430.aspx

326. Paul Suart. "Gianni Paladini: Sell me Birmingham City". Birmingham Mail. 4 March 2014. http://www.birminghammail.co.uk/sport/football/football-news/birmingham-city-latest-gianni-paladini-6768391

327. Colin Tattum. "Under-fire Peter Pannu says Carson Yeung knows that he has to sell Birmingham City". Birmingham Mail. 8 February 2014. http://www.birminghammail.co.uk/news/local-news/under-fire-peter-pannu-says-carson-6686335

328. Archbold Hong Kong: Criminal Law, Pleading, Evidence and Practice 2010 (Hong Kong: Sweet & Maxwell/Thomson Reuters, 2009), preface

329. Albert Wong. "Courts' 90pc conviction rate stirs up row". South China Morning Post. 15 September 2009. http://www.scmp.com/article/692523/courts-90pc-conviction-rate-stirs-row.

330. Legislative Council Secretariat, Research and Library Services Division, Information Note: Conviction rates in selected places, 2010, File Ref.: IN19/09-10, Fourth Legislative Council (Year 2009-2010)

331. Albert Wong. "Lawyers hope to reopen debate on jury system". South China Morning Post. 5 October 2009. http://www.scmp.com/article/694518/lawyers-hope-reopen-debate-jury-system.

332. Hong Kong Law Society, Submissions on "Conviction Rates", 23 June 2010, LC Paper No. CB(2)197/09-10(01), paragraph 19(a)

333. Patrick Yu Shuk-siu. Tales from No 9. Ice House Street. Hong Kong University Press, 2002.

334. ibid, p.11

335. ibid

336. "A century of distinction". Post Magazine. 2 June 2013. http://www.scmp.com/magazines/post-magazine/article/1248934/century-distinction

337. (2008) 232 CLR 438

338. Ibid. paragraph 101 (Heydon J)

339. Owen Bowcott. "Judiciary needs to be more diverse, peers say". The Guardian. 28 March 2012. http://www.theguardian.com/law/2012/mar/28/select-committee-seeks-diverse-judiciary

340. Hansard (31 December 1952, p. 301) (First Reading of the District Court Bill)

341. Hansard (31 December 1952, p. 303) (First Reading of the District Court Bill)

342. Hansard (14 January 1953, pp. 4-5) (Second Reading of the District Court Bill)

343. The Hon Sir Patrick Devlin, Trial by Jury (The Hamlyn Lectures, Eighth Series, Stevens & Sons Limited, 1956) p. 164

344. ibid, p.120

345. ibid, p.122

346. ibid, p.123

347. ibid, p.149

348. ibid, p.154

348. ibid, p.158-159

350. ibid, p.160

351. "First trial without jury approved". BBC News. 18 June 2009. http://news.bbc.co.uk/2/hi/uk_news/8106590.stm

352. Hansard (23 May 1973, p. 814) (Second Reading of the District Court (Amendment) Bill 1973)

353. Yeung Ka Shing Carson v. Secretary for Justice. HCAL 59 of 2013 (DHCJ Wright) paras. 28 and 34. Legal Reference System, The Judiciary of the Hong Kong SAR. 3 May 2013. http://legalref.judiciary.gov.hk/lrs/common/search/search_result_detail_frame.jsp?DIS=91734&QS=%2B&TP=JU

354. AG of Hong Kong v Lee Kwong Kut & Others [1993] AC 951 (Lord Woolf) p.964 G-H

355. Oei Hengky Wiryo v HKSAR. FACC 4/2006 (Mr Justice McHugh NPJ). Legal Reference System, The Judiciary of the Hong Kong SAR. 9 February 2007. http://legalref.judiciary.gov.hk/lrs/common/search/search_result_detail_frame.jsp?DIS=56019&QS=%2B&TP=JU

356. HKSAR v Pang Hung Fai. CACC 34/2012 (Hon Lunn JA) para. 196. Legal Reference System, The Judiciary of the Hong Kong SAR. 31 May 2013. http://legalref.judiciary.gov.hk/lrs/common/search/search_result_detail_frame.jsp?DIS=87746&QS=%2B&TP=JU

357. ibid para 13

358. Organised and Serious Crimes Ordinance (Cap. 455), Long Title

359. Security Branch, Legislative Council Brief on the Organised Crime Bill 1991, 5 August 1991, File Ref.: SCR 3/2831/87, Annex B, paras. 25-26

360. Security Branch, Legislative Council Brief on the Organised and Serious Crimes Bill 1992, 7 July 1992, File Ref.: SBCR 3/2831/87, para. 4(c)

361. Ibid, paras. 5 and 6

362. Ibid, para. 36

363. Hansard (12 October 1994, p. 124) (Resumption of debate on Second Reading of the Organised and Serious Crimes Bill 1992)

364. ibid p.140

365. Hansard (28 July 1995, p. 6491) (Resumption of debate on Second Reading of the Organised and Serious Crimes (Amendment) Bill 1995)

366. Ibid., p.6492

367. Security Branch, Government Secretariat, Legislative Council Brief on the Drug Trafficking (Recovery of Proceeds) (Amendment) Bill 1995 and the Organised and Serious Crimes (Amendment) Bill 1995, 10 April 1995, File Ref.: NCR 3/1/8 (G) VII, paras. 5 and 6

368. Ibid., Annex A, para. 16

369. Ibid, Annex B, para 13

370. Oei Hengky Wiryo v HKSAR. FACC 4/2006 (Mr Justice McHugh NPJ). Legal Reference System, The Judiciary of the Hong Kong SAR. 9 February 2007. http://legalref.judiciary.gov.hk/lrs/common/search/search_result_detail_frame.jsp?DIS=56019&QS=%2B&TP=JU

371. Au Hau Ching v HKSAR FAMC 61/2009 (Chief Justice Li A). Legal Reference System, The Judiciary of the Hong Kong SAR. 3 November 2009 http://legalref.judiciary.gov.hk/lrs/common/search/search_result_detail_frame.jsp?DIS=68338&QS=%28au%2Bhau%2Bching%29&TP=JU

372. Wong Ping Shui Adam v HKSAR FAMC 1/2001 (Mr Justice Bokhary PJ). Legal Reference System, The Judiciary of the Hong Kong SAR. 16 February 2001. http://legalref.judiciary.gov.hk/lrs/common/search/search_result_detail_frame.jsp?DIS=33901&QS=%28wong%2Bping%2Bshui%29&TP=JU

373. Jackie Liu (Principal Assistant Secretary for Financial Services and the Treasury (Financial Services))., "Letter to the Editor: "Hong Kong's efforts against money laundering". South China Morning Post. 19 March 2014. http://www.scmp.com/comment/letters/article/1452005/hong-kongs-efforts-against-money-laundering-recognised

374. Glenn Moore. "QPR Financial Results: Rangers face huge fine in top flight of debtors". The Independent. 6 March 2014. http://www.independent.co.uk/sport/football/football-league/qpr-financial-results-rangers-face-huge-fine-in-top-flight-of-debtors-9173772.html

375. Football League Statement on Birmingham City, 3 March, 2014 http://www.football-league.co.uk/latestnews/20140303/football-league-statement-on-birmingham-city_2293301_3695983

376. David Conn. "Birmingham City fans concerned at Carson Yeung's continued influence". The Guardian. 4 March 2014. http://www.theguardian.com/football/2014/mar/04/birmingham-fans-carson-yeung-influence

377. Micah Hall. "Hall Right Now: Revealed – The true story behind Ali Al Faraj". fansnetwork.co.uk. 7 October 2012. http://www.fansnetwork.co.uk/football/portsmouth/news/18346/hall-right-now-revealed--the-true-story-behind-ali-al-faraj/?scrollto=post19203

378. Daniel Kaplan. "NFL pares ownership rule". Sports Business Daily. 26 October 2009. http://www.sportsbusinessdaily.com/Journal/Issues/2009/10/20091026/This-Weeks-News/NFL-Pares-Ownership-Rule.aspx

379. James Munro. "Money Laundering Risk to Football". BBC. 1 July 2009. http://news.bbc.co.uk/sport1/hi/football/8127790.stm

380. Bill Wilson. "Football repels taxman's bid to change creditors ruling". BBC. 25 May 2012. http://www.bbc.co.uk/news/business-18208076

381. "Colin Tattum reaction to Blues victory", youtube.com, 3 May 2014 https://www.youtube.com/

14K – The third largest triad society with a membership of 25,000. Based in Hong Kong and major rivals with Sun Yee On, they are alleged to be connected to gambling, narcotics and money laundering.

Alex McLeish – served as manager of Birmingham City between November 2007 and June 2011. Left BCFC to take on the same role at Aston Villa, where he was manager between June 2011 and May 2012. Currently not in employment as a football manager.

Alternative Investment Market – AIM - is a sub-market of the London Stock Exchange, allowing smaller companies to float shares with a more flexible regulatory system than is applicable to the main market.

Andrew Lam Ping-cheung – solicitor in Hong Kong, Independent Non-Executive Director of Willie International (1999-2006) and Enerchina Holdings Ltd (2012-present), amongst several others. Acquitted on appeal on charges of witness tampering along with Kevin Egan in 2010.

Au Yeung Kai Chor - General Manager of Dragonite International Limited (also known as Ruyan Group Holdings Limited) since April 2010; he also served as its Executive Director from May 7, 2010 to October 25, 2011.

Baotou – a city of 2.65M people situated in the Inner Mongolia Autonomous Region of China. The region surrounding Baotou is known for its mines – particularly rare earths and coal.

Barker Road, The Peak – an exclusive residential road on The Peak. The road was at one point reckoned to be the second most expensive road in the world to live on.

BIH – Full name Birmingham International Holdings Limited. Known as Grandtop International Holdings Limited when they bought out Birmingham City, the company changed its name to reflect owning the club. Trades on the HKSE Main Board, stock code 02309.

Causeway Bay – a heavily urbanised area of Hong Kong Island on the eastern side of Wanchai.

Chen Lixue – Doctor to Yeung Chung. Currently being sued by Carson Yeung for breach of contract.

Cheung Chi-tai – formerly major investor in the Neptune Group, alleged to be a leader of the Wo Hop To gang of triads. Was arrested in connection with an attempted murder of a chip dealer, although charges were dropped due to a lack of evidence. Current whereabouts unknown.

Chim Pui-chung – former member of the Legislative Council of Hong Kong representing the Financial Services Functional Constituency between October 1991 and June 1998, and July 2004 and September 2012. Chim was jailed for conspiring to forge documents between June 1998 and 1999.

China Energy – Full name China Energy Development Holdings Limited, stock code 0228. Currently trades on the HKSE Main Board.

China Water – Full name China Water Industry Group Limited, stock code 01129. Currently trades on the HKSE Main Board.

Chris Hughton – former manager of Birmingham City, was until recently manager of Norwich City. Spent majority of his playing career at Tottenham Hotspur.

David Fernyhough – Former detective within the Royal Hong Kong Police, worked for five years in the Organised Crimes and Triad Bureau. Now a head of fraud investigations for AIG.

David and Ralph Gold – co-founders of the Ann Summers chain, they bought Birmingham City along with David Sullivan in 1993. Now co-owners of West Ham United with David Sullivan.

David Sullivan – born in 1949, a former porn magnate who served seventy-one days in prison for immoral earnings, bought Birmingham City along with David Gold and Ralph Gold in 1993. Now co-owner of West Ham United with the Gold Brothers.

Dongguan – an industrial city of 8M people situated between Shenzhen and Guangzhou on the Pearl River delta.

Douglas Yau Tak-hong – Born in Hong Kong in 1967, appointed judge in the District Court of Hong Kong in September 2009. Educated at the University of London (LLB 1997), called to the bar in England and Wales and in Hong Kong in 1994, appointed magistrate in 2002.

Eugene Chuang Yue-chien – managing director of Allied Welli Development between 1996 and November 2009 and Responsible Officer for Enerchine Corporate Finance between August 2005 and March 2010.

Gold Wo – Full name Gold Wo International Holdings Limited, stock code 090, forcibly wound up in September 2004

Graham Harris SC – an Englishman, Harris was called to the bar in England and Wales in 1975 and in Hong Kong in 1985. A Senior Counsel, he led Carson's defence team when the criminal case was at trial.

Guangzhou – historically known as Canton, Guangzhou is the capital of Guangdong Province, which borders Hong Kong. It is the third biggest city in China, with a population of 14M.

Hong Kong Island – Hong Kong Island is the second largest island in Hong Kong after Lantau and contains the main financial hub of the region in its Central District, along with the seat of Hong Kong's legislative and judiciary powers.

ICAC – Independent Commission Against Corruption. Established in 1974 by Governor Murray MacLehose with the aim of cleaning up corruption. Independent of the civil service, ICAC reports directly to the Chief Executive of Hong Kong.

iMerchants – Full name iMerchants Limited, stock code 08009, now trades on the Growth Enterprise Market (GEM) as Chinese Energy Holdings Limited.

Joanna Wang Man Li – Third wife of Carson Yeung and mother of his two youngest children, Camilla and Alexander.

John Reading SC – born in Australia, Reading was a prosecutor in New South Wales from 1978, and became a prosecutor in Hong Kong in 1984, and was appointed Deputy Director of Public Prosecutions in 2000. A Senior Counsel, he now works in private practice but was prosecutor in Carson's trial.

Junket Operator – a company that assists bringing high rollers into casinos by buying chips from Casinos to sell to wealthy punters, by running VIP rooms in casinos, and by organising and facilitating trips for high rollers to Macau from the People's Republic of China.

Kanstar Environmental – Full name Kanstar Environmental Paper Products Holdings Limited, stock code 08011, now trades on the Growth Enterprise Market (GEM) as Polyard Petroleum International Group Limited.

Karren Brady – former MD of Birmingham City, now Vice-Chairman of West Ham United. Appears on "The Apprentice" on BBC1, is married to former Birmingham City striker Paul Peschisolido.

Keith Harris – football financier and executive chairman of Seymour Pierce, a London-based investment brokerage. Has been personally part of consortiums in failed takeovers at Manchester United in 2012 and Portsmouth in 2013.

Kevin Egan – barrister in Hong Kong, governor of the Foreign Correspondent Club. Served as second barrister on Carson's defence. Kevin Egan was acquitted on appeal of witness tampering along with Andrew Lam in 2010.

Kingston Securities – stockbrokers run by Pollyanna Chu Yuet-wah.

Lee Yiu-tung – served as director of Birmingham International Holdings between June 2006 and January 2013. Now working as an architect.

Lian Zhuozhao – also known as Lin Cheuk-chiu, brother of Lin Cheuk-fung. Known as "the king of gambling on the high seas", linked to money laundering activites with various Chinese officials.

Lin Cheuk-fung - served as an Executive Chairman of Neptune Group Limited from June 8, 2006 to November 29, 2013 and as its Executive Director from June 21, 2005 to November 29, 2013.

Li Wing-sze – First wife of Carson Yeung and mother of his oldest son, Ryan Yeung Tsz-tsung.

Liu Xingcheng – husband of Zhou Xin and second largest shareholder in BIH.

Macau – a former Portuguese Colony, it is based thirty-seven miles southwest of Hong Kong on the other side of the Pearl River delta. Has been a Special Autonomous Region of the People's Republic of China since 1999.

Mark Pulvirenti – gave evidence in Carson's trial as an expert witness. Executive Director of Alix Partners in Hong Kong, formerly a director of Deloitte.

Mike Wiseman – honorary Vice-President of Birmingham City FC; his father Jack was a former chairman of the club and had been a member of the board since 1956; his grandfather David "Curley" Wiseman was associated with the club before that.

Neptune Group – junket operator, stock code 070, listed on the HKSE Main Board.

Peter Pannu – a former Hong Kong policeman and Barrister, served as director of Birmingham City from July 2011 to the present and as a director of BIH from September 2012 to the present. Also serves as Chief Executive and Managing Director of BIH and Acting Chairman of Birmigham City.

Pollyanna Chu Yuet-wah – CEO of Kingston Securities since April 2005, named by Forbes as the thirty-fifth richest person in Hong Kong in 2013 with a personal fortune of US$1.4billion.

Prosper eVision – Full name Prosper eVision Limited, stock code 0979, now trades on the HKSE Main Board as Green Energy Group Limited.

Raymond Yau Yan-ming – former Independent Non-Executive Director of Birmingham International Holdings, and current Executive Director of Chinese Energy Holdings and Independent Non-Executive Director of Willie International Holdings.

Ryan Yeung Tsz-tsung – born in 1994, oldest son of Carson Yeung and Li Wing-sze.

St Andrew's – the stadium where Birmingham City FC play their home games.

Sammy Yu Wai-ying – former Hong Kong footballer, served as CEO of Sing Pao Media between September 2008 and September 2009 and as director of the same company between September 2009 and August 2011.

Currently serving as Managing Director of Eastern Sports Management Ltd.

Seymour Pierce – Investment, stockbrokers and corporate financiers. Led by football financier Keith Harris, it was bought out of administration in February 2013 by Cantor Fitzgerald.

SFC – Securities and Futures Commission. An independent non-governmental statutory body outside the civil service, responsible for regulating the securities and futures markets in Hong Kong.

Shenzhen – A city of 7M people in Southern China, across the border from Hong Kong. Originally much smaller, Shenzhen grew exponentially after being made a "Special Economic Zone" by China prior to the Hong Kong handover.

Sing Pao – Cantonese langauge newspaper based in Hong Kong part owned by Carson Yeung.

SJM – Full name Sociedade de Jogos de Macau (SJM) Holdings, holder of gambling licence in Macau.

Steve Bruce – born in Newcastle, Bruce was a defender who played for Birmingham City and Manchester United among other teams before turning his hand to management. Managed Birmingham City between November 2001 and October 2007. Now manager at Hull City.

Steve McManaman – former Liverpool and Real Madrid midfielder, served as director of Birmingham International Holdings between July 2007 and June 2012.

Success Orient – Full name Success Orient Investment Limited. The company that was beneficial owner of the house on Barker Road, The Peak.

Sun Yee On – One of the biggest triad societies, with an estimated membership exceeding 55,000 worldwide. Sun Yee On is also known as New Righteousness and Peace Commercial and Industrial Guild. It was founded in 1919 and is involved in counterfeiting, gambling, narcotics, smuggling and extortion.

The Peak – a large mountain in the middle of Hong Kong Island, famed for its hyper-exclusive residential areas.

Tilton – the home end behind the goal at St Andrew's Stadium.

Triads – organised crime syndicates based in Hong Kong, Macau and China.

Tsim Sha Tsui – A densely populated urban area at the tip of the Kowloon peninsula facing Hong Kong Island, TST (as it's commonly abbreviated to) is an area of crowded markets and nightlife with a much more distinctive Chinese flavour than the more colonial Central District and Wanchai across the harbour.

Vico Hui Ho-luek – served as chairman of Birmingham City FC between October 2009 and July 2012, and as CEO and Director of BIH between June 2007 and July 2012.

Victor Ma Shui-cheong – brother-in-law to Carson Yeung, director of BIH from December 2012 to the present and of BCFC from February 2014 to the present. Also serves as the Vice-Chairman of BIH and as an executive director of Sing Pao Media.

Wanchai – a metropolitan area in the Central district of Hong Kong Island, it contains much nightlife and was the location of the District Court where Carson stood trial.

William Chan Wai-keung – served as non-executive director of Birmingham International Holdings between December 2007 and October 2012. He also served variously as director, CEO and Chairman of China Energy Development holdings between 2006 and 2009.

Wo Hop To – Triad group based in Wanchai. Their name translates to "Harmoniously United Association" and is thought to have been founded in 1908 in Sai Ying Pun as a political group against the Qing Dynasty. They specialise in protection rackets and are affiliated with Sun Yee On.

Xinjiang – officially known as the Xinjiang Uyghur Autonomous Region, it is the largest administrative division of China. It is situated in the far west of China, bordering Russia, Mongolia, Kazakhstan, Kyrgyzstan, Tajikistan, Afghanistan, Pakistan and India. It has abundant oil reserves and is the largest gas-producing region of China.

Zhou Dan – Second long-term partner of Carson Yeung

Zhou Xin – sister of Zhou Dan, wife of Liu Xingcheng

Zhou Yongkang – born in 1942 in Wuxi, China. Former Minister of Public Security in China (2002-2007), former secretary of the CPC Central Political and Legislative Committee (2007-2012), head of China National Petroleum Corporation 1996-1998. Currently under house arrest in Baotou, Inner Mongolia.

ROLL OF HONOUR

Ben Baker
Tim Beard
Robin Bradley
Colin Carberry
Bradley Coffman
Nigel Cross
Matin Durrani
Lee Foley
Nick Glynn
Jonathan Herrador
Trevor Honnor
James Hyde
Danny Kelly
Andrew McCourt
Lee McGarvie
Victor Matts
Christopher Newbold
Nicholas Peters
Chris Quinn
Qasim Razaq
Nik Spooner
Will Viles
Arthur Watson
Terry Wilcox
Robert Andrew Winmill

Simon John Baughen
Su Biela
Simon Brew
Philip Carr
Julian Coleman
Margaret Decker
Bob Eaton
Mark Gibbs
Philip Harris
Gary Hellend
Martyn Allan Hughes
JPS
George Knock
Adam McDermott
Mark Mason
Graeme Mulvey
Nathanael Peters
Chris Pegg
John Ramsay
Giles Robinson
Ray Tomkinson
Damon Warren
Adam Weaver
Craig Williams